Are Politics Local?

Are politics local? Why? Where? When? How do we measure local versus national politics? And what are the effects? This book provides answers to these questions, within an explicitly comparative framework, including both advanced and developing democracies. It does so by using a statistically based and graphical account of party nationalization, providing methodology and data for legislative elections covering scores of parties across dozens of countries. The book divides party nationalization into two dimensions – static and dynamic – to capture different aspects of localism, both with important implications for representation. *Static nationalization* measures the consistency in a party's support across the country and thus shows whether parties are able to encompass local concerns into their platforms. *Dynamic nationalization*, in turn, measures the consistency among the districts in over-time change in electoral results, under the presumption that where districts differ in their electoral responses, local factors must drive politics. Each of the two dimensions, in sum, considers representation from the perspective of the mix of national versus local politics.

Scott Morgenstern is Professor of Political Science and Director of the Center for Latin American Studies at the University of Pittsburgh. He is author of *Patterns of Legislative Politics: Roll Call Voting in Latin America and the United States* (Cambridge University Press, 2004) and the co-editor of *Legislative Politics in Latin America* (Cambridge University Press, 2002), among other publications. His articles have appeared in the *Journal of Politics, Comparative Political Studies, Comparative Politics, Party Politics, Electoral Studies,* and other journals.

Are Politics Local?

The Two Dimensions of Party Nationalization around the World

SCOTT MORGENSTERN

University of Pittsburgh

CAMBRIDGE UNIVERSITY PRESS

CAMBRIDGE
UNIVERSITY PRESS

University Printing House, Cambridge CB2 8BS, United Kingdom

One Liberty Plaza, 20th Floor, New York, NY 10006, USA

477 Williamstown Road, Port Melbourne, VIC 3207, Australia

314-321, 3rd Floor, Plot 3, Splendor Forum, Jasola District Centre, New Delhi - 110025, India

79 Anson Road, #06-04/06, Singapore 079906

Cambridge University Press is part of the University of Cambridge.

It furthers the University's mission by disseminating knowledge in the pursuit of education, learning and research at the highest international levels of excellence.

www.cambridge.org
Information on this title: www.cambridge.org/9781108400343
DOI: 10.1017/9781108227865

© Scott Morgenstern 2017

First published 2017
First paperback edition 2018

A catalogue record for this publication is available from the British Library

ISBN 978-1-108-41513-2 Hardback
ISBN 978-1-108-40034-3 Paperback

Contents

Figures

Tables

Acknowledgments

This book was inspired by my graduate training, particularly by Paul Drake and Gary Cox, who 20 years ago pushed me to add a comparative perspective to literature focusing on the US Congress. A central tenet of the academic and journalistic literature, especially of the "classic period," has been that "all politics is local." But is that true everywhere? Even in the United States, the level of localism has apparently changed. While I was in graduate school, Gary Cox and his co-author Mathew McCubbins produced their opus, *Legislative Leviathan*. Their concern in that book is how locally oriented legislators can organize themselves for collective action, and they find the answer in a collective incentive for electoral outcomes. This current book, like much of my work in the past decade, explores the strength of those electoral ties in a comparative perspective. Among my findings is that the US electoral ties are very weak comparatively, and the book therefore asks about the causes and effects of this variable.

In order to begin my exploration of those ties, Richard Potthoff helped me to write a paper in 2005 that quantified the electoral ties in a comparative perspective. Without this foundation, the current book would not have been possible. Chapter 3 is based on that original paper, and thus while he has not helped directly in the preparation of this manuscript, he deserves much credit in the preparation of that chapter. Chapter 3 also bears the marks of John Polga-Hecimovich and Peter Siavelis, due to work we co-authored about different measurement techniques. Tom Mustillo was also critical to this venture, as he, along with Sarah Mustillo, helped transform my model into a more accessible hierarchical model that runs in Stata. Chapter 6 grew from a paper with Stephen Swindle, and Chapter 7 is tied to a paper with Swindle and Andrea Castagnola; their contributions are also noted in the titles to those chapters. A key section in Chapter 9 was borrowed from a paper co-authored with Ernesto Calvo, to which Jose Manuel Magallanes and Daniel Chasquetti also contributed. I also thank Octavio Amorim-Neto Brian Crisp, Maria Escobar-Lemmon, Mark

Jones, Ekaterina Rashkova, Peter Siavelis, Ethan Scheiner, Kathleen Bawn, Andy Tow, Dawn Brancati, Allen Hicken, John Polga-Hecimovich, and others for supplying much of the data. Yen-Pin Su also deserves much credit for assisting in collecting and organizing data. Other assistants have also helped collect, organize, and analyze the data. These assistants include Ignacio Arana, Ronald Alfaro, Ronald Reha, Dana Bodnar, Ben Morgenstern, Kira Pronin, Christian Gineste, Isabel Ranner, Sofia Vera, Noah Smith, Chelsea Kontra, Emily Riley, Cindy Ling, Ben Wertkin, Christina Keller, Marina Sullivan, Clare Hoffert, Laurel Cooper, and Nathaniel Ropski, amongst others. Some of these graduate students were supported from the University of Pittsburgh's Political Science Department, some were undergraduates funded through the First Experiences in Research, and Pitt's Center for Latin American Studies helped fund the rest. Many people were helpful in setting up interviews during research trips, including Sofia Vera in Peru and Agustin Vallejo in Argentina. My friends and colleagues in Uruguay, Juan Andres Moreas, Daniel Buquet, and Daniel Chasquetti, are always helpful. Special thanks are owed to my colleagues, Barry Ames and Anibal Pérez-Líñan, who have offered friendship, support, and constructive criticism.

PART I

DESCRIBING, MEASURING, AND COMPARING
THE TWO DIMENSIONS

Dimensions of Party Nationalization: Static and Dynamic

US House Speaker Tip O'Neil famously proclaimed that "all politics is local." But politics is more local in some countries than others, and at some times than at others. Why? When, where, and how do local issues influence national elections or legislative politics more generally? How do we define and measure the degree of local influences in a manner that allows analysis across a broad range of countries? These are the questions that motivate this book.

To address these questions, I operationalize "local politics" as the inverse of party nationalization, which I measure across two dimensions, termed *static* and *dynamic*, using analyses of district-level data from legislative elections. A central thesis is that together the two dimensions provide a window into the relative importance to voters of local versus national concerns, and thus explain much about representation, legislative elections, party strategy and organization, and parliamentary politics. To explore this and subordinate theories, the book uses the data to detail the levels of localism across the world, explores sources of the variation, and evaluates the impacts on electoral accountability and collaboration among legislators.

Academic and press accounts of elections frequently, and sometimes explicitly, discuss the inverse relation of "local politics" and the "nationalization" of parties or elections. In the United States, for example, a recent theme has been whether changes to campaign finance laws have heightened the role of national politics in individual districts. Some evidence also points to the increasing partisan "waves" and a decreasing role of local factors in congressional elections. The growing importance of national advertising campaigns is also a part of the debate. The parties themselves apparently think in these terms; the Democratic Party, for example, reportedly discussed the risks involved of using the Tea Party movement to "nationalize" the 2010 midterm elections (Calmes and Shear 2010). Then, in

2016, as the Republicans were worrying about the effect on sub-national electoral contests of their party's leading presidential candidate, Donald Trump, the Washington Post cited a top aide to the Senate Majority Leader as saying: "If there are crosscurrents that are potentially harmful, the most important thing you can do is aggressively localize the race – the things that matter back home, the problems you're solving" (Gold and Kane, 2016).

The terms are also common in popular and academic discussions of elections in other countries. In Argentina, a candidate for governor in the province of Catamarca exclaimed that "luckily and by the grace of God the [gubernatorial] election has not been nationalized" (my translation; Infobae 2011). Two years later, the Argentine president worked in precisely the opposite way, centralizing the candidate selection process to name candidates who supported the "national project" (Poggi 2013). In India, news reports focus on the dominance of local issues in national elections (Sengupta 2009), and the Carnegie Endowment debated whether the 2009 election implied more of a "re-nationalization ... [or] regionalization of Indian politics" (Jaffrelot and Grare 2012). In Japan, Reed, Scheiner, and Thies (2012 p. 364) note that "Koizumi managed to nationalize the election around a single idea (reform) and to convince voters that a vote for the LDP [Liberal Democratic Party] nominee in their district was a vote for reform." Further examples come from other corners of the globe, as highlighted in the following titles: "Electoral Nationalisation, Dealignment and Realignment: Australia and the US, 1900–88" (Leithner 1997); "Elections and Nationalization of the Vote in Post-Communist Russian Politics: A Comparative Perspective" (Ishiyama 2002); and "A 'Nationalization' Process? Federal Politics and State Elections in West Germany" (Pridham 1973).

Analysts, parties, and voters raise these issues because the local–national balance dramatically changes the emphasis in campaigns and the political process. When campaigns are local, sub-national politicians (e.g. legislators or governors) can ignore mandates from their (national) political parties. Budgeting in such a scenario would emphasize district demands rather than national priorities. That production of the B-1 bomber has ties to more than 400 of the 435 US Congressional districts is a clear example of how localism overshadows concerns with efficiency (Summers p. X). On the other hand, where politics are nationalized, funds are likely to be centralized and parties can develop policies and campaigns without concern that politicians tied to a particular area will distort the broader message or block reform efforts. Large restructuring programs and other policies that yield regional shifts in economic advantages – as most do – are thus more feasible when there are low levels of local politics.

Because I am interested in the comparative study of local politics, I require precise definitions and statistically valid measures of local politics. I use a close study of electoral data for these purposes. Such data can reveal at least two particular patterns that indicate when and where politics revolve around local rather than national affairs. First, electoral data can show whether a party is equally popular around the country or wins most support from particular regions. With a bit more coding, the data can also show whether parties have more success in a particular type of constituency, such as in urban areas. Second, they can also show whether (or the degree to which) voters in all localities respond in similar ways to national issues and debates. Where they do not, I will argue, local politics must come into the voters' calculus.

Descriptions for these two-party characteristics have been presented under many names. Some of these names, such as the personal vote or incumbency advantage, have stressed the local aspect. Alternatively, those that have measured and described "national forces" or the "party vote" have emphasized the issue from the opposite angle. The most general term applied to these concepts is "nationalization," but sometimes this term has been incautiously applied to both concepts. In this book I borrow this common word, but add adjectives that grow from the statistical operationalization of the concepts that I describe in Chapter 3. I use "static nationalization" (SN) to imply the degree of homogeneity in a party's vote across a country *at a particular point in time*. "Dynamic nationalization" (DN) captures the consistency in the change in a party's vote in each district *across time*. Throughout the book, then, I am careful to use these adjectives, including them in square brackets when quoting from other authors who omit the qualifying word.

The terms "static" and "dynamic" have statistical bases, and they highlight the independence of the concepts. Not only are these concepts (almost) theoretically independent, the empirical tests I provide in Chapter 4 show very weak empirical relations. For example, while neither the US nor the UK parties are statically nationalized, the change in the vote for most British MPs (i.e. the level of DN) is much more consistent than for US members of Congress.

The US–UK comparison gives a first hint at why considering just one dimension of party nationalization provides a misleading view of political geography, localism, and the nature of politics. When SN but not DN is low, the winds of change affect a party in all corners of a country in a similar manner, regardless of the relative strength of the party in those corners. But where DN is also low, improvements in one region would not foretell a national surge. For the United States, because of the high relevance of incumbency, a legislator's retirement can sometimes cause sharp changes in the vote in a district that are inconsistent with national trends. Some districts will also respond in unique ways due to their particular sociodemographics, economic engines, employment bases, or the quality of their candidates. To provide a second example, both Spain's People's Party (PP) and the Germany's Christian

Democratic Union/Christian Social Union (CDU/CSU) alliance have important variance in their regional support (low SN), but when there is a change in support, the two parties experience that change in sharply different manners, as the different levels of DN attest. As a result, when Spain's Socialists were thrown out of office in 2011 due to the county's financial debacle, the PP was unable to take full advantage because some regions chose alternative parties. By contrast, when Germany's ruling alliance, the CDU/CSU, grew by an average of 6 points in 2013, it reaped benefits in all but 6 of the 243 electoral districts where there had been no boundary changes, and in only 2 of those districts did it lose more than 1 percent. These types of contrasts are sometimes apparent within countries. Spain's Socialists had higher SN and DN than the PP, and thus the 2011 collapse affected the party everywhere. Moving to Latin America, the three major parties in Uruguay have high DN, but regional differences are much sharper for the Broad Front than the Reds, with the National Party (Whites) fitting between the two poles. Clearly, both types of nationalization affect how the parties view politics, and thus both are essential to political analyses.

While the two nationalization concepts are independent, each has been associated with similar causes, effects, and measurements. For example, studies tie institutional variables – such as whether a system employs a presidential or parliamentary system, different aspects of the electoral system, and federalism – to both types of nationalization. Other factors that affect party systems, such as ethnic heterogeneity and parties' roots in society, are also potential explanatory variables for one or both dimensions of nationalization. Chapters 5 and 6 delve into this conundrum of using similar factors to explain independent outcomes.

The book also studies these two phenomena together, because measurements of both derive from electoral data. While other operationalizations are possible, comparative analysis prescribes measuring SN as the distribution of a party's vote across a country, and DN as the change in the district-level vote. Again, while the distribution and its change are independent of one another, because both concepts are measured as derivatives of district-level electoral data, studies of one naturally belong with the other.

Armed with these more precise definitions and a methodology to measure the concepts, the book embarks on a comparative analysis that covers scores of parties in democracies from diverse corners of the world. The descriptive analysis is useful in and of itself, since while there have been multi-country statistical studies of volatility and what I term SN, the dynamic dimension of nationalization – which is perhaps the more novel and intriguing of the concepts – has generally avoided cross-national analysis. The book moves beyond description, however, in several ways. First, the project emphasizes the importance of and means to incorporate geography or nationalization into conceptualizations of parties. Second, the book uses empirical data to corroborate the theoretic claim about the limited relation between the two aspects of nationalization. Third, the data generate criteria from which to classify parties, which, in turn, facilitate tests that can explain the source of variation. Finally, the book considers some of the consequences of the varying levels of both dimensions of nationalization. Together, these analyses provide ways to answer whether (or to what degree) party politics follow national trends rather than local issues, events, and personalities.

WHY STUDY PARTY NATIONALIZATION?

Nationalization is central to the representative process, since it shows the geographic basis of a party's electoral support. As I illustrate later in this chapter, it does so in two ways: a) as the consistency in a party's support across a nation, and b) as the degree to which changes in that support are consistent in different regions. A party is nationalized, then, if support is similar everywhere and when changes in support in one region are reflected across the country. Nationalization is a relevant description of the first dimension, since it indicates the degree to which a nation's different regions are integrated. Strong variance on this dimension, by contrast, would indicate that local factors – perhaps heightened regional identities or economic interests – drive political loyalties. The second dimension also indicates an aspect of nationalization, because when a party's support in all geographic units changes by a similar magnitude, national events must have a similar effect on all parts of a country.[1] The reverse is even clearer: if the changes (swings) are inconsistent across regions, then local factors must play a role in elections.

The geographic basis of a party's support – nationalization – influences party politics and representation by determining a party's orientation toward distribution of public resources, support for region-specific interests, and the degree of unity or perhaps the sense of purpose with which a party addresses these and other policies. When policies affect voters from distinct regions in different ways, then the legislators who represent each region might be uncomfortable teammates. Will, for example, Democrats from the US South collaborate from those in the Northeast, given that gun policy, social issues, and views on trade and welfare have very different electoral consequences in the two regions? How do Canadian Conservatives from Quebec discuss the redistribution of tax resources among provinces with their colleagues from other parts of the country? Or how do Spanish PP legislators elected in Catalonia or the Basque Country view regional autonomy in comparison with those hailing from Madrid? In some cases, the coach (party leader) may have tools or enough influence to keep the team together, but in others it will be difficult for all the players to get behind a common strategy. In political terms, this might mean the difference between coherent policy proposals that the party

[1] Below I reference and discuss Katz (1973a, b), who argues that national events can have dissimilar effects across regions (see section on "Why Study Dynamic Nationalization?").

can actively promote, and fragmented policy proposals with a lack of consensus that yields a bias toward minimal change or stagnation. Roberts (2014) concurs, explaining that internal divisions in a party "render[] the party's programmatic stance incoherent" (p. 55). Those interested in representation can then analyze whether stagnation is Pareto optimal, providing the greatest good without some players being hurt.

In spite of its clear relevance to politics and representation, political geography generally, or nationalization specifically, is mostly absent in theoretical descriptions of parties and party systems. It is not apt here to review in detail all of the conceptions of these institutions, but it is necessary to place nationalization within the context of other traits that define institutions. In this telling, even though the ideas are sometimes only implicit or lacking, I emphasize the role of geography in six classic analytical frameworks. In loose chronological order, these divide parties and party systems based on: class, the number of parties, whether they serve national rather than parochial interests, how they represent ethnic cleavages, organizational structures, and institutionalization. In this discussion I follow many other studies and move between discussions of parties and party systems. This is sometimes problematic, since some systems are composed of different types of parties. In the following section I use this reasoning to emphasize the importance of a focus on parties, but here I focus on the importance of nationalization in conceptualizing parties and the systems to which they belong.

The earliest classifications (e.g. Michels 1915) divided parties according to adjectives such as "oligarchical," "mass," and "catch all," and these terms are still prominent (e.g. Roberts 2014). These studies were concerned with the inauguration of representative democracy, and class was a more prominent concern than regionalism. The degree to which parties institutionalize (Panebianco 1988) or "integrate" potential factions (Duverger 1954) is another way theorists have classified parties, but even these well-known studies spend little time evaluating the size, shape, or influence of parties' regional bases.

The next prominent variable for classifying party systems, with clear implications for representation, is the number of parties. At one end of the scale, single party systems delineate the breach between democracy and autocracy. Among democracies, the number of parties speaks to the issues of representation through its implications for ideological diversity. The landmark studies of Duverger (1954) and Downs (1957) established the idea that two-party systems should tend to produce centrist politics, while more parties would produce a broader range of options (see also Cox 1990). Geography can enter into this discussion in several ways. First, wider ideological representation would facilitate the development of parties with a regional base. The concern, then, is with the relation among regions and their supporters. As Cox (1997) and Chhibber and Kollman (2004) ask, why and when is a single party able to gain support across regions in some countries, while in others separate parties form to represent different regions? This literature, in sum, ties representation to the number of parties, and at least the more recent versions do have an explicit tie to political geography.

Different from those studies concerned with regional representation per se, another strand of literature divides parties or party systems according to whether they serve national or parochial interests. In these studies, parties and party systems divide based on the degree of personalism and clientelism – politics that takes a local focus – on one end of the scale and, on the other, the degree to which parties provide "clarity of responsibility" (Powell 2000) or "programmatic structuration" (Kitschelt et al., 2010). The large body of work on political parties in the United States centers on this debate. It is marked at one extreme by Mayhew's (1974a) work that highlighted legislators' independence from parties and personal ties to their constituencies. While not discounting legislators' interests in pursuing policies and organizational structures that would help them with their geographically bounded constituencies, the work on both US and other world legislatures spawned by Cox and McCubbins (1993) on parties as "cartels" marks a different pole in this debate, since it provides a rationale for parties to build a structure within the legislature that would help them to pursue national as well as parochial goals.

The fourth branch of literature about types of political parties and party systems does have an explicit concern with geography, as it focuses on prescriptions for dealing with ethnic and regional divisions. Lijphart's (1977) "consociational" prescription, for example, calls for empowering ethnic or regional parties and fostering inter-party cooperation that would necessarily cross geographic lines. Horowitz (1985) takes the opposing view, arguing that electoral systems and other rules should encourage coalitions that cross ethnic (which are frequently regional) divisions. Reilly's (2002) call for the alternative vote (in which voters provide preference rankings for their choices) fits into this camp, as well. These issues are of interest, since they explicitly consider regional parties and the ability of parties to gain support in different regions. They provide useful case studies to show how different countries have succeeded or failed due to different arrangements. What they have not done, however, is to provide a general framework to compare, contrast, and measure the role of regional support for parties.

Work on the organizational structure of parties has moved away from a focus on geography. For Panebianco (1988), among the factors that define a party's organizational structure is whether the party was built from national elites "penetrating" different territories, or regional elites banding together ("diffusion"). Geography is evident in this discussion, but the extensive literature on "institutionalization" which builds from organizational theory largely ignores this topic. Mainwaring and Scully's (1995) landmark study, for example, defines institutionalization of parties or systems based on electoral volatility, roots in society, democratic legitimacy, and the stability of party rules and structures, but not (explicitly) geography.[2]

While the literature on party institutionalization largely omits discussions of geography, it does hint at the subject in discussing the importance of parties in organizing groups or, in the word of Filipov et al. (2004), "integration." These authors rationalize federalism from both economic and political perspectives. Within the political dimension, federalism allows representation of minorities, decentralization of conflicts, a means (perhaps a "payment" in exchange for autonomy) to maintain disparate regional groups within the national aegis, and a way to contain or resolve regional conflicts. They argue that parties play a central role in these processes – which can be positive or negative. Parties are motivated, they argue, by electoral systems and geography. Focusing on the latter, they continue that an ideal party in a federal system must integrate national and local elites and structures. Among other criteria for assessing integration, they query whether the party has an organizational structure at the national, local, and regional levels; whether there is a coattails effect between local and national elections; and how well the party's national platform is acceptable to the different regions. In a study of Argentina, Feierherd (2012) adds that "denationalization has weakened party integration" (p. 120; my translation).

Traditional variables have facilitated categorization and advanced our understanding of the parties and party systems that are the basis of representative democracy. But while geography and nationalization are definitional for the representative role of political parties, these traits are only implicit, if not ignored, in most theoretical discussions of party organization. The two dimensions of nationalization capture the geographic aspects of politics, and thus can add nuance to other means for categorizing parties. Studying these concepts, however, requires more precision. What is nationalization? How does it affect political parties and thereby relate to representation? A crucial first step in exploring these questions is justifying the analytical focus on parties rather than party systems.

A Focus on Parties before Party Systems

In the preceding discussion I moved back and forth between discussions of parties and party systems. This analytical laxity is sometimes problematic because, as the extensive study of rational choice and collective action has shown, components of a group do not always represent the group itself. Translating to this book, it is problematic to study party *systems* because there may be significant differences among the *parties* that comprise them.

---

[2] Their study focuses on party systems, but the organizational focus applies to individual parties. See discussion in subsequent section "A Focus on Parties before Party Systems," citing Randall and Svasand (2002), who separate measures of institutionalization for parties and party systems.

A party system, for example, can mix old and new, hierarchical and disaggregated, radical and moderate, big and small. It can also mix parties with a national focus with others whose support is regional. Critics of the institutionalization literature have taken note of this problem, leading Randall and Svasand (2002), for example, to create a model to separately measure institutionalization of parties and that of the party system. In sum, understanding parties, and the politicians that comprise them, therefore, is a necessary precedent for discussing party systems. As a result, this book focuses on nationalization of parties, only discussing party systems as the interaction of the component parties.

In many countries the most prominent parties do follow similar trends, and thus country-level institutional variables are appropriate and statements about the party system are reasonable. Further, and regardless of their differences, the parties, of course, do interact, and thus it would also be incorrect to hermetically separate them. In Chapter 7, therefore, I explicitly discuss the interaction of nationally competitive parties with those that are only prominent in a particular region. But, for the countries where parties vary in terms of nationalization, system-level labels – unless they acknowledge the variance – will be misleading. For example, are systems such as those in Canada, the UK, or Spain nationalized or regionalized, given that some parties in these countries compete only in particular regions while others compete everywhere? Studying trends in these types of systems would necessarily have to focus on the individual parties. Further, understanding the forces that led to this particular form of a system, or the effects that that system has on the political process, would require attention to the individual parties. This idea implies that while hypotheses regarding the causes or effects of system nationalization would have implications for parties, the reverse may not be true. For example, some parties may form due to national movements, while others form, perhaps at different times, as the result of rising regional demands. In short, discussing a nationalized system suggests that all parties are similar, but in many cases this is inappropriate. An analytical focus at the party level, then, increases the precision of the analysis and encourages a discussion of the interaction among parties, while system-level analysis often ignores the intricacies of the components that make up the system.

Focusing at the party rather than the system level has other advantages. First, the statistical approach I develop provides distinct measures for parties. These values quantify the variance in a party's support across time and across space, and I show that some countries house a variety of party types. Because of this variance, in Chapter 3 I argue, with supporting empirical examples, that a weighted average of the party results can yield a party system score, but such summary statistics can be misleading. Several configurations of national and local parties, for example, can yield (weighted) averages that place the "system" near the center of the range.

In sum, an average of parties (even if weighted) would not necessarily provide a good view of the system. Therefore, while there are theoretical and practical interests in the party system, the book explicitly focuses at the party level to avoid improper generalizations.

DEFINING AND DEPICTING THE DIMENSIONS OF PARTY NATIONALIZATION

Since the term first appeared in a 1959 book review of Schattschneider's work, "nationalization" has become a common word in studies of parties and party systems.[3] Its usage, however, has not been consistent. Building on Schattschneider (1960), Stokes (1965, 1967) used the term to discuss the impact of national events on elections, and thus termed an election "nationalized" if the "district effect" (defined in Chapter 3) was small. He also discussed a "national effect," which he measured as the size of the average change in party support, something close to the common notion of volatility.

Part of the definitional conflict is whether "nationalization" should apply to distributions of parties or of voters. Lago and Montero (2013) build on Caramani (2000, 2004) and Bochsler (2010) while considering both possibilities in their discussions. For the first, the level of nationalization is dependent on the extent to which a party competes or has affiliates in all districts. These and other authors measure, in a variety of ways that I detail in Chapter 3, the second aspect based on the degree to which support for the party is homogeneous across the country, which is the most common use of the concept (e.g. Rokkan 1970; Caramani 2000, 2004; Jones and Mainwaring 2003).

Part of the problem in those studies is that using "nationalization" without a modifier to describe the distribution of the vote disallows the possibility that the term has other conceptions. Some studies have followed Stokes's early conceptions, and used more careful terminology to separately describe the distribution of the vote and the consistency in over-time movements. Claggett, Flanigan, and Zingale (1984), for example, discuss "convergence" and "uniform response" as the two aspects of nationalization (see also Kawato 1987). While using separate terminology for the two concepts is a step forward, given that both refer to the local–national balance of a party's support, I prefer to maintain the base term "nationalization." My solution to the dual meanings is to add the adjectives "static" and "dynamic" to signify, respectively, the consistency in regional distributional of a party's support and the consistency in change across geographic units.

---

[3] While the notions of both types of nationalization have been bandied about since at least 1950, the term "party nationalization" has its first JSTOR appearance in 1959, in a review discussing Schattschneider's work (Goldman 1959), though Schattschneider himself first used the term "nationalization of party alignments" in a 1954 book review.

I conjure the term *static nationalization* because it describes the distribution of a party's support at a particular moment in time. In contrast to a party with strengths and weaknesses in particular regions, a statically nationalized party would have similar levels of support throughout a country. While the term "static" is apt for evaluating an event at a particular point in time, it is imperfect, since the distribution of support can change over time. An alternative term might be cross-district nationalization, but I prefer the term "static" to establish the contrast from the second concept, "dynamic."

An election for a party is dynamically nationalized when the change in that party's support across elections is consistent throughout the country. When a party with high DN gains support in one district or defined geographic unit, it would have a similar experience elsewhere. The alternative here, where support goes up in some areas and down in others, would be an election where local factors are important. For this reason, low DN implies a high "local vote."

Low DN would be consistent with at least two broad types of national politics. At one extreme, the districts could all move independently. At the other, there could be subsets of districts, perhaps from a single region or with a particular profile (e.g. urban, ethnic minorities, wealthy), that move together. While each type would produce low DN, the localism would have different impacts on representation and party organization. In the former, legislators would be independent and sui generis factors would drive voting patterns. In the latter, there might be clear factions in the party, organized around the issues that bind subsets of districts. Chapter 9 considers the latter idea, looking at whether legislators from districts that move together are more likely to cooperate in the legislature.

Figure 1.1 follows the technique employed by Mustillo and Mustillo (2012) to demonstrate these two dimensions of party nationalization, using electoral districts as the geographic unit of interest; graphs for other parties and countries are in Appendix 1 and on my personal website (www.polisci.pitt.edu/person/scott-morgenstern).[4] For a single party in each of three countries, the figure depicts the district-level legislative electoral results across several elections. Each line in the graph represents a different district, so each shows the trajectory for one party in that district from one election to the next. For example, the Social Democrats (PPD/PSD) in Portugal had support ranging from about 30 to 65 percent in 1991 across the country's 20 districts, a level of inconsistency that suggests a low or moderate level of SN. At the same time, however, a very similar percentage of voters in each district moves toward or away from the party in each election. The remarkable similarity in the change of support in each district, as indicated by high degree of parallelism among the lines, suggests that the voters who are willing to shift their alliances must be responding to national rather than local stimuli. This is the embodiment of high DN.

---

[4] Mustillo and Mustillo also discuss other dimensions, namely the idea of "fanning in" or "fanning out." I discuss this further in Chapter 3.

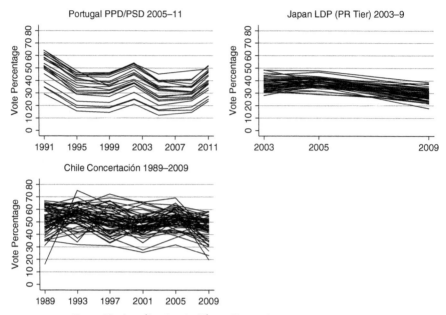

FIGURE 1.1 Party Nationalization in Three Countries

Other parties show very distinctive patterns. The second graph represents the support of Japan's Liberal Democratic Party (LDP) in the proportional representation (PR) tier of the three elections between 2003 and 2009. Japan has a two-tier electoral system, with 180 Diet members chosen through this tier, and the other 300 chosen in single-member districts. Here I focus on the PR tier, though later I show that the other tier produces a distinct pattern. The party's support in the PR tier fits within a narrow range (standard deviation of 4.7) across the 47 prefectures, suggesting a much higher level of SN than for the Portuguese PPD/PSD. The LDP lost about 10 points in the average district between 2005 and 2009, but this hit was felt with similar force in all the provinces. This consistent change, captured through the parallel lines in the figure, reflects high DN.

Finally, the graph for legislative election for Chile's Concertación coalition shows a situation with low levels of both static and dynamic nationalization. The party wins an average of about 50 percent each year, but it is much stronger in some districts than others. SN is therefore low. Note that this party's support is qualitatively different from a party whose low SN is based on having little or no support in some districts but high support in others.[5] Because DN is also low for the Concertación (as indicated by the lack of parallelism among the lines)

[5] The ideal types will become clear in the discussions of Caramani (2000, 2004) and Jones and Mainwaring (2003) that I begin to discuss later in this chapter. As noted, they use the term

there are not particular areas where the party is always strong or weak. A regional party might also have low SN, but there would be consistency in the over-time patterns, as in the graph of Portugal's PPD/PSD. That party is much weaker in the south, and thus the lines on the graph that represent southern Portuguese provinces are consistently below the others. Local politics plays a vital but different role in the two countries. In Portugal it explains why the PPD/PSD has consistently lower support in some regions, but in Chile the sharp changes in the vote both over time and among districts must indicate that localism is both highly relevant and variable. The lack of a nationally coherent pattern that is captured by the low DN could be the result of different districts reacting in dissimilar ways to national campaigns or policies, but the localism could also be the result of changing candidates who are able to focus on different local issues and whose personal qualities also vary.[6]

These pictures highlight the challenges for measurement and theoretical discussions of nationalization. Not only are there two aspects of nationalization (and other components of variance) in the party's support, outliers will bias estimates, and comparisons among differently sized parties can yield misleading results. Chapter 3 delves more deeply into the measurement challenges, and focuses on a particular hierarchical model that simultaneously analyzes the two types of variance evident in the graphs. That model, based on Stokes's original components of variance analysis, provides statistically valid measurements for SN and DN, allowing comparisons cross time and among parties. The next chapter then uses the wealth of empirical data to explore both the theoretical and empirical combinations of the two types of nationalization. Although both aspects of nationalization are measured from electoral data, they are theoretically distinct phenomena and the data confirm that the two dimensions are empirically independent. But what are the implications for democracy when parties score high on one, the other, both, or neither dimension? What factors lead to these different combinations? Those are subjects for this book. To move toward that discussion, the next section explores some questions that the two dimensions of nationalization can help to address.

WHY FOCUS ON TWO DIMENSIONS OF PARTY NATIONALIZATION

Armed with more precise definitions of party nationalization, this section moves beyond a general discussion of the importance of geography to party definitions

---

"nationalization" without qualifiers, and I thus add square brackets to add the necessary adjectives.

[6] For an explanation of the low DN in Chile, see Morgenstern, Polga, and Siavelis (2013). We argue, in general, that the electoral institutions promote personal vote-seeking activities by the candidates, as well as many changing candidacies, including independents.

to consider ways that the two dimensions, separately and perhaps in tandem, affect party organization and representation. The discussion begins with DN, with a focus on questions about the relation between parties and their legislators. Many of these questions stem from studies of the personal vote, but here I develop the idea of the "local vote." The section on SN then discusses the importance of regionalism to parties. Together, the sections explore representation from the perspective of the linkages between a national party and their legislators who represent different regions.

Why Study Dynamic Nationalization?

Beyond contributing to debates about nationalization generally, DN is of particular interest because it provides a direct measure of the degree to which legislators are electorally independent from their parties. This theme has roots in Schattschneider's (1950) concerns about weak parties and local-oriented politics in the United States, and it is also tied to more recent literature on party organization and the personal vote. As head of the American Political Science Association, Schattschneider, along with colleagues argued that US parties should develop more centralized structures, in part because he saw a "shift from sectional to national politics" (American Political Science Association 1950, p. 34). Party structures, meanwhile, lagged behind, because state and local branches had too much sway over candidate choice, committee membership, and the presidential election. In his 1960 opus, Schattschneider continues this discussion, arguing about the importance of uniformity in political opinions across the polity, which he believed would help end regional conflicts and create a national majority. Parties rooted in different regions, he argued, hampered accountability because such a system implies limited competition. To be clear, he does not expect homogeneous opinions of individuals, but nationalization implies that the parties had a relatively even number of supporters in all regions.

The degree to which legislators are independent from their parties has been a major theme in studies of US and comparative politics. Studies of the personal vote, for example, question whether more independent-minded legislators will develop coherent policy proposals, pursue constituency service, or break from their parties. As such, the party–legislator relation also influences voting patterns. If, in an effort to sway voters, legislators can rely on their personal qualities instead of just national partisan politics, then they will have incentives to provide constituency service or push for pork and particularistic politics to serve their districts (Mayhew 1974a; Cain, Ferejohn, and Fiorina 1984, 1987; Carey and Shugart 1995). Mayhew predicted that such legislators would pursue credit-claiming, position-taking, and advertising – means for building their district-level support–perhaps pursuing personal (re-election) goals rather than national or partisan priorities. Legislators' focus on personal over national interests could have negative "implications for party cohesion in the legislature, party support for the executive, and ultimately, the ability to enforce national electoral accountability in the system" (Cain et al. 1984, p. 111). Overall, the level of the personal vote provides a clear contrast between the style and quality political representation in pork-ridden systems such as Italy, Colombia, and Brazil into contrast with more nationally centered party systems such as Britain (Mainwaring 1999; Geddes 1991; Shugart and Carey 1992; Haggard and Kaufman 1995).

The idea behind DN is closely tied to these concerns, but the culprit of weakened partisan responsibility becomes the distinct characteristics and varying interests of different electoral districts rather than the characteristics and qualities of individual candidates. Every party in every country fields a multiplicity of legislative candidates each with distinct personalities, qualifications, and campaigning prowess. In some cases these characteristics influence the voters, but in others party platforms, national events, and the economy determine voters' preferences. The idea of a personal vote is meant to capture the degree to which these differences are manifested in voting. But as Katz (1973a, b) and others have argued, the personal vote literature has ignored the possibility that national level shocks have variable effects across localities. For example, a national policy to reduce farm subsidies would not affect Democrats in New York with the same force as it would in Kansas. The differential movement in the vote in these two states, then, should not be solely attributable to the personal qualities of the candidates, but also to the ethnic, social, and economic makeup of the district. As a result, Swindle and I (2005) argued that while the "personal vote" was a poor moniker for the concept that Stokes had tried to measure, it was useful to measure and study the combined impact of local and/or candidate factors on the vote. We thus apply the term "local vote" to capture the idea that voters are impacted by both candidate qualities and district characteristics. The concept of the local vote, in sum, is meant to make explicit the idea that variance in a party's district-level votes can result from candidate qualities, district characteristics, or both.

There is one other important distinction between the local and personal vote: the focus on parties in the former and individuals in the latter. Since its focus is on individuals, students of the personal vote have studied systems where parties put forth a single candidate (e.g. the United States) or voters are able to choose amongst a party's multiple candidates (e.g. Colombia, Brazil, pre-1993 Japan, or Uruguay). This focus, however, leaves aside the large group of countries where voters choose among party lists. This is an important oversight since these lists have differentiable personalities that may have strong effects on voting patterns. The local vote, then, focuses on a party's total vote in a given district, whether that vote is targeted toward an individual candidate, applied to a party list, or distributed among multiple party candidates.[7]

---

[7] A focus on parties means that the local vote is most closely related to the personal vote for countries that use either single-member districts (e.g. Britain) or closed-list PR (as in most of Europe), since there is no differentiation between a candidate's and a party's votes. In systems that

In sum, where the local vote is strong – that is, where candidate qualities or district characteristics matter for voter choices – the candidates' campaign styles, popularity, and/or the variability in the local socioeconomic structure will affect how voters feel or interpret the impact of national policies and other stimuli. For example, national decisions that address issues such as agriculture, gun regulation, trade patterns, abortion rights, or civil rights might be advantageous to a party in one district and deleterious (or less advantageous) in others. This should be true even when first accounting for a party's underlying support levels in the different districts.[8] Furthermore, where there is a significant local vote, more able candidates (as individuals or as a team) will have greater success in spinning the issues to the party's advantage or attracting the undecided voter.

Of course, the standing of the party nationally and the swings in national mood are also important to legislators, as is well described by Cox and McCubbins (1993). They argue that US legislators win by a combination of personal and party reputation. This helps explain why, in addition to pursuing the personal vote, legislators also delegate significant powers to their party leaders to shore up the party's reputation.

Testing these types of theories requires operationalization of the personal or local vote. The statistical analysis of DN resolves this concern by providing a direct measure of behavior that is comparable across countries and time periods. The main alternative, proxying the personal vote by coding electoral systems, is problematic because the measures are only indirect. Studies in this vein frequently use a coding based on Carey and Shugart's (1995) model that is carefully titled "*Incentives to cultivate* the personal vote" (my italics).[9] Among the many examples that work along these lines are two well-known studies of corruption (Kunicová and Rose-Ackerman 2005; Persson, Tabellini, and Trebbi 2003), those that focus on trade policy (Nielson 2003), and another that focuses on budget discipline (Hallerberg and Marier 2004). Focusing on East Europe, Bagashka (2012) finds that the electoral systems that promote the personal vote harm economic reform. My early work argued that personal vote electoral incentives would harm parties' voting discipline, because legislators would owe less loyalty to their party leaders (Morgenstern 2001; 2004). Incentives, however, are not the same as behavior. Legislators in most parliamentary systems, for example, are much more loyal to their parties than are those in presidential systems. Electoral incentives, this implies, must contend with other variables in explaining legislators' behavior. As Vázquez-D'Elía and

---

allow intra-party competition (e.g. Brazil, Chile, Ireland, pre-1994 Japan, etc.) there is a clearer distinction between the personal vote and the local vote.

[8] The statistical model I discuss in Chapter 2 also accounts for (or holds constant) the underlying support.

[9] Others have updated or expanded this study. See, for example, Electoral Systems and the Personal Vote Data Set (Johnson and Wallack 2012).

I (2007) explain, similar to the outside walls of a house leaving much room for variance in the interior design, electoral systems constrain but do not determine behavior. To test these theories, therefore, requires a means for operationalizing the strength of the ties among a party's legislators. DN resolves this issue by quantifying the degree to which legislators are electorally tied. In sum, the measure of DN, which is more fully developed in Chapter 3, allows tests of hypotheses about the local vote based on a direct measure of voter behavior rather than an indirect measure of incentive structures.

This measure of DN, further, is comparable across time and space. Coding electoral systems meets this criterion, but as noted it fails as a direct measure of behavior. Some studies of the personal vote have found proxies that are useful for a particular country or a particular time. Brady et al. (2000) measure the concept by using midterm elections to evaluate the difference between presidential and legislative voting. Taking a different tack, Crisp et al. (2013) study targeted government spending by looking at the similarity of districts – a measure perhaps related to the local vote – which they measure with surveys. More heterogeneity among the districts, they find, increases targeted spending. Finally, Cox and Mccubbins (1993) use the consistency of legislators' vote swings in their study, an idea closely related to the DN. The important caveat is that it is a one-dimensional measurement. As I show in Chapter 3, measuring one aspect of nationalization at a time introduces bias into the estimates.

Why Study Static Nationalization?

The study of SN focuses attention on fundamental questions about politics and representation, such as state building and the integration of a country's regions, distribution of government resources, and separatist movements. Historical studies of Europe (e.g. Weber 1976; Rokkan 1970; Caramani 2004) considered how European feudal or estate-based empires, many constituting multiple ethnic groups, developed modern parliamentary systems with regionally based representation.[10] For example, as Caramani documents, countries across Europe nationalized (in a static sense) during the 1900s, which he claims was concomitant with the shift away from regional and toward ideological divides. While his statistical models focus on what I term SN, the implications that he draws for parties' and legislators' behavior are related to DN and the personal or local vote. Specifically, he argues that as [static] nationalization increases, "local candidates ... lose their character of representing the local community. Rather they become the representatives of

---

[10] Weber's study, for example, focuses on how schools helped to integrate rural populations. He notes that discussions about the time period that he discusses (1870–1914) revolve around "civilizing" different populations (p. 5). He then goes on to discuss the move from politics that were "local and personal" toward a "concern with issues on a national and international plane" (p. 241).

the national centre of the political organization" (p. 68). This, he continues, leads the voters to shift their attention from local to national issues.

These concerns are also pertinent to US politics. Schattschneider (1960) was concerned that if parties separated on regional issues, they would fail to develop nationally oriented electorates and thus be unable to generate support for – or be accountable for – resolving national issues. Similarly, Sundquist (1973) discusses "convergence" of the party system across states, away from one-party dominant districts and regions. As a final example, Key's (1959) discussion of "secular realignments" of the vote was based on an analysis of the growing divide of the partisan vote between rural and urban districts. Interestingly, his finding of a greater salience of geography to the vote in the United States contrasts with Caramani's (2000) study of Europe, which shows a convergence in the vote among rural and urban regions.

The opposite of convergence implies pressures for separatism, and this justifies other interest in SN-like concepts (e.g. Rose and Urwin 1975). Almost by definition, parties supporting regional autonomy or irredentist movements will have regionally concentrated voters. The reverse is not necessarily true, but it would be surprising to find non-nationalized parties opposing greater regional power or autonomy. Part of the concern with regional parties is that they have little electoral incentive to serve the interests of the country as a whole. Presumably, nationalized parties, by contrast, have an incentive to serve all regions in order to build their electoral support. This suggests that encouraging parties to build national support is a way to unify the nation and reduce pressures for separatism.

Jones and Mainwaring (2003) provide additional hypotheses about the implications of [static] nationalization.[11] Most importantly, as a consequence of its effects on policy and the political process, they argue that [static] nationalization has favorable implications for the survival of democracy. This is based on several ideas. First, high [static] nationalization is indicative of strong party alignments and supportive linkages between voters and parties. Second, [statically] nationalized parties should be more unified and thus affect many aspects of legislative politics. And finally, the degree of [static] nationalization should affect public policy in terms of how parties target public funds.

Finally, SN and similar concepts are tied to specific policy or economic outcomes. For example, Lago-Peñas and Lago-Peñas (2008) find that less [statically] nationalized party systems (i.e. ones that maintain important regional parties) are bound by more rigid budgeting negotiations, thus affecting the magnitude of government transfers. Castañeda-Angarita (2013) focuses on the interplay among business groups and the local and national

---

[11] As I note in Chapter 3, their most important contribution was methodological (suggesting the Gini coefficient as a measure of the consistency in the distribution of a party's national support), but the hypotheses are also an important contribution.

governments. He finds that low levels of [static] nationalization hamper inter-governmental cooperation, thus hindering attempts at budgetary reform. Crisp et al. (2013), who I cited earlier when discussing DN, also use the distribution of the vote (aka SN) to study how governments target spending. They associate higher levels of [static] nationalization of the governing coalition with reduced targeted spending. As a final example, Hicken, Kollman, and Simmons (2016) look at health policy, and, using a broad large-n design, argue that a lack of party system nationalization "hinders states' convergence towards international health standards" (p. 573).

In sum, SN is tied to many central political questions. While some of these issues are also pertinent to DN, distinct processes are at work with different implications for the representative and political process. But as with DN, valid testing of these issues requires careful operationalization of the variables. As I empirically demonstrate in Chapter 4, the concepts do not co-vary, and thus tests should not conflate them.[12] A high level of SN, for example, will not have the same impact on democracy or regime stability in all cases, because the level of DN would be an undefined (or left-out) variable. As an example, both dimensions are necessary to show the importance of economics to an election in a particular district. The static dimension may imply differences in terms of relative importance of the poverty, class, ethnicity, and nationalism in the vote, while the dynamic dimension shows the relative weight of changing economic conditions to the vote and whether all districts react to the change in a similar way.

Data Issues

In order to fully interpret the two dimensions of nationalization, this book pays special attention to comparative methodology, data usage, and measurement techniques. To allow the broadest possible range of cases, the book focuses mostly, but not exclusively, on legislative elections. This allows comparisons across parliamentary and presidential systems. At times it is appropriate to consider the nationalization of parties as evidenced through the support for presidential candidates, but since all democratic systems have legislative elections, most of the book focuses on elections at that level. While I therefore provide some statistics for nationalization based on presidential elections, and I also consider the impact of presidentialism on party nationalization, generally the book refers to nationalization of parties in legislative elections.

The book focuses on electoral districts as the unit of analysis, because this is the level at which parties and legislators compete for seats and votes. It would be feasible and perhaps interesting to test and compare results at higher or

---

[12] One study that does consider both dimensions is Crisp et al. (2013).

lower level geographical units (e.g. states or polling places), but these are less relevant if the goal is to understand the representation which is based on electoral consistencies. For those elected, the district formally defines their representative responsibilities and the results at that level determine their fate. Parties, meanwhile, must aggregate the legislators who represent these distinct electoral constituencies. In sum, district-level electoral results drive legislators' fates and thus must condition their policy preferences and relationship with others in their party.

In a multi-year effort to apply tests to as broad a geographic base as possible, the empirical database constructed for this book (which is available at my website, cited earlier) covers about 200 parties in more than 40 countries from Europe, Asia, the Pacific Basin, Africa, and the Americas.[13] Appendix 1 and the website also include graphical representation of party nationalization for most included parties (similar to Figure 1.1). As will be explained in Chapter 3, not all of these data were usable for multivariate comparisons, but the resulting comparative database is still large. I began building the dataset with Caramani's publicly available dataset, and augmented that dataset with information on the single-member districts for Germany and France. During the course of my work, two other datasets became available: The Constituency-Level Electoral Archive (CLEA) and the Global Election Database (formerly Constituency-Level Elections Dataset). I have complemented these datasets with information I collected for Latin America, the United States, Canada,[14] Japan, and Australia and other countries, often relying on experts (such as Mark Jones and Andy Tow for Argentina, and Ethan Scheiner for Japan) to fill in holes or interpret party names and coalitions.[15] Within these broad guidelines, I only required that the party competition and district boundaries were consistent enough to allow cross-temporal and cross-district tests. This requirement eliminated, for example, New Zealand, where district boundaries have changed very frequently.

As detailed in Chapter 4, using the district-level data requires several other decisions. First, in many cases two or more parties join together in electoral coalitions. In some cases, such as the CDU/CSU alliance in Germany, the alliance is durable and joining the parties over time is not problematic. In other cases, however, parties join temporarily, and the analysis is less

---

[13] That count includes multiple observations for a few parties, such as across different time periods or for different electoral tiers.

[14] The Canadian data have two sources: the Canadian parliamentary website (www.parl.gc.ca) and the official reports of the Chief Electoral Officer of Canada. Data for Australia are available from that country's electoral commission (www.aec.gov.au). Ethan Scheiner provided the data for Japan.

[15] Thanks are owed to Octavio Amorim-Neto Brian Crisp, Maria Escobar-Lemmon, Mark Jones, Peter Siavelis, and Andy Tow for supplying parts of the Latin American data.

straightforward. Since the analysis would be distorted by changing alliance membership, in some cases the tests are conducted under the assumption that the alliance was in place for the whole period under analysis. Details of these types of decisions and other data issues are also explained in the on-line appendices.

The issue of uncontested races, especially in countries that employ single-member districts, creates another analytic problem.[16] Stokes and others simply ran their analyses on races where the two major parties won at least a minimal amount of the vote in all years. Eliminating uncontested races, however, underestimates the district heterogeneity, if not the other effects as well. While non-competition can signal a lack of geographic coverage for a party, it does not necessarily imply that the party could not win some support in that district. In single-member districts, for example, the party may concentrate its resources on winnable districts and forego others. How should the measure of nationalization account for this issue? My approach has been to consider and compare results with and without "zero districts."

Case selection was critical to the analysis, and is not without problems. My general rule was to collect data on all available countries that had at least five million people and were continuously democratic (based on Freedom House scores) during the entire period under investigation. I did make exceptions to the population rule for Uruguay and several countries in Central America. Second, with the exception of some of the regional parties of particular interest, inclusion required that parties competed in enough districts such that their overall share of the vote was above 10 percent. They also could not be so volatile as to have lost all their support in any year.[17] These case selection rules do bias the results toward stability, but the rise or fall of parties not included in the analysis will be reflected in the statistics for the included parties. What the statistics will reflect is how the changing availability of votes that results from the birth or death of a party is captured by the other parties. Further, the methodology I apply accounts for volatility (see Chapter 3) and the two dimensions of nationalization account for regional parties by measuring the degree to which support levels and change are consistent across districts.

There are several other methodological concerns. The first of these is how to obtain reliable estimates of one type of nationalization while also estimating the other. Many analyses use district-level electoral data to study one or the other aspect of nationalization, but that data is "contaminated" by

---

[16] Empirically this is not much of an issue for countries that employ proportional representation.

[17] As noted, in some cases it was necessary to conduct the analysis on alliances rather than parties. If the alliance was short-lived, we ran the model as if the two (or more) parties were in alliance for our complete time series. For some countries (such as Ireland), however, the frequent changing of parties and/or districts was too great to overcome. Details by country are in Appendix 3.

different types of variance. The solution I develop for solving this problem (though it too is imperfect) is to use a cross-sectional time series model (built from an analysis of variance) to account for the different sources of variance simultaneously.

Second, measures must consider how to handle districts of different sizes or populations. There are reasonable arguments for weighting and equally strong reasons for ignoring this issue. In this book I generally work with unweighted results, but I discuss the issue in Chapter 3.

Other issues are also important to the concepts of nationalization, but challenging to measurement. While there are techniques to evaluate the degree to which parties' support is concentrated spatially (e.g. Moran's I), most tests considering party nationalization opt for measures that do not consider the consistency in vote distribution. I have shown a few maps to highlight these issues, but continue with the regular practices. Next, when parties join electoral alliances, should we use the alliance support in the analysis, or drop the party from the analysis? These cases I have decided based on reading contextual analyses and discussing the cases with country experts. Where I analyze coalitions, the data notes clarify the choices. A final problem is that when countries modify their districts' boundaries, it is not possible to evaluate the consistency in over-time changes.

No one data selection mechanism or procedure can resolve all of these issues, and thus my inclination is to be as transparent as possible about limitations and potential biases. In Chapter 3 I highlight the virtues of a hierarchical model to measure the two nationalization dimensions, which include a) production of independent estimates of the two dimensions, b) clarity of interpretation of the statistics, and c) ease of use of a statistical model. While virtuous, I also show that the model can produce non-intuitive results under certain conditions. Overall, then, I argue for a multi-technique approach.

Previewing the Findings

This book has methodological, theoretical, and empirical/descriptive pretensions. Here I foreshadow the main hypotheses and conclusions the subsequent chapters develop in detail.

Description of National/Local Politics around the World

All politics are not local. In Chapter 2 I use the inverse of both dimensions of dynamic party nationalization to measure the degree of localism, and then use the measurements to categorize parties into four boxes: *locally focused, nationalized, unbalanced*, and *in-flux*. The first of these requires high party nationalization on both dimensions and the second the lack thereof. Unbalanced parties are high on the dynamic dimension, but score low in terms of SN. In-flux parties, finally, should be rare, because they imply high SN but not DN.

The data confirm wide variance of party nationalization around the world, among, and within countries. A regional focus underscores some trends but many exceptions. First, while there is a preponderance of nationalized parties, on both dimensions, in Western Europe (e.g. those in the Czech Republic, Germany, Finland, and Portugal), there are many other types of parties there, too. A number of that region's parties, for example, are nationalized on the dynamic but not the static dimension. This would include Labour and the Conservatives in the United Kingdom, the French Socialists, Spain's People's Party, the Finnish Centre Party, as well as parties in Belgium and Portugal. In most of these countries regional divisions and local parties hamper static nationalization, but interestingly DN stays at a relatively high level. These divisions often affect the parties that compete nationally in different ways. For this reason while the Spanish Socialists and the People's Party are both dynamically nationalized, the Socialists maintain a higher (but not high) level of SN. Finally, the Swiss FDP and SVP fall into the localized category, while the scores for some other Western European parties, such as those in France, land between the clearly identified labels.

For Eastern Europe, the Polish parties are close to the unbalanced category, the Greater Romania party is nationalized, and data for Hungarian Civic Alliance fits that description, too.

In Asia, my data covers India, Japan, and Taiwan; it excludes Korean parties due to problems with changing district names. Parties in all but Taiwan are localized, but the proportional representation tier in Japanese elections produces nationalized parties. For Taiwan, the parties have middling levels of both types of nationalization.

Across the Americas, there is more variance. Parties in the United States are not as nationalized on either dimension as a typical Western European party, but DN is moderately high, and much higher than it was in previous decades. Analysis of the USA (and some other countries) requires special attention, since at times the parties do not compete in all districts. If the analysis includes all districts, then there has been some strengthening in the SN since the 1950s, because there are fewer "zero" districts. At the same time, DN was much stronger in the 1950s. When excluding districts where only one party competes, SN looks worse over time, as does DN. This would indicate that even where the parties both compete (a figure that has gone up), then there is a greater separation of support than in times gone by.

In Canada, I formally code the Conservatives and Liberals in the ambiguous zone, but they are close to the unbalanced category. Even excluding Quebec, the parties have highly disparate levels of support in different districts, but change is felt in a surprisingly consistent manner. Support for the NDP is less diverse, but change in fortunes is also less consistent. That party therefore earns a locally focused label.

In Latin America, at least one party in Argentina, Bolivia, and Mexico has a local focus, and none in those countries is nationalized or unbalanced. There are, however, nationalized parties in Costa Rica, El Salvador, Honduras, and Uruguay. Other parties (and coalitions), including several in Chile, Brazil, and Peru, fall into ambiguous categories.

Methodology and Operationalization
The book uses the two dimensions of party nationalization to empirically identify the degree to which local factors drive elections (Chapter 4). Previous studies provide indirect proxies based only on the incentives for local behavior, or they lack a method for cross-country comparisons. Party nationalization, by contrast, is a direct measure of the degree to which elections across the country follow national trends or, by contrast, the qualities of legislative candidates and district characteristics are determinative.

Based on this idea, Chapter 3 develops a procedure for measuring static and dynamic nationalization simultaneously, based on district-level electoral data. Measuring the two dimensions together avoids statistical and theoretical bias.

Combining nationalization scores for parties into a system-level score generates another source of bias. Weighting systems can lessen the concerns, but they introduce other problems. Further, many countries include widely disparate party types, and thus a (weighted) average of these parties tells little about how the party system works. The book, therefore, emphasizes the nationalization of parties, not of party systems.

Theory
The book has three theoretical goals, and tests multiple hypotheses. The overarching emphasis is that party nationalization has two dimensions, each of which provides a distinct view of the role of localism in elections. The static dimension shows whether parties' electoral bases are widespread, and the dynamic dimension shows whether the national political/economic debate and environment plus the party's campaigns and policy proposals have differential impacts in the various regions. Moreover, the two dimensions are independent (except that when the dynamic dimensions is low, the static dimension is likely to be low too).

Second, since there are two independent types of party nationalization (qua localism), there are also two sets of factors that explain them (Chapters 5 and 6). A key distinction that I identify is that parliamentary systems increase DN while the number of electoral districts has an inverse relation with SN. Federalism and ethnic heterogeneity (taking into account the degree to which groups are geographically segregated) are also important explanatory variables. My tests for explaining intra-country variance – which consider party (rather than democracy) age, ideological extremism, and governing experience – are less successful.

Third, the degree of localism in elections influences all aspects of politics, as documented in Chapters 7–9. Where localism is more important, candidates may de-emphasize their parties' (national) campaign issues in favor of district-level concerns. At an extreme, this issue speaks to whether parties will support regional autonomy or separatist movements. As another example, localism influences whether co-partisan legislators have incentives to compete or collaborate. As others have explained, it also influences the parties' leadership structures. Finally, even if voters everywhere blame incumbents for problematic performance, localism speaks to whether voters will coordinate on an alternative – or whether no party will be able to gain advantages because each locality will favor a different alternative.

Roadmap

This book is driven by questions regarding the cause and effect of the two dimensions of nationalization, which, in turn, are indicators of the degree to which politics focus on local or national issues. The concerns are motivated by former US House Speaker Tip O'Neil's contention that "All Politics is Local." As O'Neil explains in his book by the same name (1994), local and national politics interact. He explains, in particular, that once a legislator earns respect for his or her stand and support for local issues, then they can become "'national' Congressman and vote for things that are good for the country but may not have a direct impact on [their] district (p. xvi)." The anecdotes that he provides about US politics yield interesting questions for a comparative study. Why are politics more local in some places than others? What are the effects of differing degrees of localism? The concept of party nationalization allows me to quantify the degree of localism in elections, and study the issue from a cross-national comparative perspective.

Beyond the introduction and conclusion, the book has three sections that a) describe, measure, and compare two nationalization dimensions; b) explain party nationalization; and c) use nationalization as an explanatory variable. To begin exploring the empirical data and theoretical questions, Chapter 2 develops the aforementioned typology of party types, based on the degree to which a party is statically and dynamically nationalized. The particular goal is to further develop the behavioral and organizational expectations for different types of parties. The next stage is to empirically classify parties from around the world. Chapter 3 deals with the methodological issues, explaining in detail the statistical model that I then employ to measure the two types of nationalization. The ensuing Chapter 4 then provides initial results from the analysis and uses those results in comparison with results generated by traditional methods in order to explain how extant methods are biased or misleading. It also fills in the classification of parties and party systems based on the two dimensions, and supports the contention that the dimensions are relatively independent aspects of electoral competition.

The next two chapters focus on explaining nationalization. Chapter 5 first develops a theoretical model, focusing primarily on electoral systems, executive system, decentralization, and ethnic fractionalization as explanatory variables. Building on my earlier analysis (Morgenstern, Swindle, and Castagnola 2009), a primary emphasis is that since the two dimensions of nationalization are independent, the factors that drive them must be distinct. I thus emphasize the effect of electoral systems on the static dimension and the executive system on the dynamic dimension. Different from the earlier work, the chapter introduces a new electoral system variable, the number of electoral districts, as a prime driver of static nationalization. Chapter 6 uses a multivariate model to find support for the hypotheses.

The third part of the book has three chapters that consider the impacts of party nationalization. Chapter 7 focuses on the role of regionalism in party nationalization while exploring the theoretical issues of accountability and the responsible party model. There is a clear tension between identity or regional voting and the responsible party model, and the chapter uses the concepts of nationalization to explore these themes. It argues that the responsible party model requires at least moderate levels of SN and DN, since low levels would imply that some regions are responding differently to national stimuli. The chapter also provides a typology of regional parties and a method for modeling and statistically testing the importance of states or regions.

The later chapters explicitly use party nationalization as an independent variable. The eighth chapter reviews work that discusses how the dimensions relate to legislative behavior and voter beliefs. It then uses the cases of Spain, Argentina, Bolivia, and Canada to analyze retrospective voting within the context of low levels of nationalization. How does accountability work if a party's policy stance will lead to increased support in some areas and a decrease in others? In part, I find that there is more consistency among voters in holding incumbent parties responsible (retrospective voting) than there is in coordinating on alternatives (prospective voting). Chapter 9 looks at a different impact of party nationalization, returning to the query about legislative behavior that spawned this study. Cox and McCubbins (1993) argued that the electoral tie among co-partisan US legislators was sufficient to encourage collective action. In a comparative context, however, this book shows that the US legislators have weak ties (low party nationalization). The chapter thus questions whether the weak tie is sufficient to drive intra-party collaboration. Using roll call and NOMINATE data for the United States, and then co-sponsorship data on the United States and three Latin American countries, I show that legislators are prone to co-sponsor bills with co-partisans who have similar electoral concerns; the legislators' personal electoral fates do not have much effect on roll call voting or NOMINATE scores. The first tests therefore tear at the logic in Cox and McCubbins by showing that legislators do not seem to be driven by the commonalities in their electoral fates. The second test challenges their findings in the opposite way, showing that personal concerns sometimes override partisanship in legislative decisions. Chapter 10, finally, concludes by summarizing the main arguments by emphasizing seven key findings and lessons for the study of party nationalization.

2

A Typology of Party Nationalization

Chapter 1 set forth the prime theme of this book: that party nationalization is two-dimensional concept and that each dimension, separately and together, provides a vantage point from which to evaluate the geographic basis of politics. The discussion is predicated on the idea that static and dynamic nationalization address fundamentally different party characteristics which are theoretically independent from one another. Empirically this will mean that knowing the level of nationalization for one dimension will not foretell the level of the other. Based on that construct, this chapter develops a typology based on those dimensions and provides examples of parties that fit the description. Later chapters then move from theory to empirics, developing the tools to measure the two dimensions and hence placing the parties into typology.

While this chapter focuses on static and dynamic nationalization to create a typology, I recognize that other party characteristics would add additional categories. Particularly relevant might be volatility, since estimates for it emerge from the same statistical model. Further, the degree of volatility should not be related to either SN or DN. The rise of a populist leader, for example, would yield high levels of volatility for the new party vehicle, as well as those parties from which the new leader stole support. The new party, however, could win relatively constant support across districts (yielding a high SN), or its support could be regionally concentrated (yielding a low SN). At least one existing party would also suffer greater volatility from the new entrant, but the support drop of the existing party could also be experienced relatively evenly across all districts (as in a party split) or it could be concentrated in a particular region. There is a relation of volatility, SN, and DN only in the sense that the DN captures the degree to which the change associated with the volatility is experienced at a local or national level. If a new party entrant (i.e. high volatility) increases the dispersion of parties' support across districts, then

TABLE 2.1 *A Typology of Party Types*

		Dynamic Nationalization	
		High	Low
Static Nationalization	High	Nationalized	Unstable
	Low	Unbalanced	Locally Focused

the DN must be low for the affected parties. If, however, the dispersion remains low in spite of parties average support rising and falling, then the DN would be high.

In spite of the value of enriching a typology by adding other variables, the chapter focuses on the two dimensions of nationalization in order to show that the dimensions are (mostly) independent and that the types provide useful categories for distinguishing parties. The chapter thus begins by discussing the typology based on crossing the two types of nationalization. It then discusses behavioral and organizational expectations for the party types from a theoretical perspective. It finishes by discussing empirical examples and providing some initial discussion about the party and system-level factors that might explain why parties fall into the different categories.

The Independence among Dimensions and a Typology of Nationalization

Breaking the two dimensions of party nationalization into high and low categories generates a simple 2×2 typology. Table 2.1 identifies the possible combinations and labels the different combinations of SN and DN as: *Nationalized, Locally Focused, Unbalanced,* and *Unstable.*

These ideal types imply distinctive organizational forms and behaviors of parties, all of which have direct implications for the patterns of legislative politics. In what follows I explore some of these patterns for specific parties and countries, but first provide a general discussion of those party types. These ideal-type descriptions, of course, do not attempt to account for variations within the quadrants. This is an important caveat, because parties that lie close to one or the other axis (as our empirical analysis shows that many do) may not be well described by the ideal type. The ideal types should be more reflective of actual behavior for parties that are closer to the extremes of the categories.

First, an ideal-typical *nationalized* party has homogeneous support across the nation with faceless legislative campaigners who refrain from local politicking. The expectation is that these parties will attract similar voters (middle class, minority, workers, etc.) in the various districts based on campaigns that are organized at the national level. Because changes in a *nationalized* party's support are consistent across districts, legislators (or candidates) will not differentiate themselves or call attention to local issues during campaigns. Legislative candidates in such systems, then, should be relatively unknown, and voters will focus their attention on executive candidates and party platforms rather than legislators.

As noted earlier, critics referring to what I term SN have suggested that homogeneous support could also emerge through using region- or district-specific strategies, which would require relatively personalistic and autonomous candidates, to capture a similar percentage of heterogeneously distributed voters each year so well. For the two-dimensional concept, the emergence of a *nationalized* party in the context of district heterogeneity would also require that national politics and policy have a homogeneous impact on the party's support in all districts. This complex combination of heterogeneous districts, independent candidates, and consistent patterns of voter reactions seems unlikely.

While it seems unlikely that a party could be so well coordinated as to generate similar levels of support and change by following different strategies in different districts, the fact that there are such parties (as I will demonstrate in the next chapter) requires reflection on the source of the consistent electoral patterns and behavioral implications for the parties. Perhaps these parties operate in countries with homogenous populations. Another possibility is that the groups that support the party in question – which could be based on ethnicity, class, religion, demographic, or other societal divisions – are of a similar size across the country, even if the country overall is not homogenous. In this case, some of the country's parties might be more *nationalized* than others.

Schattschneider proposed reforms to help *nationalize* parties because he lamented the manner in which local politicking distorted national policy goals. The other extreme, however, is a lack of local input into the political process. A testable hypothesis, then, is whether voters in nationalized systems feel more distant from their policy makers. Are legislators as involved with their constituents as in systems that privilege more localism? Finally, is there less pork in budgets when there is less of an incentive to target funds of questionable national value to particular constituencies?

The SN aspect of the *locally focused* category requires that this type of party have stronger support in some districts than others. Three types of scenarios will yield to low SN, and each has different implications for behavior: 1) a party could compete across a country but with varying degrees of success; 2) a party could compete in many but not all districts or regions throughout the country; and 3) a party could compete in a limited number of districts that are regionally concentrated. Under any of these scenarios the DN could also be low, thus justifying the *locally focused* category.

Concerns about the third subtype, parties whose support is regionally concentrated, are the most straightforward. These parties will have incentives to compete based on identities rather than national policies. If concentrated groups respond differently to national policies because their voting decisions are heavily weighted by the parties' or candidates' ascriptive characteristics (ethnicity, geography, etc.) then the accountability for political outcomes – the basis of democratic governance – fades. This is a theme of Chapter 7.

For the other two subtypes of *locally focused* parties, organizational structure and policy priorities are a function of whether the source of the local focus is variance in candidate qualities or of district characteristics. The low DN requires that the districts react to the national events differently. This could logically obtain if voters in different areas feel differently about policies that affect the whole country (e.g. gun control) or issues affecting the country as a whole (e.g. changing international environments) (Katz 1973a, b). This would be most likely if different groups, perhaps based on ethnicity, religion, or urbanism, are unequally distributed among districts. Locally focused parties can thus form even if the qualities of the individual legislative candidates are immaterial to an election. The idea that districts – that is, voters – may respond differently to similar stimuli suggests locally focused parties could be based on differences in district characteristics, perhaps based on voters' employment opportunities or ethnicity.

Even if a party's local focus is based on differences among districts, it is possible that there are links among some districts. Districts in a particular region might have similar types of voters, or a *locally focused* party could consistently do particularly well or poorly in a type of district that is not geographically concentrated (e.g. rural or urban). Each set of districts would be linked, even though the two sets are not.

If the local focus comes about due to variable district characteristics, but there are still consistent patterns of voting among some subsets of districts, then societal groups must be concentrated and coterminous with district lines. Further, because these are *locally focused* parties, the different subsets of districts must react distinctly to similar policies. This scenario would be consistent with a hierarchical but perhaps factionalized party structure. Assuming that they are able to act in a coordinated fashion, these types of *locally focused* parties face complicated decisions over strategies. If they have access to resources, such *locally focused* parties can choose to shower favors on districts where their support has been particularly strong, target the most competitive districts, or try to build inroads where the party has been weak. These strategy decisions would be particularly relevant in countries that use proportional representation, since a bit more support could yield additional legislative seats. The problem is that targeting policies or resources to one set of districts would reinforce rather than diminish geographic divisions.

The interest in supporting a particular region should vary with that region's political weight. For example, parties in Spain lose less by ignoring the Basque Country than do Canadian parties with respect to Quebec, because the Basque County has less than 10 percent of its country's legislative seats while the comparable number for Quebec is almost 25 percent. The district magnitude also matters: where it is low, parties can ignore individual districts. Local and regional strategies, therefore, will not be the same for parties where some or all districts return just one or a few legislators than in countries that have high district magnitude in all regions.

The other pattern of politics that would be consistent with a party that has a broad presence across the country but a local focus is one where candidate qualities are important to voters. If the politicians that represent the different districts are independent from their parties, then the rise and fall of those parties' support would be based, at least partially, on the politicians' personal merits. This type of independence would suggest a party that is much less hierarchically structured than the type of system that produces a locally focused party due to differences in district characteristics. Of course, these two sources of a local focus – district characteristics and candidate qualities – are not mutually exclusive. The point to emphasize is that both can yield locally focused parties, but they have different implications for party organization and the focus of policy.

Implications for parties that are based on candidates who are relatively autonomous from their parties have been the subject of much discussion under the label of the "personal vote" (Cain et al. 1984, 1987; Carey and Shugart 1995; Cox and McCubbins 1993; McCubbins and Rosenbluth 1995; Samuels 2002; Golden 2003; Hallerberg and Marier 2004; Morgenstern 2005; Primo and Snyder 2010; Bagashka 2012; Crisp et al. 2013; André and Depauw 2015; Preece 2014; Shin 2017). As I emphasized in Chapter 1, the personal vote and the local vote are akin, but the former assumes that the different voting patterns that define *locally focused* parties result from independent candidates with distinct qualities, ignoring the possibility that the patterns could also result from differences in the characteristics of the districts. The personal vote literature thus does not explore the possibility of ties among groups of a party's legislators, who might be grouped due to geography or other interests. Still, that very broad literature has developed a number of themes that define the expectations for *locally focused* parties.

Much of the personal vote literature considers political implications for parties where legislators' own interests dominate those of the party. These include the likelihood of legislators to dissent from their party, the importance of constituency service, pork barrel politics, how candidates raise money, the constant campaigning, and the organization of the committee system, among many others. A central idea behind these theories is that if voters focus on the legislative candidates' qualities rather than just party characteristics, then politicians will face continual decisions about supporting their party versus meeting the district's needs. Given the need to attract local votes, candidates will construct their political strategies based on the exigencies of the particular constituency that they are competing to represent. Legislative campaigns for *locally focused* parties, then, will emphasize district issues and the candidates' personal qualities and experience. Further, legislators of such parties will demand more control over political resources essential to their electoral success than would legislators representing *nationalized* parties. This may additionally imply that legislators in *locally focused* parties will put more effort into their constituency service than will legislators serving in nationally focused parties.[1] Where parties are locally focused it will be more difficult to construct legislative coalitions, and party discipline should also suffer.

The *locally focused* label implies that national issues have a lower priority, but certainly these parties and their candidates will take positions on themes important to the country. As Cox and McCubbins (1993) explain, since legislators get benefits (electoral and other) from their party (or else such politicians would either run as independents or join groups at the center of the district), they are concerned with building the party's image. With each issue that puts district interests in contrast to the party's national policy positions, then, the legislators must re-evaluate the cost of dissenting based on the value of the party's national image with relation to the legislator's electoral strategy. The stronger the link between districts, the less common will be these tensions. This is because the link between districts is equivalent to the degree to which legislators from different districts view promoting the party's image as more important than voting in favor of local issues. Of course, as the number of legislators who view the importance of promoting their party's national image rises, the degree of local focus in elections will necessarily decrease. When the links are particularly strong, the change in the party's support would move in a more homogenous pattern and the party would land in the *unbalanced* category.

In sum, locally focused parties do not all resemble one another. Organizational frameworks and behavioral patterns for these parties will be based on a) the relative importance of national issues in legislative elections, b) whether the local focus is a function of district characteristics or candidate qualities, and c) the importance of individual districts to the party's national total, which is largely based on the district magnitude. Of course, the size and focus of locally focused parties also matters. Following Strom (1990), those that compete in multiple regions and try to win control of the legislature would behave and organize differently from parties whose support is concentrated in one or just a few regions and are trying to emphasize their ideological positions (especially those with a local focus) rather than trying to maximize the number seats they could win in the legislature.

Unbalanced parties have unequal levels of support in the various districts, but the changing fate of these parties in any election is reflected similarly in all districts. As perhaps typified by the British case, though a party's base level of support across districts may begin at disparate levels, the high salience of national issues leads the party's vote share to rise and fall at similar rates across the districts.

The unbalanced category houses two or perhaps three distinct patterns, based on differences in the geographic distribution of the parties' support.

---

[1] Though nationally focused parties may still have an incentive to serve local constituents, their interest in doing so is for their collective benefit rather than for the benefit of an individual legislator.

First, parties can have support in just one or a few regions of the country. Spain's Basque National Party or the Bloc Quebecois in Canada would provide examples. These parties do not fit the typology well, however, since their support in one region is unhinged from others (where they remain at zero support). More interesting for the typology are the parties in these countries that have a national reach – for example, the People's Party in Spain or the Liberals in Canada – and these are likely to display lower (but above zero) levels of support where the regional parties are strong. The alternative pattern of support resembles a checkerboard, where the party has inconsistent support across the nation and within the various regions. Within England, for example, the Conservatives' support ranges from about 6 percent to 60 percent for 2005, and in Ontario, support in 2011 for Canada's Liberals varied from under 10 percent to almost 50 percent.

Either of these patterns can accompany consistent cross-time movements in the parties' support (otherwise they would fall in the *locally focused* category). As examples, the graphs in Appendix 1 show that the change in support for the Conservative and Labour parties is consistent across England, as it is for Spain's Socialist Workers' Party (PSOE).

These two unbalanced patterns have very different implications for politics. Most clearly, parties with regionally concentrated support would be much more likely to face calls for separatism than would those whose voters are distributed in a checkerboard pattern. Both types could face conflicts over resources and constituents who demand responsiveness to particular (rather than national) issues. The difference would be the degree to which the demands are couched in regionalist language.

The final category I have labeled *unstable*. This label is appropriate because while low levels of SN are compatible with any level of DN, if SN is high then it can only be sustained if DN is also high. A high level of SN implies uniform support across districts, and this would change if there were strong differences in how districts change across time (low DN).[2]

As expected, Chapter 4 shows that there are very few parties that fall into the unstable box. When the parties do earn such a label, it must reflect localized electioneering in the context of one or more electoral contests that produced relatively homogeneous support. That consistent support level could be the result of heightened but fleeting national salience of particular issues, such as might occur in response to national referenda on constitutional reforms, economic reforms, or controversial leaders. This party type, however, is unstable because either the low DN would lead them toward the *locally focused* category or the limited role of localism would lead the party toward the *nationalized* box. Of course, though the ideal type defines stark distinctions

---

[2] Since the statistics are based on averages it is possible to conjure up a set of districts where the heterogeneity is zero and the district-time effect is greater than zero, but the empirical basis for such a case seems very weak.

among categories, empirically the differences are more of degree. Some parties will maintain a combination of relatively homogeneous geographic support with some amount of local focus.

Ideal and Actual Types

In this section I rely on interviews and secondary sources to summarize the organizational and behavioral characteristics of several parties that typify different categories of the typology. I also use the discussion to outline institutional and sociodemographic features of the countries involved to foreshadow later discussions (in Chapters 5 and 6) about country- and party-level factors that drive parties into different categories. Those chapters provide specific hypotheses and tests, but here the purpose is heuristic – to highlight similarities within categories and differences across them – rather than strictly analytical, and thus I am less concerned with case selection here than in later parts of this book. In Chapter 4 I provide data that more carefully categorizes the parties and other chapters apply more direct comparative tests and careful methodologies. Here, however, I rely on eyeball analysis of the parties' electoral behavior (which the printed and on-line appendices display in graph form, in ways similar to Figure 1.1) for all the parties that undergird the analysis for the book.

Nationalized Parties (and the Japanese Exception)
To begin, Figure 1.1 of the introductory chapter offered the proportional representation (PR) tier from Japan's LDP as a close approximation of a nationalized party. In 2009, Japan's LDP won between 20 and 40 percent of the vote in all 47 PR districts, with one minor exception. Further, when the party lost votes that year, it lost a similar percentage everywhere. Among other medium or large parties that closely approximate this ideal type are Spain's PSOE, several in Central America, and one or more parties in Bolivia, the Czech Republic, the Dominican Republic, Germany, Hungary, Paraguay, Sweden, and Uruguay. By and large the graphs for this group show more geographic dispersion in the support (less SN), but strong consistency in the movements of the vote over-time (high DN). In terms of the parties' organization and behavior, as well as the countries' institutional and sociodemographic framework, this group shares several characteristics, but overall it is a diverse group. The set includes parties in both parliamentary and presidential systems, but all of the latter countries are relatively small and unitary. An important similarity is that most countries use proportional representation and, though Spain is a partial exception, very few electoral districts; the German and Japanese parties do not make the list when using the single-member district tier and Spain shows a bit more dispersion (lower SN) than the others. In terms of sociogeography, Alesina and Zhuravskaya's (2011) index (see Chapter 6) that codes countries based on the geographic segregation of a country's ethnic or language groups indicates that all except

for Spain, Bolivia, and the Central American cases are relatively homogeneous societies. In terms of behavior and organization, most have centralized structures, but factions are prominent in Uruguay and Japan. These factions, however, are not geographically based.

While the graph for the PR tier of Japan's LDP suggests high nationalization on both dimensions, a complete picture of the party is more complex, and suggests tensions of national and local forces. It also suggests a pause when looking at data for just one tier of an electoral system, and perhaps a concern for contamination among different levels of elections. The tension is first evident in the contrast of the electoral support patterns for the party in the single-member district tier of the elections with that of the PR tier. In 2009, the LDP's vote in the 300 single-member districts ranged from 0 percent (in 10 districts) to 70 percent, and, as a graph of the party (see Appendix 1) shows, there is little relation in the up and down movements in the different districts. This localism reflects or is the result of several factors. First, the LDP has traditionally performed much better in rural areas than in cities, and its support has been based on personal relations and expensive clientelism. In part for this reason, the LDP's SN is rather low when considering the single-member districts, which allow parsing of the country into more internally homogeneous and externally heterogeneous pieces. Traditionally the LDP has been factionalized, and the rural–urban divide in the party is palpable, but Scheiner (2012) also highlights the importance of political centralism. In short, he follows Chhibber and Kollman (1998, 2004) to argue that in spite of localizing attractions for legislators or factions, plus divided ideological positions within the party, Diet members have a strong common interest in working together to control the strong central government. Given the end of one-party dominance, he also explains that the post-1993 electoral reform reduced intra-party competition, thus heightening policy issues (of national content) in campaigns (Rosenbluth and Thies 2010).[3] The tension of local and national politics is also evident in Scheiner's (2006) book on the failure of the opposition, which he explains as the result of the combination of clientelism – which is based on locally based relations – and "fiscal centralism."

A key question for the analysis is whether the legislators from the (nationally focused) PR and (locally focused) SMD tiers behave differently. For the case of Japan, evidence suggests that they do not. Carlson (2006) explains that the PR and SMD legislators frequently rotate, so all candidates are worried about retaining their local bases. He does find some evidence for changes in the expenditures on campaigns, but overall PR legislators seem to behave as if they were running for SMD seats (see also Koellner 2009). One study of

---

[3] Prior to 1993 Japan used a single non-transferable vote system that encouraged factionalism. Rosenbluth and Thies argue about the interplay of economic policies, interests, and political institutions. Economic pressures led to reforms of the political system, which in turn led to new economic policies.

Japan does find that the parties distinguish among legislators and give opportunities to distribute particularistic goods to those who are electorally vulnerability and need to develop local ties. They also find, however, that the ties between the tiers limit the differences among legislators (Pekkanen et al. 2006).[4] Studies of other countries do find differences in the behavior of legislators at the two levels. A study comparing legislators in the parliaments of Scotland, Wales, and two German states, for example, finds legislators from the SMDs spend more time on constituency service, while PR legislators are more interested in working with interest groups (Lundberg 2005). Thames (2001, 2005) found a difference in party discipline between the two tiers for Russia, but not in other East European cases. For Mexico, discipline has remained very high within the parties, so there is little evidence for differences among legislators elected from the two tiers, but Kerevel (2010) shows that the Mexican parties use different processes to choose candidates in the two levels, and they are different in terms of their control over leadership positions.

The limited differences in behavior for the Japanese legislators indicates that, at least in this case, the PR tier of elections provides a misleading view of party nationalization. For Japan, this may be the result of the strong ties between the two tiers. It could also imply, however, that using electoral data that collapses single-member districts into larger regions, as some studies of nationalization have done (e.g. Jones and Mainwaring [2003], who do this for Chile and the United States) could unreasonably reduce variance in the data and thus produce misleading impressions of high nationalization on one or both dimensions.

Spain's PSOE is another large party that has moderately high levels of nationalization on both dimensions. The PSOE does worse in the Basque Country than in most other regions, and it is very strong in a few other places, but overall the standard deviation of its support in the different electoral districts was just 5.4 points in 2011. As the graph for the PSOE in Appendix 1 shows, their DN is also very strong, in spite of the regionalism. This was even the case during the economic crisis of 2011, in which the party suffered everywhere, with a consistent fall of about 15 points. Spain's party *system* is not nationalized, however. As I describe in Chapter 7, the votes lost by the PSOE in 2011 were distributed to different parties in different regions, thus emphasizing the disjuncture between party and party system nationalization. The People's Party (PP), the country's second largest force, has much lower SN owing to its much weaker support in the Basque Country and Catalonia than in other regions. The figure also shows that its DN is weaker; in 2011, for example, the PP gained in most provinces, but not in the four Basque Country districts.

---

[4] Moser and Scheiner (2012) show that the tiers can have differential impacts on the number of parties and the number of women elected. The impacts, however, are conditioned by context, including whether the country is an established democracy or not. Their book, however, focuses less on the behavior of the legislators.

The PSOE's high level of SN, and perhaps its high DN, is surprising given the country's political decentralization, which is supported by cultural divides and a particular institutional framework. The country is cut into 17 autonomous regions, 3 of which have a special "nationality" status and use Spanish as a second language. Further, since the country is cut into 52 electoral districts for its 350 lower-house members, where voters only choose a small number of representatives (the district magnitude is 5 or under in than one-half of the districts, but over 30 in Barcelona and Madrid), there would be opportunities and incentives for legislators or parties to tailor personal or partisan appeals to their districts. This certainly enables the survival of separatist parties or other parties in the Basque Country, Catalonia, Galicia, and other regions. Perhaps counteracting these trends is the parliamentary system, which has been headed by one of the two main parties (or the PP's forerunner), sans a significant coalition partner (though this may change after 2016), since democratization. Further, Ajenjo and Molina (2011) explain that the legislators are subject to strict party discipline, and cannot vote independently, or even submit amendments without working through the parties.

Several factors contribute to the Spanish parties' moderately high level of static and dynamic nationalization, in spite of the strong regionalism. First, the PSOE and PP operate through centralized structures. As in other parliamentary democracies, elections and policies are focused on the prime minister, and individual parliamentarians are not free to pursue Mayhewian credit-claiming for policy initiatives. Montero (2007) explains that in spite of the "archetypal, decentralised structure" of the party system, power has not devolved to sub-national elites. He explains this contradiction through a discussion of the bifurcated regional and national "political class[es]," between which there is "little circulation." Interviews suggested that this advantaged the PSOE over the PP, because the former had a message more sympathetic to federalism. A PP party leader in the autonomous region of Galicia told me that the centralization hurt his party because it was not able to moderate its message in the Basque Country or Catalonia. Perhaps this was a bit self-serving, because he implied that the decentralization did help the party in his region. Specifically, he argued that the party had been more successful in Galicia, since it organized later and learned from its mistakes.

The graphs from the main parties of the Czech Republic suggest that the Social Democrats (CSSD), the Civic Democratic Party (ODS), and the Left Bloc are all nationalized. Support for each fits in a narrow band, with Prague being the exceptional district for the CSSD and ODS, while the Left Bloc is a bit stronger than elsewhere in the industrial center of *Usti nad Labem*. In 2013 a new party emerged, the ANO-2011, and won 47 of the 200 legislative seats. The high level of nationalization of the major parties sustained itself, as this new party received a remarkably similar level of support across the 14 electoral divisions (ranging from 16 to 22 percent). The parties divide on ideology, and though Moravian independence was briefly a prospect, this cleavage has not endured (Hlousek and Kopecek 2008). Hlousek and Kopecek also note that a party formed to support rural interests, but it failed to meet the requisite quota. In keeping with the idea that nationalized parties will resist the influence of regional politicians, Kopecky (2006) reports that "there are few viable obstacles to party influence in all major areas of the Czech government" (127), but he also notes "local politics . . . is in the hands of elected independents" (128). This does not appear to affect parliamentary elections, however, as Kopecky interprets electoral results such as the fall of the ODS in 2002 to their focus on "national issues."

Three final examples of parties that display high levels of static and dynamic nationalization are the Netherlands Christina Democratic Appeal (CDA), their Labour party (PvdA), and their Liberal Party (VVD). An oddity in their system – while voting takes place in 40 districts, legislative seats are allocated based on a single national constituency – forces me to exclude the country from my comparative statistical analysis in later chapters, but it is still useful as an illustrative case. Together these three parties earned about two-thirds of the votes in the period under study (1994–2010), and each displays especially high degrees of DN (based on the 40 districts). The VVD, the smallest of the three, is the most statically nationalized, with a range of support measuring only about 10 points, but the others also display consistent levels of support, falling within about a 20-point range.

The center-left PvdA was formed after World War II, and has been a central player in Netherlands politics, frequently controlling between 20 and 30 percent of the parliamentary seats and participating in many cabinet governments. Except for a significant low-point in 2002, its support has generally been concentrated between about 18 and 40 percent. Graphing its cross-time and cross-district support (see the on-line appendix) also suggests two prominent features. First, the distribution of support is not uniform; the party wins a considerably higher percentage of the vote in 5 of the 40 districts than others. Second, the over-time movements exhibit a phenomenal degree of homogeneity.

The Christian Democratic Appeal was formed in 1977 as the result of a long in the making merger of three Christian Democratic parties. Today the party is considered centrist. It has a center-left leaning, but has also participated in a minority center-right government (2010–12). On average, its support has grown marginally between 1994 and 2006, from about 22 to 26 percent. Since DN is high, the support across districts has consistently stayed within about a 20 point range. Its support is weakest in Amsterdam and other northern provinces, consistent with the traditional regional division that divided Protestants and Catholics. Perhaps the party's position favoring a more limited European Union (while it hosts the International Criminal Court and International Court of Justice) also harms its support in Amsterdam.

The high static and dynamic nationalization in the Netherlands is somewhat surprising given three factors that might have pushed toward lower levels on one or both dimensions. First, the country was formed from largely independent regions. The union of the regions resulted from the common fight first against the Spanish and later to protect against other threats. They have also continually faced a common geographic challenge. Second, the Netherlands has a large number of immigrants (about 20 percent). Third, there are linguistic variants and different religious traditions that are concentrated geographically (with Catholics in the South and Protestants in the North).

Several other factors, however, have countered this potentially low level of nationalization. First, bolstering one or both dimensions of nationalization is that the country is unitary, and comprises only about 17 million people. Bax (1990, 1995) describes the country's tradition as a melting pot, having overcome geographic divisions through a plan of centralization beginning in the Napoleonic regime. He adds that the system known since World War II as "pillarization" has helped to "manage" minorities within the multi-ethnic society, though this system has broken down in recent decades. Next, while there is a traditional divide between Protestants in the North and Catholics in the South, the country is largely secular. Linguistic dialectical differences exist, but neither they nor religion has seriously divided the country. Perhaps this is due to the incomplete separation of the religions; Lijphart (1969) reports that while the South was 90 percent Catholic, they made up 40 percent of the North. Lijphart, however, credits the continuing politics of accommodation to important compromises worked out during World War I. Also, the country is highly urbanized, with only about 4 percent working in agriculture. Overall, these factors contribute to the country's consociational governments, where power sharing is more the norm than are divisive appeals.

A final factor is the electoral system. As noted, because the Netherlands bases seats allotments on a national distribution of the vote, in essence it has only a single national constituency. Parties, as a result, mostly use the same names on all of their electoral lists (personal communication, Netherlands Electoral Council). The country does allow citizens to choose among candidates on the (open) list, but unless a candidate receives at least 25 percent of the electoral quota, the party's rank ordering is not altered.

Locally Focused Parties

Politics looks very different for the parties that typify the locally focused category. In this section I focus on those parties that have a national reach, but whose cross-time and cross-district support is highly variable. Parties such as Canada's Bloc Quebecois or the Basque Nationalist Party (BNP), however, arguably fit into this category, too. The BNP, for example, only competes in four districts, all of which are contained in one geographic (and political) region. In some sense the party fits more easily into the *unbalanced* category, since movements in the party's support follow very similar paths in those four districts. But since those changes are uncorrelated with the lack of change elsewhere – staying at zero – the party can fit into this category.

Moving to the parties with broader reach, Argentina's Peronists, the Justicialist Party (PJ), provides a first example. Its support varies considerably, ranging from about 15 percent to about 80 percent in 2011 (plus one district where it did not compete), and this has widened over time. The PJ has significant difficulties in organizing its regional wings. Candidate choice is decentralized, and in many districts the party does not even run under its nationally recognized name. For example, in 2011 it dropped its traditional Justicialist title in some, but not all provinces, opting instead for the name of "Front for Victory" (FpV). In 2009 there were more anomalies; for example, it allied with Popular Encounter in the federal district, and in Cordoba there were both FpV and Justicialista lists. A senate staffer and compiler of election data, Andy Tow (personal communications), explained further that often two or more lists for the legislature support a single presidential candidate. Historically, independents have won in many provinces, and many of these later join the PJ after the election.

This decentralized electoral process was palpable in interviews with legislators from several parties. In tones reminiscent of academic discussions of personal vote seeking, legislators highlighted their frequent trips into their districts, and their intention to use "mouth-to-mouth" contact: meetings with neighborhood groups, speaking in bars and other public places, and with local NGOs. Another point of discussion was the influence of governors, mayors, or other important politicians – and these politicians' relations with the president – in influencing elections for the national legislature. As underscored by Jones (2008), the governors are highly influential in choosing candidates and directing legislative elections. The influence of the governors leads him to categorize the legislators as "provincial-party loyalists" (see also Eaton 2002; Jones 2002). This adds to the local flavor of the elections, since not all are tied to the president, even if they formally belong to the same party. Gervasoni (2010) adds that some provinces are so highly controlled by provincial bosses that they challenge the democratic label.

Argentina's electoral decentralization, however, does have limits. One representative of the Radical Civic Union (UCR), the other traditionally important party, complained (personal interview, 2012) that the local representation was only for electoral purposes. She argued that parties were "nationalist" and that once the elections were over, the (decentralized) federal system ceased to exist. As one example, she explained that legislators were free to co-sign proposed legislation that passed through their offices, but in later stages after committees dealt with the bill, then the parties made decisions and the individual legislators were more restricted. Another representative who had been in the UCR earlier but is now with a new party, argued that there are two types of legislation: local and party. She was particularly unhappy with the top-down "imposition" of party policy. These interviews match broader studies of legislative behavior. This has led Jones (2002, 2008), among others, to seek explanations for the very high party unity in legislative decisions in spite of the importance of region to some political decisions. Studies of roll call voting show very few examples of intra-party dissent, though there are clear examples of dissenters abstaining to express displeasure or even deny their party the necessary quorum. Jones and Eaton (2002) also mention occasional groups of legislators forming a geographic bloc. Overall, however, the PJ and the UCR have been successful at managing roll call voting, through their influence over candidate choice, future careers, electoral resources, and political capital. The control, however, is far from complete. Zelaznik (2012) discusses, for example, important dissents, and the formation of "sub-blocs" within the PJ whose members have manifested dissent by "absenting themselves from the floor, abstaining, or ultimately voting against the party" (p. 67, my translation). In 2005, he explains, the divisions within the party brought the congress to a standstill, and the party also suffered defections in 2008 and 2009. Overall, then, the statistics substantially overestimate the degree of party unity, in large part because controversial legislation is not brought to a vote.[5]

The United States' parties provide another pattern for locally focused parties. These parties do not compete in all districts, and in others they run either giants or sacrificial lambs. Different from the Spanish BNP, however, the support patterns are not as clearly marked by geography. The Democrats, for example, do garner many votes even where the Republicans win, and vice versa. While the range in support is clear, there are debates about the commonality in the parties' electoral trends. The on-line appendix graphs, which show results for the 1980s–2000s, suggest significant heterogeneity along both dimensions. Support levels vary greatly, and a good year for a Democrat in one district does not guarantee that another Democrat, even in a neighboring district, will also do well. This is consistent with the long-discussed idea that all politics is local in the United States. At the same time, it does not deter Cox and McCubbins (1993), whose well-regarded book develops a theory of collective party action based on the idea that co-partisan legislators are clearly concerned with the fortunes of the party as a whole.[6] The local focus, then, does not imply that there is a complete absence of partisan swings or that legislators and voters are unconcerned with events, policies, and conditions at the national level. The variation in district-level returns, however, does imply a premium for local factors in explaining electoral outcomes.

Patterns in the vote for India's National Congress Party (INC) also suggest a locally focused label. The country has more than 500 single-member districts, and the party's vote ranges from 0 to over 70 percent across them. Even in individual states there is instability in the pattern of results. For Delhi, for example, the party gained more than 35 points from 1999 to 2004 in the Chandni Chowk district, but its support was essentially flat in South Delhi. Of

---

[5] As elsewhere (Morgenstern 2004), I use the term "party unity" in a generic manner, which can result from some combination of imposed discipline and ideological cohesion.

[6] See also Jacobson and Kernell (1983) who explain that the parties' electoral fortunes drive retirement patterns.

course India's politics are highly decentralized, with dozens of parties competing in different states. Further, as Chhibber and Kollman (2004) explain, different parties compete at the state level than at the national level. They attribute this distinct pattern to particular aspects of the country's federal system.

These examples suggest a solid relation between decentralized electoral and political structures and low levels of the two dimensions of nationalization. The United States, India, Canada, and Argentina are all decentralized federal systems, and all but Argentina use single-member district systems. There are exceptions among other decentralized systems, such as the Spanish PSOE, which I discussed as a case of unbalanced support. The Spanish use a parliamentary rather than a presidential system, however, and use proportional representation rather than single-member districts. The British parties work within a system that combines a parliamentary form of government and single-member districts, but the country is unitary and Labour and the Conservatives do not compete in Northern Ireland.[7] It is notable that the set of *locally focused* cases includes parties in both presidential and parliamentary systems. Most parties in parliamentary systems, however, appear to have high DN, even if their SN is low (see Appendix 1 graphs for the German, Portuguese, and South African parties). The parties in presidential systems, meanwhile, have lower DN (see graphs of parties in Chile, Mexico, and Peru).

Unbalanced Parties

As noted, the different levels of support that typify unbalanced parties can be within or among regions. Perhaps the best examples of parties that manifest both types of variance, plus consistent over-time trends, are Labour and the Conservatives in the United Kingdom, but the Canadian Conservatives and Liberals also approximate the ideal type. Only the latter of these countries is federal, but the United Kingdom also has distinct regions. Both countries use single-member districts, within parliamentary frameworks. The maps (Figures 2.1–2.4) show that both countries sustain regional parties (which is characteristic of a locally focused category), but also have parties that compete nationally. Within the regions, both the regional and national parties have checkerboard patterns of support. For example, while the Bloc Quebecois gets all its support in Quebec, the Conservatives also compete well in many of the province's 75 districts. Similarly, while Sinn Fein only wins votes in Northern Ireland and the Scottish National Party only competes in its home country, the Liberals, Conservatives, and Liberal Democrats compete countrywide.

To show the diverse support of the national parties, the first map (Figure 2.1) highlights the Conservative Party in Canada for 2011, though it is somewhat misleading to the eye since large provinces dominate the geography, but the population (and the number of electoral districts) are concentrated in smaller provinces. The second map (Figure 2.2) thus focuses on the party's support in the most populous provinces, Ontario and Quebec. Within these provinces, the

---

[7] The graph excludes Scotland, due to the frequent changes of constituency borders.

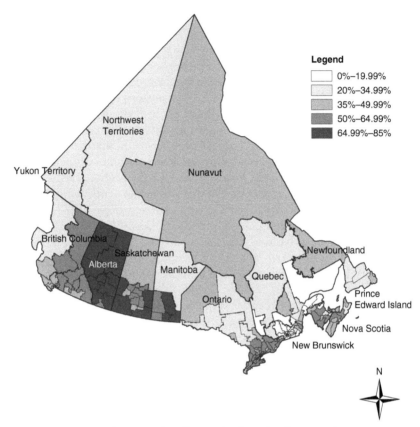

FIGURE 2.1 Mapping Static Nationalization in Canada: Conservatives 2011

Conservative Party also has pockets of strength and weakness, and especially in Quebec, neither latitude nor longitude are determinant. This shows, then, the two potential types of unbalanced parties: support can vary among or within regions (or both).

The United Kingdom has a similar pattern (Figures 2.3 and 2.4). Even ignoring Northern Ireland (where the Conservatives are represented through an alliance partner) and Scotland (which redistricted, thus making the over-time comparisons difficult), support for the Conservatives varies from under 10 percent to over 50 percent, and the range for Labour is even greater. In spite of the wide spread in values, Figure 2.5 shows that the lines connecting the district-level support are virtually parallel, typifying very high dynamic nationalization.

The graphs for the Canadian Conservatives and Liberals are similar (see Appendix 1), but show a bit more localism on both dimensions. The Conservatives are present, but weak in most of Quebec, and in a few districts they have won more than 80 percent of the vote. The degree of parallelism for

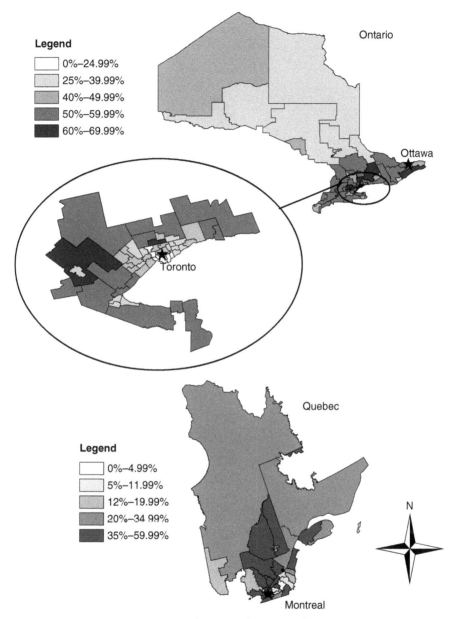

FIGURE 2.2 Mapping Static Nationalization in Two Canadian Provinces: Conservatives 2011

the graph's lines are not nearly as confused as in Argentina, but neither are they as parallel as in the Netherlands or even the United Kingdom. In 2006 the Liberals' support ranged, in an evenly spread pattern, from under 10 percent to

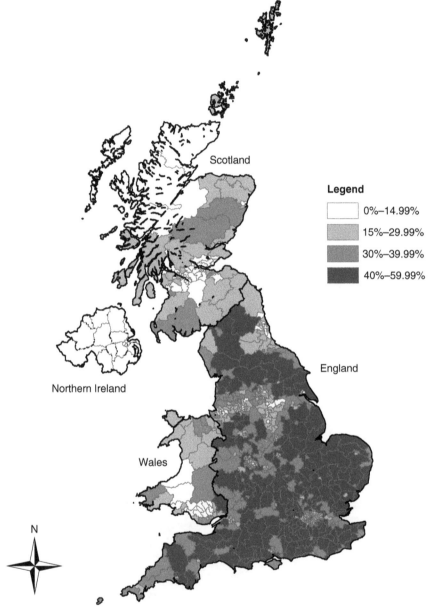

FIGURE 2.3 Mapping Static Nationalization in the UK: Conservatives 2001

over 60 percent, but this range narrowed by 2011. On the dynamic scale, the
Liberals' support shows a regression to the mean – support fell more where the
party had been strong than in other districts. In sum, parties in these countries

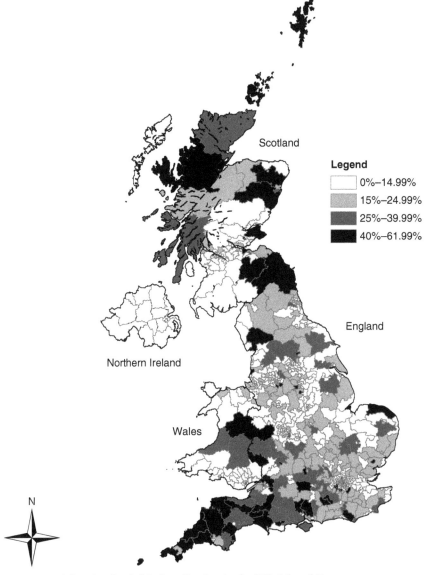

FIGURE 2.4 Mapping Static Nationalization in the UK: Liberal Democrats 2001

fit into the unbalanced box, regardless of whether the regional issues are considered.

As expected, the two parts of the heterogeneity in electoral support (within and among regions) have had different impacts on politics in these countries. Consistent with the parties' weakness in some areas, regional issues have

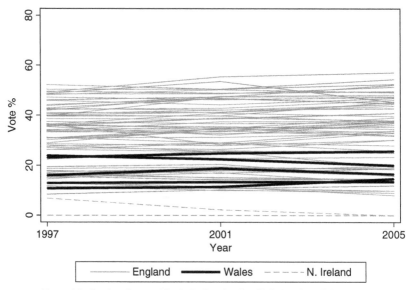

Every 8th district; does not include Scotland or N. Ireland coalition partners.

FIGURE 2.5 Party Nationalization: UK Conservative Party 1997–2005

provided constant political wedges (most significantly, but not only including the irredentism in Northern Ireland and Quebec). The checkerboard pattern, by contrast, reflects, at least for these countries, a politically significant, but much less dramatic pull toward district-centered politics. Specifically, it implies concerns with the geographic concentration of ethnic or religious minorities, layered within a sometimes tense relation between national and local level party leaders.

What appears to drive the differences in SN (at least within rather than among regions) is the small units into which the country is cut. In other words, if the candidate has limited impact on the vote choice, then the range of support within a region must be the function of how that region is carved into units that do not all resemble one another. In these countries, electoral districts do have unique identities, but are too small to allow regional appeals.

As an example, among the 106 federal ridings (districts) in the Canadian province of Ontario, the Liberals won between 7 and 50 percent in 2011. There is some geographic pattern to the party's strength, but what are more marked are the emphatic differences in the makeup of the different ridings. The checkerboard pattern of partisan support reflects the polyglot population, which is geographically concentrated according to ethnic minority status, religious affinities, and wealth (see Blais 2005, Gerber 2006, Harrel 2013). To highlight the effects of these categories, Figure 2.6 shows the support for the Liberal Party and demographic data for four ridings in Ontario. In Oshawa and

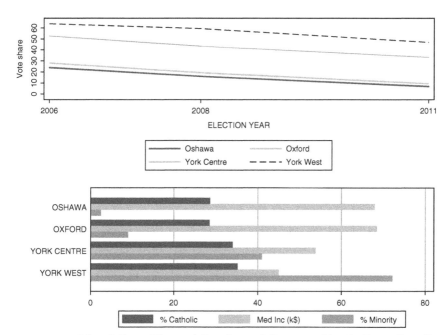

FIGURE 2.6 Liberal Party Electoral Results and Demographics in Four Canadian Ridings

Oxford the Liberals won less than 10 percent in 2011, while in York Centre and York West the party has traditionally been much stronger. In all four ridings, however, the party has lost a similar portion of its vote since 2006. The demographics for the two sets of ridings are starkly different. In Oshawa and Oxford, where the party is weaker, there are fewer Catholics, the medium income is higher, and the percentage of what the census succinctly (but perhaps inelegantly) terms "visible minorities" is much smaller.[8]

The unbalanced parties in Canada and the United Kingdom face pressures and politics from the national and local levels. A first place this is evident is in the processes for the selection of legislative candidates. Cross and Young (2013) explain that while local party associations are highly involved in the Canadian candidate selection process – to the point of discussing them as autonomous– national parties have increasingly inserted themselves in the candidate selection process through the appointment of candidates and general interference with

---

[8] Demographic data taken from: www12.statcan.gc.ca/nhs-enm/2011/dp-pd/prof/details/download-telecharger/comprehensive/comp-csv-tab-nhs-enm.cfm?Lang=E. Income data taken from: www12.statcan.gc.ca/nhs-enm/2011/dp-pd/prof/details/download-telecharger/comprehensive/comp-csv-tab-nhs-enm.cfm?Lang=E.

"local" processes (p. 26). In Britain, national leaders are able to impose candidacies in particular districts, which they might do as rewards or for other strategic reasons.

While the parties are present at the local level, the high DN implies that support levels change in response to national rather than local issues. Blais et al. (2003) report that candidates themselves have a small, but significant impact on the choice of voters in Canadian elections (though others they cite find almost no impact). Thus, while nominations do take place at the constituency level, the decentralization itself would seem to have limited impact on the low static nationalization.

Behavior of legislators also shows how national politics dominate, but do not erase localism. As Cox (1987) describes, British Members of Parliament (MPs) do not freely vote their conscience, but delegate that authority to their parties. Cain, Ferejohn, and Fiorina (1984, 1987) partially contest the "textbook" view of British MPs, which posits them as "faceless troops in the party ranks who vote in accord with the party whip" (1984, p. 114). In this view, they are almost powerless in shaping legislation or seeking benefits for their districts. Cain et al. (1984, 1987) show a more nuanced view, where most MPs have come to conduct regularly "surgeries" (meetings with constituents), but they still find that the legislators' personal reputations have a much smaller effect on elections than in the United States. Studies of Canada have presented similar findings. Eagles (2013) does show there are some free votes that allow Canadian legislators to pursue constituency issues, but these focus on a limited set of (usually moral) issues. "Party politics," he concludes, "dominates the House of Commons, even when controversial moral issues, which may cause extraordinarily high constituency pressure to be brought to bear on an MP, are at stake" (p. 85).

These studies give weight to the view that the high DN stems from the parliamentary system. As Lijphart (1999) and many others have noted, in parliamentary systems voters can only register their views about the executive through their votes for their parliamentarian. Cain et al. (1984) confirm this hypothesis by showing that support for the UK prime minister has a much greater impact on the vote than does support for the president in US elections. In Canada, most evidence points to the prevalence of parties and perhaps the popularity of the prime minister in explaining district-level election results (Johnston 2002; Blais et al. 2003). This is not to deny that localism is irrelevant, however. The differences in districts' (or regions') population filter messages about national politics, and issues can have differential impacts on these groups. One study of the personal vote in Canada finds that the legislative candidate has a "decisive" impact on 5 percent of voters (and less in Quebec) (Blais et al. 2003). Ferejohn and Gaines (1991) also find some evidence suggesting that the personal vote can play a role in Canadian legislative elections, though they also point to contradictory data. When the UK Conservatives collapsed in 1993, the party fell by more than 30 points in

92 of the country's 295 districts, but in some districts it held relatively steady.[9] Cain et al. (1984) reported that the swing in 1979 was less consistent in Britain than had generally been the case. In most years, however, the rise and fall of the parties in both countries follows a very consistent pattern, suggesting a limited impact of candidates. It also suggests that even if district characteristics affect a party's base level of support in these countries, it is national events and politics that drive marginal voters and hence changes in the parties' level of support.

The preceding discussions of ideal types and examples have revealed potential hypotheses about causes that lead a party into a particular category, as well as expectations about behavior. Among the lessons is that one or the other dimensions by itself is insufficient for categorization. Also, as I emphasized in the discussion of the locally focused category, the levels of the two dimensions of nationalization are continuous, rather than discrete variables. Behavioral interpretations that focus on ideal types, therefore, must take care to avoid a sole focus on the extremes. The US–UK comparison is exemplary. Both have low levels of SN, but while the lines in graphs for the UK parties are relatively parallel, they are jumbled for the US parties, suggesting much lower DN for parties in the latter country. As I quantify in later chapters, the US parties have middle-range scores on the dynamic scale, however, and this common element in the vote should encourage some collaboration among party members. At the same time, since the British parties are not at the extreme low end of DN in a comparative context, we might expect a bit more focus on local politicking there than elsewhere.

Conclusion

This chapter has focused on a typology based on the two dimensions of nationalization in order to highlight the (almost) independence of the dimensions and consider the behavioral expectations of parties typified by the different categories. In so doing, the typology underlines how studies that ignore the two-dimensional nature of party nationalization will necessarily jumble together a number of very different party types. Reaching conclusions about the relation of democracy with one of the dimensions – which sometimes go under the guise of party nationalization or the personal vote – therefore, could be quite misleading. As an example, the impact of the "personal vote" on campaign styles or government spending patterns will vary according to how parties' support is spread across the country. Further, the next chapter explains that failure to account for each concept simultaneously can lead to misleading, if not biased statistical indicators.

Based on the theoretical typology developed in this chapter, the next two chapters work toward quantifying the dimensions in order to place parties more

[9] Specifically, it fell by less than 5 percent in 5 districts and less than 10 percent in 12 districts.

carefully into the categories. Chapter 3 develops a statistical model to measure static and dynamic nationalization, advancing from a components of variance model developed by Stokes in the 1960s. Chapter 4 applies the model to dozens of parties from across the world and demonstrates the utility of the statistical and theoretical models. The remainder of the book then moves toward explaining the factors that lead a party to land in a particular box and the consequences to a political system for the placement of a country's parties. Many of the roots of these explanatory models are found in the party descriptions from this current chapter, which explained how country-level factors such as the executive and electoral systems, plus political decentralization, should be related to one or both types of nationalization. There are also differences among parties within some countries, but the explanations for this variance appears more sui generis and the cross-country differences are more significant. The behavioral explanations of this chapter presage the last part of the book, where individual chapters look at facets of party behavior and organization by considering the accountability of parties across regions and the relations among a party's legislators.

3

Measuring Static and Dynamic Nationalization*

Chapter 1 portrayed graphs for three countries that set out the problematic: parties have support that varies across the nation and changes over time. The statistical goal is to estimate these two patterns simultaneously. To do this I first justify use of a simple hierarchical model that Tom and Sarah Mustillo (2012) developed as an equivalent (and more easily applicable) form of a components of variance analysis that I developed with Richard Potthoff (2005). I then discuss other techniques, but argue that they are inferior. Within that discussion, I show how to adjust or weight the model and discuss when this is appropriate.

The graphical data using district-level electoral results suggests a means for analytically separating and evaluating volatility, and the two types of nationalization. The Morgenstern and Potthoff (M&P) model, which builds on work by Stokes (1965, 1967), accomplishes this task. It does this by decomposing electoral data in a way that not only allows measurement of the phenomena (which will allow empirical comparisons), but also suggests the proper interpretation of the concepts. As I explain in this chapter, the model calculates SN and volatility directly, and I argue that the residual measures the impact of district characteristics or candidate qualities, which I define as the inverse of DN. The sense of the model is that once we have accounted for the underlying support of a party in a district and the movement over time in that party's base support, the remaining movement in a party's support must be attributed to district-level factors.

While based on Stokes's work, the alternative model that Potthoff and I set forth corrects a flawed statistical assumption in his model and allows analysis of a much broader set of countries. Our model, like that of Stokes, also has the advantage of providing results at the party level, which I have argued is superior

---

* This chapter relies on and borrows from two papers I co-authored. The first was with Richard Potthoff (2005) and the second with John Polga-Hecimovich and Peter Siavelis (2013).

to studies that conflate different parties into a sometimes misleading country aggregate. Finally, while explaining the algebra behind our model involves multiple lines of equations filled with Greek letters (details are in Morgenstern and Potthoff 2005), the technique is intuitive and easy to apply using standard statistical packages.

In this chapter I rely on my earlier work with Potthoff to explain the Stokes model and our alternative specification, then turn to the Mustillo and Mustillo improvements; finally, I offer a criticism of other techniques. The following chapter then applies the methodology to a large database of parties to offer a first look at the results. The discussion uses the results in two ways: first in a critique of extant methods, showing the degree to which different techniques provide misleading statistics, and second in the creation of a typology of parties.

COMPONENTS OF VARIANCE AND A HIERARCHICAL MODEL

In addition to the conscious focus on parties, the terminology that I have chosen for this book grows from an attempt to develop statistically precise definitions. The methodology is based on dissecting district-level electoral data into three "pieces." A first piece is the distribution of the party's vote around the country. Potthoff and I called this "district heterogeneity," and here I term it "static nationalization" to capture the idea that it measures the distribution at a particular point in time (or as an average over several time periods). A second piece measured the average change in the party's national vote. This provides a measure of volatility.[1] Having accounted for these two pieces, we labeled the residual the "district-time effect" to capture the idea of unexplained variance both in the districts and across time. Swindle and I (2005) later renamed this cumbersome term the "local vote," arguing that it captured effects of either candidate qualities or district characteristics. While the local vote is a useful term because of its intentional relation to the personal vote,[2] in work with Polga and Siavelis (2012, 2014) we used the term "dynamic nationalization." This phrase, as noted earlier, allows precision in discussions of nationalization and calls attention to the independence of the concept's two dimensions.

In order to clarify the concepts and move toward a means for measuring them through an integrated model, Table 3.1 portrays the results for a single party in two hypothetical countries (C1 and C2). Each of these countries has three equally sized electoral districts (D1, D2, and D3), and we will consider the results across two election years (Y1 and Y2). In the first election year (Y1), the parties' electoral support is identical in both countries. That is, the party of

---

[1] As noted, this operationalization for volatility adds another layer of confusion in terminology, because Stokes labels this the "national effect."

[2] Katz (1973a) rightly pointed out that some indicators of the personal vote ignore the possibility that district factors may drive differences in the district-level vote. We chose the term "local vote" to account for this idea.

TABLE 3.1 *Hypothetical Support for a Single Party in Two Countries*

	Country C1			Country C2		
District	Y1	Y2	Avg	Y1	Y2	Avg
D1	59	49	54	59	43	51
D2	53	43	48	53	49	51
D3	47	37	42	47	37	42
Average	53	43	48	53	43	48

interest is assumed to have won 59 percent of the vote in D1, 53 percent of the vote in D2, and 47 percent of the vote in D3 in both countries.

The variance in the party's support across districts is the basis for SN. In the second election year (Y2), the average support for the party dropped by 10 points in both countries. That change, or more generally, the variance in the movement across time, provides a measure of *electoral volatility*. The distribution of that loss, however, varies from one country to the other. In C1, the party loses exactly 10 percent in each district, while in C2 the 10-point total loss between the two years is distributed unequally among the districts. Since the change in support – the swing – is identical for all districts in C1, district characteristics or candidate qualities must have played no role in the election, while in C2, alternatively, district characteristics or candidate qualities did affect the election. The degree of consistency in the district-level swing, therefore, is a proxy for DN.

In sum, the notion of SN is meant to conjure an image of the degree to which a party has (in)consistent support across districts. The degree of variance is relatively high – implying low SN – for the US parties, since their support varies greatly between rural Kansas and metropolitan New York. DN addresses the localism issue that concerned Schattschneider and Stokes. Having once accounted for movement over time and among districts, what is left are the idiosyncratic qualities and characteristics of candidates and districts. Katz (1973) and others (Brady et al. 2000) have argued that these idiosyncrasies may also yield systematic (but not uniform) responses of the districts to national events. New gun control legislation, for example, might harm the Democrats in the South, but help them in the North. It would therefore be incorrect to attribute all of the effect to candidates, as implied with the term "personal vote." I therefore apply the term DN – or its opposite, the *local vote* – to capture the degree to which variance in the change of a party's electoral fortunes is accounted for by characteristics particular to districts or candidates.

This solution may not satisfy the authors who desire a measure for non-uniform responses to national phenomena. While such measures would be useful, Stokes, before turning to a criticism of Katz's methodology, argues in a rejoinder that he tested for non-uniform responses and found them to be negligible.[3] He argues further that uniform responses are interesting phenomena that inform analyses of congressional behavior. Claggett, Flanigan, and Zingale (1984) concur, as the consistent responses indicate the degree to which "the distinctive regional political cultures and traditions are being replaced by a more similar mixture of political sentiments across the nation" (p. 80). Further, the absence of uniform responses must imply the presence of local forces in explaining electoral outcomes. In sum, measuring the DN through this type of data decomposition provides a useful window on the political process.

To measure SN, the challenge is to consider it within the larger electoral context. For any particular point in time (or an average), the standard deviation of a party's success across districts, the Gini coefficient, or the index of variation could provide measures of SN. Such simple measures of dispersion, however, are problematic for C2, because a second type of variance is also driving the parties' geographic support. In other words, while country C1 has no local effect, it is significant for C2. Proper measurement, therefore, must account for the different types of variation simultaneously.

Stokes's approach to this problem was to study district-level electoral returns through a components of variance model that broke down the electoral changes into what he referred to as district, state (or regional), and national components. His basic approach can capture both the static and dynamic aspects of electoral change. The modified version of his model that Potthoff and I proposed thus captures, in terms of country C1, the perfect parallel of cross-time movement among districts, the moderate range in the party's support among the districts, and the degree of over-time change of party P1's aggregate electoral returns.

While Potthoff and I favor the Stokes approach for its ability to account for the multi-dimensional variance in electoral support, the specific model he uses requires two important adjustments. First, we transformed his fixed effect for districts to a random effect. In this case, our goal was to use the districts as a categorical variable and examine the variance among the multiple districts.

Second, for comparative work, the model requires an adjustment since many countries do not divide their states (or their equivalents) into smaller electoral districts. Potthoff and I therefore transformed Stokes's model from three levels to two, because all countries have districts, but not all have states.[4] We argue further that Stokes's "national component" should be reinterpreted. When expressed as a percentage of the total variance in the system that component captures, to a degree, the uniform responses that Stokes and others discussed.

---

[3] Potthoff and I investigated the statistical reasoning and techniques Stokes used to reach this conclusion, but found them to be unclear. Although he briefly indicates that he somehow tested covariances and correlation coefficients, such tests are not standard in variance components analysis and it is not clear how they could have been suitably done.

[4] The state level can go back into the model, as I show in Chapter 7. For a discussion of nesting, see Morgenstern and Potthoff (2005).

But, as a raw figure it signals the level of change in a party's overall support. As such, it is an indicator of electoral volatility.

Stokes's intuitive model begins with the question of the effect of national, state, and district politics on a party's vote. To test for these impacts, he begins with the distribution of a party's votes among the various states and at the level of the electoral districts. He then examines the changes over time in the state- and district-level vote, and decomposes the data to extract the different sources of variance.

The M&P model is as follows:

$$y_{ik} = \mu + A_k + B_i + C_{ik} \quad (i = 1...I; \ k = 1...K)$$

Here, y_{ik} is the percentage of the total vote (received by the political party under consideration) in the election in district i at time k; K is the number of elections, or years, covered by the analysis; I is the number of districts; A_k is a nationwide random effect for time k, assumed to have mean 0 and (unknown) variance σ_A^2; B_i is a random effect (covering all years) for district i, providing for SN, and assumed to have mean 0 and variance σ_B^2; C_{ik} is a residual (or random interaction) effect, for district i and time k, assumed to have mean 0 and variance σ^2; and μ is a fixed effect representing the overall unweighted mean of the party's vote percentages across all districts and elections. The original paper (Morgenstern and Potthoff 2005) details this and other models, and provides formulas for estimating the components.

The substantive interpretation, and hence the labeling, of these components is critical. Stokes labeled what we call σ_A^2 (the variance component attributed to A_k) the national component, arguing that it captures the average or national movement of a party. As noted, we reinterpret this component. In the example above, the σ_A^2 would relate to the 10-point aggregate change for the party, not the degree of uniformity of response in the districts (which is captured in the residual). The interpretation given by Stokes is somewhat justified by considering σ_A^2 as a percentage of total variance, since it would then reflect the importance of the aggregate or national change in terms of other factors. This is problematic in comparisons, however, since countries with a small total variance might appear to have a higher local component than those with much more total change.[5] As a raw number, however, this component reflects the magnitude of a party's change in support, and is thus better interpreted as a measure of volatility.[6] For country C2, our model would attribute the 10-point aggregate swing largely to σ_A^2 and use the differences in each district from that

---

[5] For example, if a country had a local component of 10 within a total variance of 20, it would appear to have a larger local effect than a country with a local component of 50 and total variance of 200.

[6] Stokes even uses this component to discuss the variability of electoral strength (see 1967, p. 189).

average (-6, +6, and 0) to estimate the residual component.[7] A focus on percentages alone would miss the magnitude of that change. If, for example, there was a 20-point average change, with residuals also twice as large (i.e. if σ_A and σ both doubled), the ratio of σ_A^2 to the total variance – and hence the figure for the "national effect" – would remain the same. The magnitude of σ_A^2, however, would be much larger, correctly capturing the idea of greater volatility. As a result, Potthoff and I label σ_A^2 our "time" or "volatility" component as it captures the variance of the party over time.

While not a focus of this book, this measure of volatility is a useful advance over traditional methods. Most studies have settled on the Pedersen index, which as Mainwaring and Scully (1995) explain, is calculated

by adding the net change in percentage of seats (or votes) gained or lost by each party from one election to the next, then dividing by two. An index of 15, for example, means that some parties experienced an aggregate gain of 15 percent of the seats from one election to the next while others lost a total of 15 percent. (p. 6)

The Pedersen index, however, suffers from problems similar to studies of SN or DN that employ electoral data without breaking down the sources of variance. For example, Roberts and Wibbels's (1999) report of minimal volatility between the 1993 and 1997 elections in Chile ignores the heterogeneity across districts and neglects the very sharp changes in support that our analysis uncovers at the district level. Similar problems would arise in applications to the United States or the United Kingdom. Studies of volatility based on the Pedersen index or similar measures also have a problem in that they aggregate all parties in the calculations and statistics and therefore fail to reflect the relative movements within the system. By contrast, our method can provide separate scores for each party, alliance, or "block" (Bartolini and Mair's [1990] focus). Further, studies of volatility are generally mute on the subject of whether the changes are experienced differently around the country, which could be quite important to conclusions about the relation of volatility and cleavage structures. Lastly, the Pedersen index distorts volatility scores, in that all variance in elections is attributed to this one party characteristic, rather than the three that we have identified.[8]

---

[7] For simplification this discussion ignores the issue of district heterogeneity.

[8] Bartolini and Mair (1990), for example, calculate a "total volatility" score of 13.5 for the period 1978–81 for France. Their principal argument, though, is based on calculating "block volatility," which they find to be 6.3 between those two election years. When we apply our model to blocks, our method bears out the relatively low block volatility. For the Socialists and Communists combined into a block, the standard deviation of the national-level electoral movements (i.e. the square root of the variance component for volatility) is 4.1 points. But our method can also differentiate among parties. When we apply it to the Socialists, Communists, and Gaullists individually for the 1978–81 period, we find their respective standard deviations to be 8.7, 4.6, and 2.8 points, thus indicating a substantial level of instability for the leftist parties.

Returning to our particular components of interest, the B_i's in the model capture the variation in a party's average returns across districts, and thus provide an estimate of SN. Stokes then interpreted the residual, C_{ik}, as a measure of the "district effect," reasoning that since other components accounted for time (national), state, and district effects, the residual would include variance attributable to the local/ephemeral qualities of candidates or idiosyncratic characteristics of districts. This latter term is also somewhat imprecise, however, since the residual has both a time and a district subscript. In other words, the residual captures the idiosyncratic movements of districts *and time* that are unaccounted for by heterogeneity in support among districts or national-level volatility. The residual should be interpreted, therefore, as capturing both non-uniform responses to national policy, as well as the importance of candidate characteristics and district peculiarities to the election. This led Potthoff and me to adopt the phrase "district-time effect," though I have now adopted the terms "dynamic nationalization" (DN) or the "local vote."

Mustillo and Mustillo (2012) offer several important modifications to this model. They first show that the M&P model is equivalent to a hierarchical model with random effects for districts and time. Specifically, the Stata command for this model is:[9]

mixed vote%|| _all : R.district || year :, var

In dialogue with Tom Mustillo, he argued that this model "under-specif[ies] the temporal structure (the fixed effects) by failing to account for the fact that a party's performance in a given district is correlated over time" (personal communication 6/12/12). This leads M&M to argue in favor of adding a fixed effect to model the trends in voter support. Because the time trends are not necessarily linear, they propose adding a squared time term (for three years of data; presumably higher order polynomials would be appropriate for longer time trends) to the model to account for changed slopes.

Their other important change is to account for two other potential sources and types of variance. The first is systematic but non-uniform responses of the districts, which could produce a "fanning" pattern of the data.[10] The other captures "variability in the mean rate of change." As they explain, this too could be systematic, and hence a part of a local effect.

---

[9] In this model, mixed refers to a "Multilevel mixed-effects linear regression" with vote%, the dependent variable defined as the district-level vote. "District" is based on a continuous count and Year is defined similarly. Variables before the || are fixed effects, and those after are random effects. The colon refers to the nesting structure.

[10] Mustillo and Mustillo (2012) focus on a "fanning in" pattern, but "fanning out" would be possible if parties consolidate their support in one or a few regions.

To capture these two potential sources of variance, M&M develop a multilevel model that that nests time within districts. The calls in Stata for the two models are as follows:

$$(1)\ \text{mixed vote}\%\ \text{time time}^2\,||\,\text{district}:,\ \text{mle variance};$$

$$(2)\ \text{mixed vote}\%\ \text{time time}^2\,||\,\text{district}:\text{time},\ \text{mle variance covariance (unstructured)}$$

While similar to the M&P model, these two models differ in interpretation, because they estimate variance around the curve (i.e. the mean vote trend) while the M&P model estimates variance around a point (i.e. the average level of a party's support across districts and time).[11] The M&M model has other advantages as well, providing excellent balance in the goals for a statistical indicator of the two types of nationalization: ease of application, directly interpretable statistics, and accounting for multiple levels of variance. It is also adaptable to different types of systems.

Mustillo and Mustillo explain that the choice between their two models should be based on theory and empirics. While theoretically possible, their empirical tests showed that the second of these models did not pick up significant amounts of extra variance in most cases; still, it is pertinent to unique circumstances. In my tests I also find that the first model is usually adequate, but in a few cases (e.g. Austria's FP from 2002 to 2008 and Brazil's PMDB if measured from 1990 to 2006) the more parameterized model provides better results, both in terms of the amount of explained variance as well as the intuition behind the results.

RESULTS FOR HYPOTHETICAL CASES

The simple hypothetical three-district example shows the plausible results that this model produces. To review, the model measures the variance in a party's support across time and across districts, and thus large values for SN imply inconsistent support across districts. The time component of the model is analogous to indicators of volatility, and large values of this component therefore imply that a party's national vote share is inconsistent over time. The residual component, finally, measures the inverse of DN. Larger residual values imply greater inconsistency in the change of support for the different districts across elections, having accounted for the other effects.

In the example, for C1 there is a perfectly tandem movement of the party's district-level support and the residual in the model (DN) is therefore zero. In this case other effects follow directly. Volatility is the variance in a party's average overall vote change. From Table 3.1, the volatility for C1 (and C2) would be the variance of 53 and 43, or 50; the square root of which, 7.1, represents the standard deviation of those numbers. SN is the variance of a party's average votes across districts. For C1, then, the SN would be calculated as the variance

[11] Tom Mustillo, personal communication (6/12/12).

of 54, 48, and 42, which equals 36. Again, the square root of this number (6) represents the standard deviation of the three values, so if the sample were larger, we would expect that that about two-thirds of districts would fall within 6 points of the mean district-level support.

Where DN is not zero, as in C2, the model has a residual and the calculations require more math. In this case, the model returns values of 44 for volatility, 18 for SN, and 18 for DN.[12] The values for volatility and SN are lower than for C1 since, in a sense, the model attributes some of the cross-district and cross-time changes to the residual.

The alternative models, as detailed in M&P (2005), provide misleading or incomplete results. For both countries C1 and C2, Stokes's model would yield the same values as ours for $\hat{\sigma}_A^2$ and $\hat{\sigma}^2$ but would not produce a $\hat{\sigma}_B^2$ at all. In a prominent paper, Kawato (1987) provides another model that measures the two dimensions, but it ignores $\hat{\sigma}_B^2$ and for both countries it would calculate $\hat{\sigma}_A^2 = 38$ and $\hat{\sigma}^2 = 36$.[13] The associated bias yields very misleading results (as he underestimates σ_A^2 and overestimates σ^2 for both countries). Another problem with the Kawato model (as with the Caramani and Mainwaring/Jones models that I discuss in the section on "Static Nationalization Measures") is that it yields identical results for countries C1 and C2. In contrast, the M&P model accurately reveals important differences between the hypothetical countries.

Finally, the model reveals the problems with standard calculation of volatility. The Pedersen index only accounts for the movement at the national level and thus would return the same value (10 if there were just two parties) for both countries. But, variation attributed to the SN and DN effects should be taken into account when estimating volatility, and doing so yields different indicators for these two countries. The values of the variance components for time (50 for C1 and 44 for C2), or their more directly interpretable square roots (7.1 and 6.6), are more defensible as indicators of volatility.

Results from Illustrative Cases

To demonstrate the utility of the model, I now return to the three examples from Chapter 1. The graph of Portugal's PPD/PSD suggested a moderate level of SN, given the wide range in the party's support. The lines, however, maintained a remarkable level of parallelism: that consistent pattern yields low values for the DN in the statistical analysis, and thus the party is highly nationalized on the dynamic dimension. The results of the M&M model, when estimated for the full time period, returned values for SN and DN of 55.9 and 1.1 respectively. The statistics for the Japanese LDP, calculated across the 47 provinces for the PR tier of its elections, indicate that the vote distribution among districts is very tight and that movements in the party's support across time that were closely

---

[12] When applying the stata's mixed command to generate these estimates, these results require the REML option.
[13] See Morgenstern and Potthoff (2005) for details.

parallel for all districts. The statistics tell this story very well; the static score is just 12.0 and the dynamic score was 7.3. The Chilean Concertación showed the most uneven distribution and movements, and this too is reflected in the scores. Its static score was on par with that of Portugal (51.9), but its dynamic score was many times that of these other parties (182.4).

Figures 3.1a and 3.1b provide examples of the patterns that generate different levels of SN and DN. The first set of graphs focuses on how the patterns change as SN decreases. To emphasize the change in the static dimension, I have chosen cases that hold DN under 20. Recall that lower values on the scores for either dimension imply higher levels of nationalization, because the statistics are essentially measures of the degree of variation. As the static values rise from about 10 to 170, the width of the bands increases (implying lower SN). The second set of graphs shows rising values on the indicator for DN (thus indicating more heterogeneous movements or lower DN). For those graphs the static score is always between 40 and 70. Here, as the dynamic score rises from 15 to 182, the degree to which the lines are parallel decreases sharply. To put it another way, while the support for the MNR in Bolivia follows a similar path in most districts, it would be hard to predict whether the Colombian Liberals improved in 2006 over 2002 in one district simply by knowing whether they improved in another. The graphs also highlight the influence of outliers. Excluding one outlying district from analysis in the Dominican Republic would decrease its

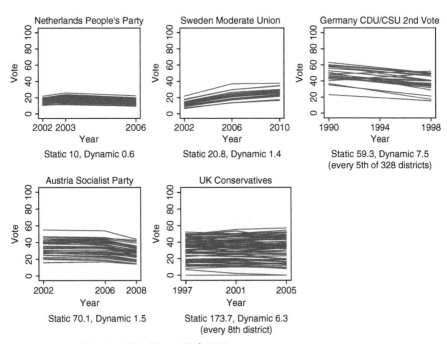

FIGURE 3.1A Varying SN, Given High DN

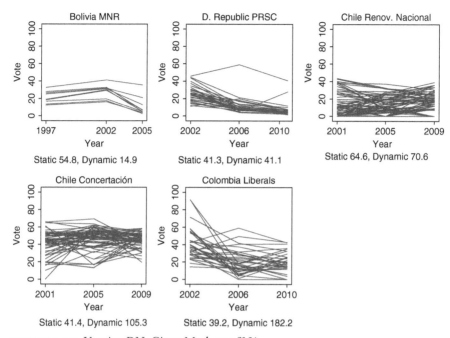

FIGURE 3.1B Varying DN, Given Moderate SN*
* Low SN or DN implies more statistical variation, and vice versa.

static score dramatically, from 41.3 to 5.0; that party's dynamic score, however, is not significantly affected by the outlier (removing it changes the DN value from 41.1 to 35.9).

In Chapter 4 I will analyze all the parties in my database and place them into the typology of nationalization types as outlined in Chapter 2. The graphs suggest that the Dutch Peoples Party is representative of a "nationalized" party, as the degree of variance is low for both dimensions.[14] The best example here for a "localized" party would be the Colombian Liberals, because the raw scores from the analysis would be high on both dimensions. The pattern shown for the UK Conservatives approximates an "unbalanced party," since it has low scores for SN but high scores for DN.

Alternative Approaches for Measuring Nationalization

While I find significant advantages in the M&M (or M&P) approach, it is not without flaws. In this and the subsequent section, therefore, I rely on my work

---

[14] As noted, the Netherlands reports statistics for 40 districts. But because they use a single national tier to distribute seats, I exclude the country from the explanatory analyses.

with Polga and Siavelis to review alternative measures.[15] The discussion highlights the utility and weaknesses of each measure, and also includes a section about weighting population, the number of districts, and the size of parties. The purpose of the discussion is to show that because each methodology emphasizes different aspects of one or the other dimension of nationalization, the measures are poorly correlated and studies of nationalization may therefore be dependent on the choice of measure. Thus, while I do have a preferred approach, this discussion suggests validating conclusions by considering alternative methods. In what follows, I first discuss those methods that focus on SN, and then those that develop concepts related to the dynamic concept. Within the discussion of SN I also discuss weighting and the translation between parties and party systems, though these are concerns for both dimensions. Similarly, I discuss how studies should deal with districts where a party fails to compete within the DN section, though it is pertinent to the other dimension, too.

Static Nationalization Measures

The most prominent comparative studies related to SN are Caramani's (2005) historical study of Europe and Jones and Mainwaring's (2003) study of the "nationalization of parties and party systems" in Latin America, both of which only address the homogeneity of support across districts.[16] These are both important works that offer compelling findings and useful methodological innovations. The results, however, do not always provide intuitive indicators of the spread of a party's support. Further, because these methodologies do not parse the sources of variance in the data, they conflate the different dimensions and produce biased results.

In the first of these studies, Caramani uses the coefficient (or index) of variation[17] to consider the spread of electoral returns to each party in each district. If the returns are relatively consistent, then the party is considered nationalized. He finds important variation across the countries of Europe, but his main finding is increased homogenization of districts over time. For both hypothesized countries in Table 3.1, the standard deviation for party P1 in both years is 6, and thus for both countries he would calculate a coefficient of 6/53 in Y1 and 6/43 for Y2, numbers that would indicate relatively high levels of (static) nationalization (but lower in Y1). There are several problems here. First, they reflect the component that Potthoff and I use to indicate SN plus the residual component (reflecting DN) combined.[18] Especially if the variance

---

[15] Caramani (2015) also provides a review of different measurement techniques.

[16] Caramani (2015) applies these ideas to Europeanization.

[17] Coefficient of variation = Standard deviation/mean.

[18] Note that for both countries C1 and C2 the sum of our $\hat{\sigma}_B^2$ and $\hat{\sigma}^2$ is 36, the square root of which (6) is the standard deviation of the party's vote percentages across districts that Caramani's method would obtain for each year.

around the dynamic component is large, these types of measures could be misleading.

Second, though his weighting by the average support has some validity, it can also produce misleading results.[19] As I discuss in more detail in a subsequent section that focuses on weighting, without a weighting system small parties will almost always look more nationalized than bigger parties, simply because smaller parties must have smaller standard deviations. At the same time, weighting the standard deviations by the average vote can have the opposite result, leading small parties that have minimal absolute divergence in their support to very low [static] nationalization scores. For example, because relative rather than absolute values drive the statistics, a variance of one would yield a very low SN score for a party with average support of two percent.

Mainwaring and Jones have a similar goal in their tests for Latin America. Instead of the coefficient of variation, they argue that the Gini coefficient, a measure typically applied to measure the equality in the distribution of income, provides a better measure of inter-district homogeneity. Like the coefficient of variation, the Gini coefficient yields a scaled statistic that is useful in comparing results among countries or over time for a single country.

While useful, their measure, which they labeled the Party Nationalization Score (PNS), has important limitations. First, as with the standard deviation or coefficient of variation, it effectively conflates the different sources of variance in the data. A second problem with their approach, as well that of Caramani, is that offsetting district support levels would go undetected. That is, because they are static, these two approaches would not detect the differences if P1's vote totals for D1 and D2 were interchanged for any year.

The implicit scaling of the Gini coefficient can lead to awkward results in other cases, as well.[20] If the party gets all its votes in one or a small number of districts (as some regional or ethnic parties do), then the model returns identical results regardless of the size of the party in the one district where it won support. That is, if the party wins zero votes in districts 1 through 3, then regardless of whether the party wins 1 percent or 100 percent in district 4, the model returns the same value (here 0.75).[21] Table 3.2 shows these and other awkward results. The first two

[19] As an example where weighting does provide better comparisons, consider a party in a 4-district country that has no support in 3 districts and wins 12 percent in the fourth district. These values also produce a standard deviation of 6. Conceptually this party is much less nationalized than are those in the example of Chapter 1, so simply using the standard deviation would be misleading. Applying the index of variation, the parties of Table 1.1 have values of about 0.1, while the 4-district party here described scores 2, correctly indicating that this is a much less nationalized party.
[20] Another problem, which is most evident with the index of variation, is that the results are dependent on which party the investigator chooses as a reference. For example, the index of variation would be different for the Democrats and Republicans in the United States, even though one is a reflection of the other. If besides P1 there is only one other party (P2) in the example of Table 1, then in either country the coefficient of variation for Y2 is 6/43 for P1 but 6/57 for P2.
[21] The index of variation has a similar problem; in this example it produces a value of 2 regardless of the size of the support in the one district where the party won support.

TABLE 3.2 *Hypothetical Problems for Gini Coefficients and the Index of Variation*

District Numbers	Party 1 % Vote	Party 2 % Vote	Party 3 % Vote	Party 4 % Vote	Party 5 % Vote	Party 6 % Vote	Party 7 % Vote
1	10	1	0	0	0	10	10
2	10	1	0	0	0	10	10
3	16	1.6	0	0	12	10	10
4	17	1.7	0	24	0	10	10
5	18	1.8	0			0	20
6	19	1.9	0				
7	20	2	0				
8	21	2.1	0				
9	22	2.2	0				
10	30	3	24				
Average	18.30	1.83	2.40	6.00	3.00	8	12
St. Deviation	5.83	0.58	7.59	12.00	6.00	4.47	4.47
Gini	0.16	0.16	0.90	0.75	0.75	.18	.12
Index of Var.	0.32	0.32	3.16	2.00	2.00	.56	.37

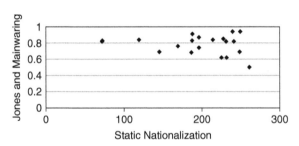

FIGURE 3.2 Two Measures of Static Nationalization

columns show the vote for two parties that differ by a factor of 10 in each district. Again, the Gini coefficient and the Index of Variation produce identical results for the two parties, even though the consistency in support for Party 2 is much greater than Party 1. A comparison of Parties 3 and 4 shows how the Gini coefficient is dependent on the number of districts. If there are four districts in a country and the party competes in one, the Gini coefficient is 0.75, while a similar scenario in a 10-district country yields a value of 0.9. Finally, the parties in the last two columns have perfect consistency in support in four districts, but Party 6 gets 10 percent less than elsewhere in District 5 while Party 7 gets 10 percent more. The Gini coefficient, however, produces different results for the two parties.

To illustrate the extent of this problem, Figure 3.2 graphs the Jones and Mainwaring values against those produced under the M&P technique for the

South American cases.[22] The figure shows a striking disjuncture for many cases. For example, of the ten parties that hover around a score of 0.8 for Jones and Mainwaring, the Morgenstern and Potthoff values range from a very low 32 (Bolivia's MNR) to over 150 (e.g. Mexico's PAN). Overall, the Gini-based measure produces very limited variance in the results, while the components of variance approach shows stark differences in the cases. This higher level of variance seems appropriate when examining the data. For Chile during the period they study (1989–2001), the Jones and Mainwaring method produces values for the leading coalition, the Concertación, that imply almost perfectly even levels of support (at least 0.9).[23] The data, however, show significant variance; in 2005 the Concertación won an average of 52 percent, but less than 44 percent in 9 districts and greater than 60 percent in another 9 districts. Overall, the standard deviation was over 7, thus implying that the coalition is not equally strong in all areas.

To provide further comparisons, Table 3.3 provides another set of hypothetical data and results from different indicators for a five-district country across two elections, and Figure 3.3 presents the results graphically.[24] The different indicators yield widely differing views of the extent of SN for these parties.

The most basic indicators of SN, such as Rose and Urwin's (1975) number of uncontested legislative seats or Caramani's (2004) territorial coverage (TC) index, measure the percentage of sub-national units in which a party runs candidates. One version of this index created by Bochsler (2010) weights uncontested districts by population while leaving contested districts unweighted. If parties do not compete in small districts their scores are only minimally affected, while if they fail to field candidates in large districts, their nationalization scores shrink significantly. Still, while these calculations capture the options parties present to voters, they do not differentiate cases where parties receive few votes from those where parties are competitive or dominant.

Subsequent indicators, which I discussed earlier, focus on variance in parties' district-level support. These include the standard deviation (SD) of the vote across districts from the parties' mean vote share, the mean absolute deviation (MAD) of vote share which Rose and Urwin (1975) label the "index of

---

[22] I exclude the US from this analysis, since Jones and Mainwaring use state-level rather than district-level results. I discuss this issue later in this chapter. They use a similar technique for Canada. Their data also includes Central America, which I have excluded here. In other places in the manuscript I reverse the M&P values, but here higher numbers imply more variance and hence less static nationalization.

[23] Jones and Mainwaring provide a country score rather than a party score, and also aggregate the 60 districts into 13 administrative regions. For comparative purposes I recalculated the scores at the district level. Their scores, however, are remarkably similar to the scores I report.

[24] This discussion is borrowed directly from Morgenstern, Polga, and Siavelis (2014). See also Bochsler (2010) and Caramani (2004) for detailed discussions of the different techniques.

TABLE 3.3 *Examples of Static Nationalization Measures*

Election 1	Voters	Vote Share				
		Party 1	Party 2	Party 3	Party 4	Party 5
District 1	10000	44	0	10	10	0
District 2	1000	42	42	2	12	0
District 3	1000	30	40	1	12	4
District 4	1000	40	44	5	10	0
District 5	50	0	30	0	70	0
Mean vote share		31.20	31.20	3.60	22.80	0.80
TC		99.62	0.23	99.62	1.00	0.08
MAD		12.96	12.96	3.12	18.88	1.28
SD		18.25	18.25	4.04	26.40	1.79
CV		0.59	0.59	1.12	1.16	2.24
PNS		0.74	0.74	0.47	0.57	0.20
wPNS		0.97	0.23	0.83	0.95	0.08
sPNS		0.85	0.00	0.44	0.81	0.00
Election 2	Voters	Party 1	Party 2	Party 3	Party 4	Party 5
District 1	10000	50	2	0	10	0
District 2	1000	40	45	0	12	0
District 3	1000	55	30	0	12	10
District 4	1000	45	48	0	10	0
District 5	50	50	30	10	10	0
M&P Static		0.00	15.91	0.00	0.00	2.46
M&M Static		0.00	15.91	0.00	0.00	2.53

Indicators defined in text.
Both the M&P and M&M statistics are the square root of the results. The Mustillo and Mustillo data is run without a year^2 term.
Source: Morgenstern, Polga, and Siavelis (2014).

variation," and the Lee Index, which takes the absolute difference between district scores and the national mean and divides it by two instead of the number of regions (Lee 1988). However, because these indicators are based on deviations from the party's mean vote share, large parties are likely to have higher variances and lower levels of nationalization (Blalock 1972; Allison 1978; Caramani 2004, 2015); the MAD and SD scores suggest that the three larger parties, 1, 2, and 4, are much less statically nationalized than Parties 3 and 5, even though the first three maintain significant support in all districts and

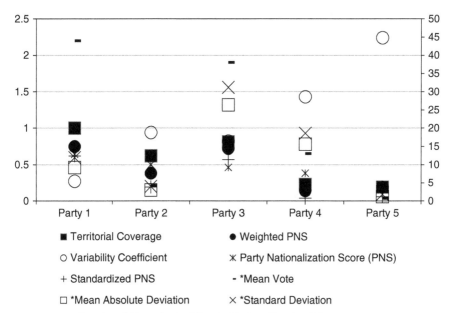

FIGURE 3.3 Graphs of Hypothetical Static Nationalization Measures
* Uses axis on the right.

Party 5 has support in only one. Furthermore, these measures do not take into account the distribution of voters across districts, as Parties 1 and 2 appear equally statically nationalized, even though Party 1 earns zero votes in a 50-person district and Party 2 wins zero votes in a 10,000-person district.

The next row displays the Party Nationalization Score (PNS), as discussed earlier. Again, Parties 1 and 2 have equal PNS, even though Party 1 earned a large share of the vote in the large district (1) while Party 2 did not win any support, and the reverse is true in the tiny district (5). Moreover, this type of model produces equal results for a party that wins a single vote in one district and none elsewhere as a second party that wins thousands of votes in one district but none elsewhere. Failure to adjust for district vote shares also suggests that small parties are more statically nationalized than larger ones, since small parties necessarily have little variance in their vote shares. It can be highly misleading, therefore, to calculate SN scores without adjusting (weighting) for heterogeneity in party or district size.

Before turning to the weighting issues which define the next two indicators in the table (wPNS and sPNS), I move to the bottom part of the table. To calculate the M&P or the M&M SN scores, the table displays a second year of data. In this example, Party 2's results imply that for about two-thirds of the districts, the party's support falls within about 15.9 points of the mean. With only two years of data, this model does not perform particularly well, strangely suggesting that Party 1 (as well as Parties 3 and 4) is nearly perfect on the static dimension. Adding a third year of data that parallels the vote in Year 1, however, does yield a reasonable estimate for SN of about 64. Still, even using just two years of data the model does provide reasonable estimates for Parties 2 and 4. In this example the M&M results are similar to those of M&P (only Party 5 has a slightly different score).

Despite the important statistical and theoretical advances that the M&P or M&M models provide, they have two weaknesses: 1) higher data requirements (at least two years of data with consistent district boundaries) and 2) a lack of control for biases in party size, district size, and number of districts. While the first limitation is offset by the improved estimation produced by using more data, the latter is only corrected through weighting. Simple commands in statistical programs such as Stata and R allow frequency weighting, but due to the problems noted earlier regarding the validity of comparing relative rather than absolute differences in the party's vote across districts, the results are not always satisfying.[25]

In sum, each measure of SN measures requires tradeoffs. The hypothetical data suggests that the choice among measures is consequential, since there is little statistical relation among the results. This implies, as my co-authors and I emphasize, that analyses should consider multiple techniques.

Weighting

This discussion suggests that variance in party size, district population, and the number of electoral districts can produce nonsensical SN scores. As a remedy, several authors suggest weighting systems. Caramani uses the Variability Coefficient (CV) to correct for the difference between large and small parties by dividing the SD of the vote score by the national mean vote share. Dividing by the party size, however, will lead to coding small parties with small absolute deviations as poorly nationalized. Table 3.3 highlights this problem in its comparison of Parties 1, 2, and 3. Party 3 is small, and all its votes fit into a range of just 10 percent. However, it has a CV that indicates much poorer SN than Parties 1 or 2, whose scores range over 40 percent. This outcome is misleading if SN is meant to capture the consistency in a party's support.

As Bochsler's review of the literature notes, several authors, including Ersson, Janda, and Lane (1985) and Rose and Urwin (1975), have proposed weighting systems to account for the difference in the population of districts (see also Caramani 2004, p. 63). The logic here is that if a party is strong in all the larger districts but weak in a small one, its nationalization score should discount the small district. Bochsler's solution, the Weighted Party Nationalization Score (wPNS), weights the district-level vote by the log of the district population and

---

[25] The Stata weighting command for the M&M model is - mixed *vote year year²* ||*district*:, mle var fw(*pop*)-, where *pop* is the number of voters in each district. For M&P, we use: mixed *vote* || _all: R.*district* [fw=*pop*] || *year*:, var.

then applies the Gini-based index.[26] In our hypothetical example this measure discounts the small District 5; as a result, the wPNS is much higher than the PNS for Parties 1 and 4, because they had consistent representation in all districts except District 5. For Party 2, the wPNS falls sharply from the PNS, because the process puts more weight on the lack of votes in the large district. A small alternative to this model would be to focus on the district magnitude rather than the population, given that parties are concerned with the number of seats in a district, not the population.

While the population (or district magnitude) of the districts is an intra-country issue, Bochsler is also concerned with how the number of districts affects inter-country comparisons. Static nationalization must be infinite (or undefined) if there is just one district, and with many districts it would be more likely that a party could build a following for a particular district. In other words, there is likely to be more variance in the support of Democrats in the 435 congressional districts than when those districts are aggregated into state-level averages. Further, when districts are larger, the party will have more incentives to develop a broad-based constituency that would cover, for example, both rural and urban populations or perhaps different ethnic groups. Thus, while there is no necessary relationship between the number of districts and [static] nationalization (except when there is just one district), Bochsler reasoned that scores for the latter should be weighted by the former. As he does with regards to population, Bochsler proposes a logarithmic transformation of the data to indicate an increasing heterogeneity of the vote as the number of districts rises, but with a decreasing marginal effect of the number of districts. For example, splitting a single district into two should almost always have a greater effect on decreasing SN than moving from 50 to 51 districts (or even 50 to 60). When weighting the wPNS by the log of the number of districts, he generates his "Standardised Party Nationalization Score" (sPNS).

This methodology does provide an important adjustment to the unweighted scores, but it too can provide some awkward results, for both theoretical and empirical reasons. The theoretical problem is that Bochsler attempts to preserve scale invariance, arguing that if a party were split in two, then each new party should have the same variance as the original. But if a large party were split into equal sized pieces that averaged just a few percent of the vote in each district, the small absolute deviations in those parties' district-level votes would be magnified in a manner that misleadingly implies low [static] nationalization.

A second problem with sPNS (and, by extension, the wPNS) results from the curvilinear nature of the Gini index. As a result, weights have a differential impact on parties depending on their level of SN. In the example, even though all the calculations are based on five districts, the ratio of sPNS to wPNS differs significantly among the parties. Note too that some of the results that the model

[26] On his website, Bochsler provides an Excel file with a built-in macro that calculates the TC, the wPNS, and the sPNS: see www.bochsler.eu/pns/index_us.html.

produces do not provide an intuitive view of the system. For Party 2 Bochsler's model yields a sPNS value below 0.01, which does not clearly identify a party with significant support in four of the five districts that include about one-third of the population. Many other distributions also fail to yield intuitive values.

In sum, weighting mechanisms have justification for SN scores, but they are imperfect solutions. With regard to the number of districts and the population of the districts, there are questions about the functional form of the weights, their differential impacts at different levels of nationalization, and whether the weights distort the concepts. The problems are most evident with regards to weighting by party size, where transformation can change small absolute deviations in a party's vote percentages across districts into large relative differences. This suggests that it is perhaps more reasonable to compare parties that are all of at least moderate size and countries with a similar number of districts than to apply weights.

Bochsler applies his weighting system to the Gini-based measure of Jones and Mainwaring, but of course this or other weighting schemes are applicable to other measurement techniques. Weighting the SD by the population, for example, would yield a much reduced value (indicating higher nationalization) for Party 1 since the outlier in terms of votes is in the very small district.[27] The empirical problem is that the weighting systems must assume a particular functional form that is not always appropriate. For example, though he recognizes that there are many potential functional forms, Bochsler chose a logarithmic function to model the expected positive relation between variance in the party's district-level support and the number of districts. Depending on how the district lines are drawn, a country with two districts, for example, could have separate regional parties, or it could have parties that compete well in both districts. The likelihood of regional parties may increase as the number of districts rises, but there is not a necessary relationship.

Perhaps because of these types of concerns, some analyses of the United States aggregate data at the state or regional level to calculate SN scores (Schattschneider 1960; Sundquist 1973; Sorauf 1980; Jones and Mainwaring 2003), but as Claggett et al. (1984) warn, this masks parties' more heterogeneous support in individual districts. For the US parties, applying the analysis to legislative elections aggregated for the 50 states, rather than computing it for the 435 districts, yields a 15 percent difference in (static) nationalization scores for 1998 and 2000 (the PNS scores were between 0.70 and 0.72 for the two parties in the two years when measured at a district level, but between 0.81 and 0.85 when measured at a state level). Similar differences appear in analyses of DN for the same data.

A related problem occurs in two-level electoral systems: should nationalization be measured for the larger proportional districts or the

---

[27] The weighted standard deviation is easily calculated by first creating a weighted average, then weighting each squared deviation by the population, and finally taking the square root of the sum and dividing by n (or n-1).

smaller single-member districts? Furthermore, there is nothing sacred about the district level. Analysis could consider party support at the precinct or any other level, too. At its extreme, every household could have its own measurement, making parties' support appear heterogeneous (present in some, but absent in many other households). In comparative perspective, this implies that countries with few electoral districts will likely have higher nationalization (on both dimensions) than countries with many.

In sum, Bochsler offers an important contribution to the methodology of [static] nationalization by forcing researchers to consider the impact of the number of districts and district size. As the examples in Table 3.3 have shown, comparing parties of different sizes can also yield misleading results. Here again weighting is possible, and Bochsler reviews several measures that deal with party size. He then argues that methodologies that indicate that small parties are poorly nationalized are often correct. As my examples show, however, it is not always clear how to evaluate results for these parties. At the party level, then, it is probably most appropriate to consider parties of similar sizes. But the weighting becomes important for models that aggregate scores for the parties to generate a value for system-level party nationalization.

Parties and Party Systems
While the work I have been reviewing focuses on parties, some authors are concerned with party systems. The party system analyses add a layer of complication, since they require another level of weighting; how much should small parties count with respect to the larger parties? Jones and Mainwaring solve this problem by simply weighing the scores of each party by their average share of the vote. Under this scheme, a party that is strong in one district and weak everywhere else would have a very small weight. Regional parties, then, would be undervalued in this scheme, even though it was created to capture the degree of localism in the system.

Another prominent measure of [static] nationalization is the "inflation" index, which measures the relation between the number of parties at the district and national levels. Chhibber and Kollman use this to compare the party system in the United States, which has a similar configuration in all districts, with that of India, which presents a variety of structures. Kasuya and Moenius (2008) further develop this concept, adding that the model should also account for the contribution of each district to the national party system (what they term "dispersion"). Bochsler, however, correctly notes that this is an indirect measure of nationalization, with numerous problems. It does clearly separate the Indian and US party systems, but the translation of the effective number of parties at the district level depends on the electoral system. In sum, inflation indices are useful indicators for indicating the consistency of district-level party systems, but they are incomplete indicators of the distribution of votes for individual parties.

A final concern with party system measures is that they may fail to account for correlations among the parties' scores. As long as there are more than two parties, there is no necessary correlation between static (or dynamic) scores in one party and another. Still, there is some dependence in the sense that one or more parties must adjust when the support for another changes. In the static sense, all the parties' scores must add to 100 percent, so while no one party is necessarily correlated with another, there is a dependence among the parties in the system.

These problems are not insurmountable (see King et al. 2000; Alemán and Kellam 2008, pp. 197–98), but because they add complexity to an already complex issue, it seems best to focus on parties rather than party systems for comparative analyses.

Alternative Approaches for the Study of Dynamic Nationalization

There are also various methods to measure the dynamic aspect of nationalization, although this dimension has been less explored than the static. Again borrowing from my work with Polga and Siavelis (2014), I focus on two sets of models. The basis of the first set is that parties that experience uniform district-level movements are dynamically nationalized, or have a small local vote. I then turn to another set of studies, some of which criticize the idea that uniform swings measure personalism or localism. While some of these studies do provide other methods for measuring the degree of personalism, most focus on a single country and are inapplicable in a comparative context.

Studies Relying on Uniform Swing

The SD of party support across districts provides a measure of SN, and in a similar manner the SD of a party's district-level swing – the change in the electoral returns for a party across two elections – provides the most straightforward measure of DN (Butler and Stokes 1969; Johnston 1981; Kawato 1987).[28] The SD of the district-level swing would give a sense of the degree to which districts move together and hence could be interpreted as measuring the importance of local factors in an election. If all districts gained or lost a similar proportion of the vote across two elections, then the SD would be small. This would indicate that national events have a similar impact across districts. By contrast, if district-level swings are inconsistent, then candidate qualities or district characteristics must play an important role in the elections. In the example from Table 3.1, for country C1 party P1 had a swing of –10 points between year Y1 and Y2 in all districts, and thus the SD of the swing was zero. By contrast, the swings in C2 were not consistent, and thus local factors must have played some role in that election.

---

[28] Caramani (2015) uses the concept of uniform swings at the country level to discuss the degree of Europeanization.

TABLE 3.4 *Examples of Dynamic Nationalization Measures*

	Swing of vote share				
	Party 1	Party 2	Party 3	Party 4	Party 5
District 1	6	2	-10	0	0
District 2	-2	3	-2	0	0
District 3	25	-10	-1	0	6
District 4	5	4	-5	0	0
District 5	50	0	10	-60	0
Mean vote (2 years)	39.6	31.1	2.8	16.8	1.4
Mean swing	16.8	-0.2	-1.6	-12	1.2
SD swing	21.1	5.7	7.4	26.8	2.7
Correlation yr1–yr2	-0.4	0.9	-0.5	-0.4	1.0
Swing SD weighted by party size	30.5	8.4	131.6	58.8	95.8
Swing SD weighted by district pop	9.8	4.1	16.8	0.5	1.0
M&P dynamic	13.5	3.6	3.9	17.8	1.9
M&M dynamic	12.1	3.6	3.8	16.7	1.7

Both the M&P and Mustillo and Mustillo statistics are the square root of the results. The Mustillo and Mustillo data is run without a $year^2$ term.

To provide other examples for this conception of the local vote or DN, Table 3.4 provides the swings implied from the same hypothetical parties depicted in Table 3.3. Party 2 provides a good example of the utility of this method, because while its average swing was negligible (-0.2%) the change in one district was substantial and in a different direction than in the others. The SD of the swing, therefore, gives a sense of that inconsistency.

The next row in the table considers a related method: the correlation of the district level vote across two elections (Converse 1969; Hoschka and Schunck 1978).[19] While also reasonable, the procedure produces very different

---

[29] A related method could use a regression of the district vote on the vote in previous elections. Adding a time element to the regression provides information about both types of nationalization. Still, Wittenberg (2008) argues that the results are misleading unless the regression line between the two sets of data yields a slope close to 1 and an intercept close to 0. His alternative is the "concordance correlation coefficient" (Lin 1989, 2000). However, it has a drawback, since restricting the intercept to zero ignores potential volatility where all districts move together with a similar magnitude (i.e. high dynamic nationalization). When there is volatility, the concordance statistic is inapplicable. One could subtract the average vote change before running the analysis, but this creates other biases. For concerns about dynamic nationalization, then, the correlation coefficient seems superior to the concordance measure, assuming analysts consider the effects of outliers and the slope of the regression line.

impressions about the relative DN levels. The SD of the swing, for example, suggests an important gap between Parties 2 and 3 on the one hand and Party 4 on the other, while the correlation coefficient would group Parties 3 and 4 as similar.

As in the case of SN, it is possible – and perhaps reasonable – to apply weights based on party size, district population (or magnitude), and/or the number of districts. Again, the last of these is only important for comparing countries with different numbers of districts, but Table 3.4 shows results for one method for weighting the SD measures in order to highlight other concerns. Here, the weight by party size is calculated by dividing the SD of the swing calculation by twice the average vote of the party.[30] The population-adjusted measure is calculated by multiplying the district-level vote by the relative size of the population, and then calculating the swing and its SD.

These adjustments yield starkly different results. First, because small parties necessarily have small variance in their vote returns and hence small swings (and high correlation coefficients), the weighted results distort the comparisons of Parties 3 and 5 with the others. While the weighted swing suggests that those parties are the most affected by local forces, it is Party 1 that experienced the widest swings. This again suggests that absolute rather than the relative sizes are more appropriate. When weighting by population, votes and swings are most important in District 1 and negligible in District 5. Therefore, the large swing for Party 1 in District 5 is discounted and the indicator shrinks from 21 to 10. This is less problematic than the weights based on party size, but care is still needed when applying them.

Of course, a model looking solely at SDs or correlations in the swing would suffer from the same incompleteness as the studies on SN. The next systems are more involved computationally, but in part because they do consider multiple sources of variance in the vote, they offer some analytical advantages. As reviewed more fully in Morgenstern et al. (2013), Alemán and Kellam (2008) use a compositional data analysis to estimate systematic and random components of the vote. They use these to represent, in turn, national forces and district-level effects. The technique has some useful properties, but its applicability is limited to two-party systems. It is also limited by failing to account for heterogeneity in district size or number of districts across countries. Finally, it is a highly complex procedure.[31]

The last statistics in the table are those that result from my preferred, but still flawed methods that were discussed at the outset of this chapter: those of

---

[30] As such, a party winning about 50 percent would have a full weight.
[31] Despite the authors' generous provision of their algorithm, my colleagues and I were unable to apply the model.

Morgenstern and Potthoff (2005), and Mustillo and Mustillo (2012). In these examples, the results for Party 1 imply that approximately two-thirds of the districts would have a variation in the change in their vote of −16.8 ± 13.5 percent according to the M&P model or −16.8 ± 12.1 percent according to the M&M model. The values pertaining to Parties 2, 3, and 5 are smaller, indicating a smaller local vote (or higher DN).

As we note in the SN section, these models do not adjust for party size or take account of Bochsler's concerns. Still, these models could be adjusted by restricting comparisons to similarly sized parties, or adjusting the final scores by the parties' average vote. To account for differences in district population, models can apply frequency or sampling weights. The weights, however, produce more reasonable estimates for some of the parties than for others. This again suggests the need for care in their application.

In sum, with or without weighting systems, all static and dynamic nationalization measures are imperfect and require tradeoffs. As a result, they can provide starkly different views of a party's profile. Choice of the measure, therefore, yields different results and will lead to different conclusions about causes and effects. Thus, while I find the methods that use hierarchical models the most compelling, where possible it is important to consider how conclusions would vary when applying other methods.

Other Measures of the Personal Vote and Non-Uniform Response

One of the reasons that DN is a particularly useful concept is that it is akin to the personal vote, a concept that has spawned considerable debate. As Swindle and I (2005) explain, the "local vote" is a broader concept than is the personal vote, but it captures the concepts that concerned Cain et al. and Carey and Shugart. Techniques that measure the personal vote, therefore, can be alternatives to those discussed earlier.

Despite Stokes's early foray into the theme and the long interest in the personal vote and related concepts, there have been few attempts to measure this phenomenon, especially in a comparative framework. The pioneering work of Cain, Ferejohn, and Fiorina (1984, 1987), which built, to some extent, from the idea of the incumbency advantage in the United States, is an important exception. The incumbency literature (Mayhew 1974a; Alford and Brady 1988; Gelman and King 1990) did attempt to separate and quantify the personal and partisan aspects of the vote, but the techniques developed do not measure the full phenomenon that DN is meant to capture. Further, while Cox and Morgenstern (2001) did show that these models are applicable to multi-member contexts, they are intended for other ends. Cain et al.'s work, however, does have more promise for studies of DN, because they have a statistical method for establishing a difference in the personal vote for the two countries in their study, the United States and the United Kingdom. Their primary evidence that the personal vote was larger in the United States than in its former colonizer were regressions for each country that tested for relations between a voter's choice for legislator and their support for the incumbent executive, plus incumbency and partisan identification. They show that while voters in both countries were driven by partisanship, the job rating for the executive was important to the British, while US voters were not influenced by the presidents' approval rating. Interestingly, incumbency was important in both models, but the influence was stronger in the US case.

While the Cain et al. model provides a useful starting point for the analysis of DN, it is not applicable for a large-n study. Their two-country model relied on separate surveys, and the direct comparability is therefore questionable. Further, they lack a direct measure of voters' choices, relying on self-reports. A large-n study would also have to contend with the changing conditions in different countries that would affect the executive's approval ratings, and would require data on incumbency which is difficult to collect for multi-member districts. Among other challenges, extending their technique would require internationally comparative surveys across multiple years. In short, while this type of analysis provides useful data for individual countries, it is inapplicable to broad comparisons.

Still, Cain et al.'s attempt to measure the personal vote in a comparative context is an exception. Most studies fail to provide a direct measure, and instead rely on Carey and Shugart's "Incentives to Cultivate a Personal Vote," which provides a coding of electoral systems based on whether they should induce legislators to make personal or partisan appeals. But as the title of the article suggests, and the authors emphasize, incentives to cultivate a personal vote are very different from the actual personal vote.

The other strand of the literature on measuring the extent of personalism in vote choice has entered into a debate about the validity of using the uniform swing as a measure of personal (or local) voting. As noted in Chapter 1, Katz (1973a) argues that non-uniform swings could be a logical response to a nationally oriented party. Stokes (1965, 1967) and Claggett et al. (1984), however, find value in studying the degree of uniformity. I agree with this latter view. It is conceivable that voters could respond in non-uniform ways to national stimuli, as Katz suggests. But if they do, then non-uniform swings would still suggest an important role of localism in politics. The localism might emphasize district characteristics over candidate qualities, however. For this reason it is more appropriate to discuss the "local effect" than a personal vote.

Brady et al. (2000) are also interested in non-uniform responses, and argue for a regression model of [dynamic] nationalization that includes as predictors the vote for the president (which is supposedly national) and that for the member of Congress in the district in the previous (midterm) election. Their measurement, however, still conflates the two dimensions of nationalization. Further, their measure may still fail to capture the differential effect that some policies would have in different districts. If the president became identified with a policy (such as gun control) that drove support in different directions, then the coefficient on the vote for the president in the previous election could be near zero, since the regression (roughly) computes the average effect. Aside from these issues, the Brady et al. (2000) model is not applicable to countries that, unlike the United States, do not employ midterm elections. As such, their model is incapable of addressing comparative issues.

Handling of Uncontested Districts

In addition to the weighting issues, an important concern in calculating the two dimensions of nationalization is how to deal with districts where a party does not compete. Caramani (2000, 2004) uses all districts in his analyses, regardless of whether a party participates in an election or not. This does show the change in the degree to which parties compete in districts. It is problematic, however, in a comparative perspective since the incentives to compete are different for systems with small versus large district magnitudes. When the district magnitude is large, the party gets seats for winning even a small percentage of the vote. But when few seats are awarded – which includes not only US- or UK-style first-past-the-post systems where only one candidate wins, but also the many systems that include some districts that award just two or three seats – only the largest parties may have an incentive to run candidates. And even large parties may decline to run where regional parties are strong.

Authors have chosen various ways to deal with this problem. Caramani's decision to use all districts without regard to whether a party won any votes is defensible, since part of his interest was to show increasing levels of coverage for the parties. But, the model will obviously overestimate the degree of variability for the United States, Great Britain, or other countries where the use of plurality rather than proportional electoral rules (i.e. single-member districts) leads major parties to refrain from competing sometimes, but not always, in particular districts.

The opposite extreme is to use just the districts where parties compete in all included elections. Morgenstern and Potthoff (2005) argue that this is the most reasonable strategy for the United States, since parties' support in the districts that they do not compete is certainly larger than zero. The strategy, however, leads them to eliminate over 200 of the 435 districts for the 1980s.

In a third strategy, Jones and Mainwaring's (2003) use states or regions as electoral districts, aggregating all the votes for each party across all districts in a state or region. This, too, is problematic. First, it bases its measures on fictional geography, because electoral seats are allocated at the district level, not at the level of states or regions. Second, in reducing the number of districts substantially, the statistics will (almost) necessarily suggest more nationalization under this methodology. As noted earlier, this problem led Bochsler to devise a weighting system to account for differences in the number of districts in cross-country comparisons.

In a set of papers, King and his co-authors propose alternative techniques to deal with uncontested districts, based on estimating the expected vote for parties that declined to participate (see especially Gelman and King 1994 and Katz and King 1999). In addition to their computational complexity, these techniques are not easily adaptable to broad comparisons, because they apply only to two-party systems or may require models specific to each case.

Conclusion

While the concepts and graphical depiction of the two dimensions of nationalization are straightforward, capturing them statistically is not. In this chapter I have argued in favor of a hierarchical model that decomposes the variance of the district-level vote as the best method. That conclusion is based on the model's simultaneous measurement of the different types of variance, its flexibility in allowing for different levels of variance (state, region, district) and weighting systems, and the wider variance it produces in comparison to other models which seems more in tune with the empirical reality. Like all others, the model is still imperfect. Part of the problem is that differences in party size, the number of districts, and the population of districts make direct comparisons invalid. Weighting can aid this set of concerns, but weights can also generate misleading results. Comparative studies also face the problem of dealing with parties that fail to compete everywhere. This too can generate biased results in statistical measurements, and there is no clear solution for resolving it. Thus, while I will focus on the hierarchical model approach, it is appropriate to apply other methods for robustness checks. To avoid concerns about weighting, in most of this book I focus on parties of at least moderate size and consciously discuss biases that arise from variance in district size and the number of districts. Finally, I generally apply the model to districts where parties compete to avoid overemphasizing volatility in district-level changes. The next chapter applies these techniques to parties in dozens of countries and uses the results to build a typology of party nationalization.

4

Applying the Model: Patterns of Static and Dynamic Nationalization

The models defined in the previous chapter allow cross-national comparisons of the two dimensions of nationalization. In this chapter I apply the M&M hierarchical model to a large database of parties from around the world. The empirical data illuminates many important features of individual countries and provides much fodder for comparative analyses. In so doing, the data supports the idea that the two types of nationalization – static and dynamic – are empirically (as well as theoretically) independent. The result is placement of the parties into the three categories: *nationalized, locally focused,* or *unbalanced.*

Beyond categorizing the parties and exploring the typology, the chapter uses the empirical applications to explore methodological issues about the overall face-validity of the findings, concerns about intra-country variance, the impact of changing the levels of analysis, and how to handle non-competitive districts. It also shows that analyses of electoral data at the district level are fraught with challenges. This chapter tackles – or at least addresses – many of these challenges. I addressed three of these problems in the previous chapter, arguing that while imperfect, weighting can resolve some concerns about the varying size of districts, the number of districts in a country, and the size of the parties. In addition, analyses must contend with parties that do not always compete in all districts, and the alliances that regional-level parties forge in the legislature. These challenges lead me to look at the data in multiple ways.

THE DATA

The database covers parties in over 40 countries and thus gives an extensive view of nationalization around the world. In this first look at the data, I present statistics for the period of approximately 1990–2010, though the time period is shorter if there was redistricting or an electoral system changed. The regression analysis of Chapter 6 uses a subset of this data and details about the specific elections used is in the data appendix and on-line country notes at my website.[1] I have compiled data for this project from multiple sources. Some came directly from electoral administrations in the respective countries. Much data, however, is now available from the comprehensive databases compiled by other academics working on issues of nationalization. The "Constituency Level Election Archive" (CLEA), led by Ken Kollman, Allen Hicken, Daniele Caramani, and David Backer, was the most important source of my data, though I have had to update many countries and verify district boundaries. Before CLEA became available, I built from the data Caramani (2000) provides for Europe. Another comprehensive database that was important to my data collection was the Global Election Database (GED) compiled by Dawn Brancati.[2] To complement and cross-check these broad data sources, I have used the European Election Database, other data have been generously provided by scholars, and my research assistants have been invaluable in collecting and coding more data. Data not available at CLEA or GED is now on my website.

There were three main selection criteria.[3] The first was continual democracy, which I operationalized by choosing only those countries that scored no more than a three on either dimension of the Freedom House index during the entire time period under study. The second criterion was that there was a population of at least five million. I did make an exception to this rule for Uruguay and Costa Rica, the two longstanding democracies in Latin America, plus the final Central American country with a small population, Panama. In the regression analysis, I do run tests with and without these countries to assure against bias. The third necessity was data availability. Data are available for many developing and less-developed countries across all regions of the world. For some countries the data are easily accessible and are included in the aforementioned databases. Other countries, however, do not provide district-level data. As I have argued, the

---

[1] www.polisci.pitt.edu/person/scott-morgenstern
[2] Caramani's data set is available on CD with the accompanying reference volume. I corrected several important errors from that database, especially for the United Kingdom. Kathleen Bawn provided the data for Germany, and the French data came from the Centre d'Informatisation des Données Socio-Politiques; my research assistants, Dana Bodnar and Christian Gineste, helped to organize the complex French data. Other assistants helped to collect and format data from other countries, including Yen Pin Su, Ignacio Arana, and John Polga. Many others, including Peter Siavelis, Mark Jones, Daniel Buquet, Ekaterina Rashkova (who helped with the "Project on Political Transformation and the Electoral Process in Post-Communist Europe" at Essex), David Lublin (see his "Election Passport"), and Andy Tow have supplied data and answered questions about how to code them.
[3] A fourth criterion is that the country had more than one electoral district. This eliminates Israel and the Netherlands. The decision about the Netherlands is not straightforward, however, since it has 19 administrative electoral districts (and the European Electoral Database provides data for 40 divisions). But, since seats are allocated at the national level, the electoral districts are politically inconsequential. Tests at this level could prove useful, but it would be equivalent to testing sub-district polling places in other countries.

electoral district is a key level of analysis, since it is the basis on which parties and candidates fight for legislative seats. Another problem that left some countries (e. g. Italy, South Korea, and New Zealand) out of the analysis is that district boundaries (and/or the district names) have changed so frequently that it was not possible to construct a time series of their electoral results, which is necessary for my analyses. This is not generally a problem for countries that use states or provinces as electoral constituencies, but for countries that divide territories into smaller units for elections, redistricting is common. I have carefully reviewed each of these cases and constructed datasets based on the time periods between redistricting. In a few cases, such as the United Kingdom and Germany, redistricting occurred in just one or a few regions (e.g. Scotland), and thus I dropped that region or affected districts from the analysis.

Finally, consistent with the recommendation of the previous chapter about comparing parties of a significant size (rather than weighting the statistics by party size) the data only cover parties that won an average of at least 10 percent of the vote nationally for the entire period under consideration. In the descriptive sections and in Chapter 7, which focuses on regional parties, I soften these restrictions. I also provide more historical data in later sections, in order to show trends for individual parties and countries. The on-line appendix gives details about each of the countries, how I resolved data issues, and why a country or party was excluded.

These selection criteria are not without complications. First, requiring that the parties gain at least 10 percent of the vote over the whole country and period of time eliminates important regional parties. However, because their participation has a direct impact on the other parties, their impact is still influential in the analysis. That is, if a regional party does well, then other parties will score poorly in that region, thus driving down SN. In turn, changes in the regional party's vote will affect the DN of other parties. Finally, as noted, I do include an exploration of regional parties in Chapter 7. There is a second problem with the data selection criteria: since parties have to compete in three successive elections, the database is biased toward the more stable systems. The result is that volatile Eastern European systems, as well as some parties in Latin America and other regions, are excluded. The case of Bolivia is exemplary; CONDEPA won an average of 10 percent of the vote in 1997, reaching 40 percent in the capital city. In the next election CONDEPA's average vote was under 1 percent (and it only reached 1.8 percent in La Paz). Again, these types of empirical realities do not undermine most of the data analyses. For cases such as Bolivia, the rise and fall of "flash" parties is reflected in the changing support of the parties that do have continual support. If CONDEPA has relatively high SN, its participation would have a consistent impact on other parties. But if its impact is strongest in one or more regions that would mean that one or more of the parties would have low SN. By extension, other parties' DN would reflect the fall of the "flash" party. Further, I do discuss patterns for some of these parties with highly volatile support in the country-level descriptions.

In terms of hypothesis testing, these types of exclusions could be consequential. If, for example, the goal is to study the institutionalization of systems, then excluding the volatile systems would be akin to selecting on the dependent variable. For the institutional hypotheses I explore in Chapter 5 or the impacts of nationalization that are the subject of the last part of the book, however, excluding these parties is less consequential.

Working with party-level data creates two other problems. The first regards name changes and coalitions. If two parties form a coalition in one year but not in another, the choice is to either eliminate both from the analysis (because they do not appear separately in the first year) or conjoin them for the full analysis. In most cases I have chosen the second route, and documented this in the on-line data appendix.

A second problem noted in the previous chapter is how to handle cases where a party fails to compete in some of the districts. Should the party receive zero for its support, or should the district be eliminated from the analysis? Generally, for countries that employ proportional representation electoral systems I have used all districts, though as I noted in Chapter 3 this might be problematic in countries that have some small magnitude districts. For the single-member district countries using all districts is problematic because under two scenarios a party could decide not to put forth a candidate in a particular district: it may lack support in a particular region, or it may prefer to husband its resources instead of wasting them in districts where they cannot win a majority. At the same time, it might make a different decision in a subsequent election, and thus the swings could look very large. At the same time, eliminating all districts where a party does not compete is problematic if the parties are consistently absent in particular districts, as is common in India, the United Kingdom or Canada.[4] It seems incorrect, therefore, to apply a blanket methodology, either including or eliminating the zero districts for all countries or parties. In some cases, then, I examine two sets of data for these countries, based on inclusion or exclusion of the "zero districts."

Two other countries provide problems for dealing with the non-competitive districts. First, in Chile the district magnitude is just two for all its 60 districts.[5] The parties are forged into two main coalitions, and the rules strongly encourage the parties to compete as part of the coalitions (Siavelis 1997). Since there are more than two parties in each coalition, the parties are unable to compete everywhere, even though the coalitions do appear in each district. Thus, I have used all districts to calculate the values for the coalitions, but eliminated zero districts for the

---

[4] Including zero districts will generally magnify statistics that show the homogeneity of the distribution of a party's vote, and thus bias the results toward less static nationalization. The statistics could generate a view of more static nationalization for parties that compete in relatively few districts (since there would be many homogeneous results). They may suggest stronger dynamic nationalization, however, because successive zeros in many districts will provide the impression that the many districts are moving in a parallel fashion.

[5] Chile has passed an electoral reform that will take effect for the 2017 election.

parties. Second, in Germany the CDU does not compete in Bavaria, but it is in a long-term coalition with the CSU, which only competes there. I therefore count this as one party, and no zeros appear. It may be reasonable to apply a similar methodology to other cases, perhaps using party families. This would greatly alter the data for Belgium, where parties divide into either the Flemish or the Dutch regions, but they have clear affinities with parties in the other. In general, however, I leave these types of analyses to country specialists.

A related concern about which parties to include is the dependent relationship among the parties' static and dynamic nationalization scores. When there are more than two parties there is no necessary relationship between any pair of parties; the heterogeneous support of one party could be absorbed by one or multiple parties. Still, there is a necessary relation among the full complement of parties, and if there are two parties both will have identical scores.[6] To account for this problem, the multivariate analysis in Chapter 5 first uses multiple parties for each country (unless there is only one with the requisite 10 percent average or there are only two parties in the system), but then runs the analysis using just the largest party for each country as a robustness check.

EMPIRICAL RESULTS AND NATIONALIZATION TYPES

In order to view the results of the analysis and place the parties into the typology, Figure 4.1 displays the estimates from the hierarchical model described in Chapter 3, using the last three available elections for each country and the case selection criteria previously discussed. It labels the points by the party's country, to give a first view of the geographic coverage in the data. As explained earlier, the scales are reversed so that lower values imply less nationalization on both scales. The figure jitters the results to avoid overlaying the observations (thus explaining the small negative values in the figure) and truncates the axes at 100 not only for display purposes, but also because very high values add little analytical value and bias averages. Values near zero imply high consistency in the changes among districts, but there is clearly less information in differentiating among cases once they have reached some (arbitrary) high level. In short, localism is a central driver of elections for all cases with values over 100. Figure 4.2 blows up the northeast (*nationalized*) and southeast (*unbalanced*) sectors for better visualization of the cases. For countries where there are two-level electoral systems (Germany), the plot includes estimations when using results from both levels. For the United States, United Kingdom, and India, the plot includes one observation that includes all districts and another (indicated by *) that eliminates uncompetitive districts. For the United States, the graph includes separate observations for several decades. Subsequent statistical analyses include only one observation per party to avoid bias. Appendix 2

---

[6] The scores would be identical if there are just two parties, since the standard deviations of their support would be the same and their swings would mirror each other.

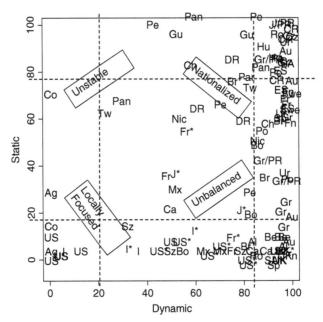

FIGURE 4.1 Nationalization around the World

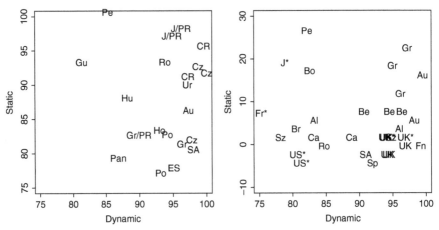

FIGURE 4.2 Nationalization around the World: Nationalized and Unbalanced Quadrants

provides results for each party and country, and, as noted, the printed and on-line appendices offer graphical representation of the data for each party.

In positioning the cases, the graphs shows wide variance on both dimensions of nationalization and give empirical evidence to the claim that there is no necessary relationship between the two types of nationalization, except that where SN is strong, DN cannot be particularly weak. The largest concentration of cases is in the *nationalized* corner, where parties have limited spread in their support around the country (SN) and any changes in district-level support are relatively parallel (DN). There are also multiple cases where the parties have low scores on each dimension, landing them in the *locally focused* category. Finally, there are a large number of cases in the *unbalanced* category, where there is significant spread in the parties' district-level support but changes in their support have low variance among the districts. As predicted, at least in the long run, high SN is incompatible with low DN, so no cases fit at the extremes of the *unstable* box. A few cases come close to fitting into that quadrant. Among these, Peru's UPP has a very high static score and relatively low DN, because it changed from an essentially regional party in the first year of the data to a national competitor in the second. In the last year (2011) it was part of a coalition but still saw its average support fall almost 20 points. The instability in Peru's party system also places another of their parties, Peru Posible, into that quadrant of the graph when applying the restricted model. Accounting for fanning, however, lowers the party's static score from the top to the middle of the scale. That party collapsed from 25 percent of the vote in 2001 to 3 percent in 2006, before recovering in 2011 with 17 percent. The label *unstable* clearly fits. The others that are close to the northwest quadrant – Taiwan's KMT, Panama's MOLIRENA, and the Colombian Conservatives – have levels of SN that are low enough such that they are not incompatible with lower values on the dynamic scale. This provides an empirical caution against drawing the margins for the categories at the center of each scale.

This example raises a wider concern about category boundaries: that broad generalizations mask variance within the categories. Empirically there are multiple cases in the center of the graph, or at the extreme on one dimension but not at the other. As foreshadowed in Chapter 2, behavioral interpretations that focus on ideal types, therefore, must take care to avoid a sole focus on the extremes. The US–UK comparison is exemplary. Parties from both countries (when excluding uncompetitive districts) fall into the lower right quadrant of the graph, but while the British parties all have dynamic scores very close to the maximum, those scores for the US parties are about 20 percent lower.[7] The breach in how these two sets of parties organize and behave suggests that the cutoff for labeling parties should not be at the center of each scale. Even dividing the scales into quarters or thirds, as suggested by the dotted lines, may be insufficient. Perhaps a different type of empirical evaluation could determine the level along the scales that generates enough motivation for parties and legislators to concern themselves with local rather than national politics.

---

[7] Exclusion of uncompetitive districts has little impact on results for the United Kingdom, but it moves the US cases far to the left in the graph. US parties in the 1970s through the 1990s had lower dynamic scores than in the 1950s and 2000s.

EXPLORING THE RESULTS

Do the results from Figure 4.1 provide a reasonable summary of the politics in these countries? Do they separate different types of parties? In order to evaluate these basic questions, I now provide some descriptions of the parties under investigation.

First, the *nationalized* quadrant groups a very diverse set of parties. The category includes several European and Eastern European parties (from Austria, the Czech Republic, Hungary Netherlands,[8] Romania, and Sweden) plus parties in Japan using the PR tier of the election. From the Americas, there are only parties from small countries (Uruguay and several in Central America) plus one (in Peru) that received just over the minimum average vote for the analysis. Importantly, several parties from countries that Caramani (2005) and Jones and Mainwaring (2003) identify as nationalized do not appear in this quadrant. For example, Caramani highlights pre-unification Germany, while Uruguay scores high on Jones and Mainwaring's scales. Here, the German CDU/CSU and the SPD look *nationalized* if using the PR tier of the elections, but they both fall closer to the unbalanced box using data for the SMD tier. For Uruguay, if the data is run for the last three years that Mainwaring and Jones use, the Colorados score at the margins of the *nationalized* box, but the Blancos and Frente Amplio score too low on SN for that category. Since Jones and Mainwaring focus on the static scale, this finding is contradictory to theirs. Another finding that partially contradicts other studies regards Japan. The highly regional and clientelistic nature of the Japanese parties would suggest that the parties would have a local focus. But, while the data from the single-member districts places the LDP into and the DPJ close to the *localized* box, the data from the PR tier of their elections suggests high nationalization for both the LDP and the DPJ. This finding suggests that electoral systems do have consequences for political behavior.

Next, five different countries – Argentina, Colombia, India, Japan, and the United States – have at least one locally focused party. The United States data represented here is for the 2000s, but other decades yield similar results. Note, however, that without uncompetitive districts the US parties land closer to the unbalanced category.[9] The other countries in this set comport with received wisdom; the Japanese parties (in the single-member district tier) have a locally focused reputation, as do the Colombian parties, especially for the period included (1994–2002). The Argentine parties function within a system where provincial politics are very important, and each election produces multiple and different provincial parties. Coalitions form, but voters often

---

[8] As noted, the Netherlands have only one real electoral district, and therefore I excluded them from much of the analysis in this book. Electoral data, however, is reported for 40 divisions, and the statistics here are based on those divisions.

[9] Becasuse, as noted, both will have identiacal scores, when there are just two parties in the system, I only include one party in the analysis.

face ballots with different party names from province to province and election to election.

While these findings are consistent with general expectations about the countries, not all the main parties in Argentina, Colombia, or India fit into this box. This supports the idea that the analysis should focus on parties rather than party systems. Most of the intra-country distinctions, however, are not particularly large. For Colombia, the graph places the Liberals in this box, and the other main party, the Conservatives, would qualify in terms of DN. Its static numbers, however, are only moderate. Similarly, the Argentine PJ fits in the box, and while its other main party, the UCR, has low DN, its static score is a bit too high for it to qualify as *locally focused*. The Indian party that does win the *locally focused* label is the Indian National Congress. The BJP fits in terms of static nationalization, but while its dynamic score (about 35) does not suggest highly consistent movements, it is too high to qualify the party for the *localized focused* category.

In addition to these parties, traditional analyses might suggest several others that should win the *locally focused* label but do not have the statistics to support that classification. For example, the Spanish Socialists or People's Party do not fit, and neither do the parties in countries with newer or less-stable democratic or electoral politics, such as Bolivia, Peru, El Salvador, Poland, and Romania. Many of these countries do have parties that suggest an important role of localism on one dimension, but they fail to qualify on another. As noted earlier, other types of analysis would have to show whether parties with moderate degrees of localism behave substantially differently from those that have high scores on either dimension.

There are some surprises with respect to the *local-focused* category. First, while the post-1989 overall support for the Chilean coalitions has been extremely consistent, the data point to important variance at the district-level. Further, the coalitions have different profiles; each had one very high and one moderate score, but these scores were on different dimensions. At the party level, scores are generally lower, even when excluding districts the party did not put forth candidates in one or more years. Second, for the period 2002–2010 the main Brazilian parties, including the PT, PMDB, PSDB, and PFL, were relatively high on the scales for both dimensions. This marks much greater consistency in the vote than was evident in earlier years.

Finally, the *unbalanced* category also has a diverse group of parties, including parties from the United States (the 1950s and 2000s, when uncompetitive districts are excluded), the three main UK parties (regardless of inclusion of uncompetitive districts), the two largest parties in Canada, as well as one or more parties in Australia (Coalition, Labour), Austria (SPO, OVP), Belgium (CD&V, PS, MR), Bolivia (ADN), Brazil (PFL), Finland (Kesk), Germany (SPD first vote), Romania (SD), South Africa (ANC), Spain (PP), and Switzerland (CVP, SP). Most of these parties are known to have variable strength around their respective countries. It may be less well known that the district-level support moves in a similar fashion. This means that a good year for any of these parties is manifested nationally, not just in the districts where it is strongest. For Belgium, the parties do not compete everywhere. This generates the low levels of SN. But, as is clear from the graphs in Appendix 1, changes among the districts hew closely to one another.

Again, there is more to glean by analyzing intra-country differences. For Canada, the Liberals and the Conservatives fall into the *unbalanced* category, but while the NDP also has regionally oriented support, it displays less nationalization on the dynamic scale. For Germany, the database has both the first and second vote (PR and SMD tiers) for 1990–98, but there was redistricting afterwards; for 2002–2008, the data covers just the PR tier of the elections. For the earlier period, the CDU/CSU coalition falls close to the *unbalanced* category, regardless of the electoral tier (the graph shows just the SMD tier), with its static score a bit too high to cleanly fall into the box. For the 2000s, the graph uses the PR tier and shows that again the CDU/CSU is close to the *unbalanced* box. The SPD, however, shows an important change. It is *unbalanced* in the earlier period, but as clearly shown in the Appendix 1 graph, the party's SN moved sharply higher for the 2000s. The Left (Die Linke), finally, is dynamically nationalized, but its SN is moderate.[10]

PARTY OR PARTY SYSTEM?

Jones and Mainwaring use weighted averages of a party-level analysis to create aggregate system-level scores. Chhibber and Kollman (2004) are also interested in party systems, and their measure, in effect, is a weighted average of party effects as well. While useful, averages can obscure intra-country variance. But, by looking at that variance, we can determine the degree to which the party-level findings are generalizable for country-level analyses.

To conduct this analysis, Table 4.1 categorizes countries according to whether the parties are similar or different on the two nationalization dimensions. It is biased toward finding similarities by excluding small (less than 10 percent average vote) and demonstrably regional parties (as in Spain or Canada). The cutoff point for difference in the table is 30 points for either dimension, but it also counts as similar all parties that have scores above 100 (on either dimension), based on the logic that such parties are not nationalized and thus statistical differences amongst them are substantively unimportant. While the analysis finds limited intra-country variance in about one-half of the sample, in the other half parties vary on one or both dimensions. In a few countries, (Bolivia, France, and Panama) moreover, parties stand apart from others on both scales.

This analysis is intentionally favorable to finding system-level patterns, because similarities among parties would justify aggregating party-level scores in order to discuss party systems. In showing that there are many intra-country

---

[10] Die Linke was created as a merger in 2007; the data thus uses the PDS results for 2002 and 2005.

TABLE 4.1 *Intra-Country Constituency on Two Dimensions*

	All same for static*	With one or more different on static
All same for dynamic*	Australia	Argentina
	Belgium	Austria
	Brazil	Colombia
	Costa Rica	Finland
	Czech Republic	Germany PR
	Dominican Republic	Portugal
	El Salvador	Romania
	Germany	South Africa
	Ghana	Spain
	Japan	Uruguay
	Mexico	
	Netherlands	
	Peru	
	Sweden	
	UK	
With one or more different on dynamic	Canada	Bolivia
	Chile	France
	Guatemala	
	India	
	Nicaragua	
	Switzerland	
	Taiwan	

*"Same" implies all values fall within a range of 30 or all are above 100; Honduras, Korea, Paraguay, and USA excluded, since only one party included in the database.

distinctions, however, the analysis suggests the importance of focusing on parties rather than the system level.

VOLATILITY AND CHANGES IN NATIONALIZATION

While the focus of the above comparisons is to separate parties at a particular period of time, the methodology is applicable for studying in-country change, a concern that drives the work of Caramani (2000, 2005) and Polga (n.d.). As Polga argues with reference to the Latin American cases, while there is a presumption (stemming from Caramani's work) that parties should nationalize over time, some parties have shown a move toward denationalization. My data includes multiple time periods for just a few parties, and thus in the remainder of this book I do not dwell on intra-country change. It this section, however, I explore a few countries to show that while the scores show general stability in most countries, change is evident in others. The subsequent section then explores changes in the United States.

Where volatility is significant, whether it results from the appearance of new parties or change among existing ones, nationalization scores are likely to change. The M&M model (and its predecessors) provides estimates for volatility and can help to contextualize the analysis. Two countries from Latin America and two from Eastern Europe provide tests for the changes in nationalization levels in the context of democratization and changing party dynamics. In Latin America, several countries (e.g. Argentina) that transitioned to democracy in the third wave did so with party systems that, at least initially, looked similar to what they had prior to their dictatorships. Others (e.g. Chile) added new parties to a base that looked similar to the pre-dictatorship period. Bolivia and Brazil fall into a third category, with new party systems. They thus provide the best opportunity for studying nationalization trends in a manner that is similar to the countries of Eastern Europe, which also developed new parties after the fall of the Soviet Union.

In Bolivia, the once-ubiquitous MNR shrank to irrelevance in some, but not all provinces by 2005. The result was decreasing static nationalization and an increase on the dynamic dimension. Figure 4.3 shows this graphically, and the M&M scores are listed in Table 4.2. The sharp drop in support in 2005 generated the lower dynamic score (implying more nationalization), but since the party retained support in a few districts, the static score remains high. The table also lists the statistics that estimate the parties' average support (the constant) and volatility (year and year squared). These large values for volatility imply significant shifts in support. In this case the shift left the party with unbalanced support, but this is not a necessary outcome.

The other Latin American case in this group, Brazil, democratized in 1985. Its first few elections produced high levels of volatility, but in recent years that has ebbed. Most interesting is the trajectory of the Workers' Party (PT), whose leaders held the presidency between 2003 and 2016. The party won just 8 percent of the vote across the districts in 1990 and its support was under 3 percent in 6 of the 27 states. Support then grew and held steady at between 12 and 14 percent for the three elections in the 2000s (2002, 2006, 2010). This growth was partly the result of increased support where it had been non-existent before, but in 2010 it still won less than 5 percent in 2 districts. The M&M scores, therefore, show little change. Using 1990–98, the model returns a static score of about 23.8 and a dynamic score of 9.9. For the 2000s, the respective scores were 28.9 and 8.4.

Moving to Eastern Europe, the Czech Republic provides another example of a volatile system, but some Czech parties have moved toward nationalization.

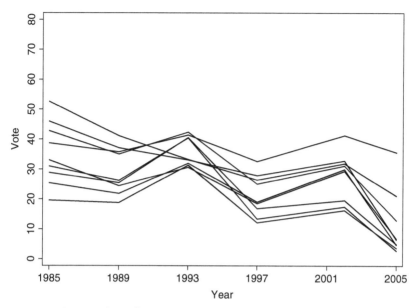

FIGURE 4.3: Support for Bolivia's MNR, 1985–2005

TABLE 4.2 *Evolution of Nationalization: Bolivia's MNR* *

Year	M&M Constant	M&M Year	M&M Year Squared	M&M Static	M&M Dynamic
1985–1993	35.3	–12.0	6.2	29.4	28.8
1989–1997	29.5	17.3	–10.7	19.5	20.1
1993–2002	36.1	–25.4	10.6	19.2	22.7
1997–2005	22.3	–5.0	1.9	54.9	14.9

*Higher numbers indicate less nationalization.

Analysis of these parties is complicated, because few that competed in the inaugural democratic elections of 1990 have continued to compete in subsequent years under the same name, and the country has continued to witness the birth and death of parties ever since. Some of the new parties, moreover, have won significant shares of the votes; the "Top 9" won 16 percent on average, with a range from 10 to 27 percent in 2010, while the largest party, the Social Democrats (CSSD), only averaged 22 percent. Further, the Czechs changed the districting system before the 1996 election, moving from 8 to 14 multi-member constituencies.

While the constant changes complicate the analysis, the country's Social Democrats have competed in each election since 1990. They started off very small, winning just 4.5 percent in the country's 8 electoral districts in 1990. They did not gain much in 1992, but in 1996 (when the country re-divided the electoral districts) the party's support grew to 26 percent, on average. They then grew a bit more for the 2002 and 2006 elections, before falling back to 22 percent in 2010. There was not much of a trend for SN during this time. Excluding 1992, when the small size of the party necessarily produced a large PNS (1-GINI), there was a small movement toward static nationalization after 1996. The more interesting change occurred with DN, though subsequent elections will be necessary to confirm the trend. The standard deviation of the swing fell from over 4 for between 1992 and 1996, and 2.3 between 2002 and 2006 (the district changes prevent tests for 1996–2002), to just 1.0 for 2006–10. If this low number is sustained, the Czech Social Democrats will have moved among categories in the typology, from *locally focused* to *unbalanced* or perhaps *nationalized*.

Hungary also allows a test of how parties nationalize after democratization, but here the statistics suggest that the patterns established in early years have not changed substantially, at least for the larger parties. Working backwards, three parties dominated the 2010 election: the Hungarian Civic Union (FIDESZ), the Socialists (MSZP), and the Movement for a Better Hungary. The last of these parties was new to that election, while the Socialists and Civic Union had competed since the inauguration of democracy in 1990. In 1994 the Civic Union was still small, winning just 7 percent on average in the country's 20 proportional representation districts. That support was consistent around the nation, ranging from about 5 to 10 percent. While it has developed some areas of particular strength, its growth has been relatively consistent, such that the range of its support fit into a band of 45 to 62 percent in 2010. The Socialists won 32 percent in 1994, 33 percent in 1998, 41.6 percent in 2002, 43.3 percent in 2006, but only 18.6 percent in 2010. The standard deviation of the support was over 4 for each year until 2010, when it fell to just 2.8. Since the SD shrank at the same time as the average vote, the party must have dissolved everywhere, rather than retaining strength in some districts. A measure of DN confirms this. Table 4.3 lists the swing and its standard deviation for the FIDESZ and the MSZP. The parties had smaller swings in the first two years than in the latter,

TABLE 4.3 *Swings and their Standard Deviations: Hungary*

	Civic Union		Socialists	
	Swing	SD of Swing	Swing	SD of Swing
1998	22.7	4.1	0.3	3.0
2002	13.0	3.8	8.8	3.6
2006	0.1	6.1	1.7	5.1
2010	11.1	5.5	−24.7	4.9

and the biggest standard deviations were in 2006, even though the actual swings were much smaller that year. That the high swing to the FIDESZ in 1998 or the negative swing against the Socialists in 2010 did not produce higher standard deviations implies that there is no particular trend toward a regional pattern of competition. Finding that for 2010 the MSZP as well as the new party, the Movement for a Better Hungary, each gained at least 10 percent in all regions, and a maximum of 28 percent, confirms that local effects are strong, but parties do not seem to be concentrating in particular regions.

TRENDS IN THE UNITED STATES

My most extensive over-time data is for the United States, and it allows a consideration of rough hypotheses about factors that may be driving change. Many journalistic accounts of US politics argue that politics have become more "nationalized," perhaps owing to campaign financing that the parties or nationally organized interest groups direct. Academics, further, have shown that the parties have become more internally centralized and externally polarized, thus also suggesting an increased element of political nationalization.

The data do not give full support to the idea that the politics have become more nationalized, but they do highlight some important changes. Figures 4.4 A and B graph the results of the M&M model for US House elections using the last three elections for each decade (excluding the 1960s, when there was wide-scale redistricting not only at the start of the decade). Higher values on these graphs indicate lower levels of nationalization, as they are indicative of larger degrees of variance. Because the high number of districts where one of the parties does not participate data are skewed by the lower line in each of the graphs therefore excludes districts where one of the parties receives less than 10 percent.

The wide differential in support around the nation (and within states or regions) of the parties yields very high values in the static graph (i.e. low SN); the square root of values when all districts are included roughly indicates a standard deviation of about 20 for the votes for each of the parties. The results for just the competitive districts show somewhat smaller values (indicating higher nationalization), but the values still range from about 14 in the 1950s to 18 in the 1980s. Note that the two lines move toward convergence in the last two decades, which is mostly explained by the smaller number of districts where one party fails to compete. These results hardly change if the analysis is run on all elections in each decade or on off-year elections sandwiched between two presidential elections. The result, overall, is that while it is not stable, SN for the United States is very low.

For DN, an analysis of M&M values using all districts yields values growing from moderate levels in the 1950s to very high levels in the 1980s before falling back somewhat in the 1990s and 2000s. The values from the analysis that uses just the competitive districts is parallel, except for the 1980s when the analysis shows a decline for the competitive districts instead of the

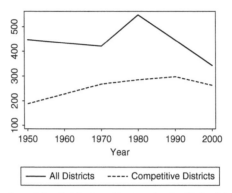

FIGURE 4.4 A Evolution of Static Nationalization in the United States

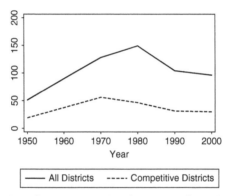

FIGURE 4.4 B Evolution of Dynamic Nationalization in the United States

sharp rise. That reduction is significant, with the values falling by almost one-half (from 55 to 30). The takeaway is still that the US parties have low DN, but there is evidence that localism is less severe than in earlier decades.

LEVELS OF ANALYSIS

How do different levels of analysis affect the results? There are two concerns. On one level, it may be more reasonable to compare results from the executive rather than legislative contests in presidential systems when comparing across regime types. This is because presidential systems allow voters to separate their choice for a local representative from the national executive, while parliamentary systems disallow this choice. Elections in parliamentary systems, then, are de facto executive elections. Second, if there is interest in understanding the depth to which parties have national roots, then local or municipal elections are also of interest. The most nationalized parties might show similar patterns for these parties as for legislative or executive elections. Others, however, might show much greater influence of local politics. In this section, I review executive elections in the United States and Argentina to show that these contests do suggest greater nationalization (on both dimensions) than do the legislative contests. I then use data from Chile to show that municipal elections highlight the role of localism.

To test for the relation between presidential and legislative elections in the United States, I ran the model on the three presidential and congressional elections that were held concurrently in 1992, 1996, and 2000, a decade that had the added advantage of holding three presidential elections between redistricting. As in other tests on US congressional elections, this sample suggested that localism was very important. The static statistic was approximately 260 and the dynamic value was over 60. The presidential election showed more homogeneity in the district-level support (SN), with a value of 167, but that still suggests a high degree of localism. The important difference in the models was along the other dimension, which returned a result of only 12 for the presidential election, putting it in a league with some of the most highly dynamically nationalized countries. These results confirm the findings of Vertz et al. (1987), who show that US presidential elections are nationalized, congressional elections are "localized," and both Senate and gubernatorial elections have state-level effects.

The Argentine data tell a somewhat different story. Argentina also has midterm elections, so I ran the tests for the congressional and presidential elections for the years 1999, 2003, and 2007. Even for a country that has experienced large electoral instability, this period was exceptional, given the wild rotation of presidencies in the 2001–2002 period. Still, regularly scheduled elections did occur, and the Peronists (Partido Justicialista; PJ) continued to win wide support. The model returned static scores that were considerably lower (implying more nationalization) in the presidential elections than in the congressional contests (77 versus 187), but unlike the United States, here the dynamic scores suggested less nationalization in the presidential elections (yielding values of 140 versus 113). But, given that these values are still very high, it would be misleading to argue that the presidential elections are less nationalized.

Going in the other direction, Chilean municipal data helps to clarify the reach of the parties to the local level. Further, these data avoid some of the complications in Chilean legislative data, because parties are able to compete everywhere. In legislative elections, by contrast, the coalition dynamics combined with the two-member district system prevents the parties from competing in many districts (see Morgenstern et al., 2012, for details). In the post-dictatorship era (1990–2010), the parties showed very high static and dynamic nationalization for the municipal elections, on a par with data for the presidency. Legislative data suggested, generally, a greater local effect.

In sum, there is not a necessary relationship between the level of an election and either dimension of nationalization. Presidential elections do not always elicit more nationalization than congressional contests, and municipal elections can show strong signs that national politics or alignments are more important to voters than local issues or personalities.

Methodological Choices and the US–UK Comparison

The US–UK comparison has been at the forefront of studies of party nationalization since the days of Schattschneider. He, as well as Stokes and Cain et al., has worried about the intense localism in US politics. This comparison has spawned important debates (and methodological innovations) about the relative and absolute sizes of the national vote in the two countries, and the trends. Are politics local in the United States, as claimed by Speaker of the House Tip O'Neil and political scientists such as David Mayhew (1974a) – or do legislators concern themselves with national party reputations, a thesis that drives the work of Cox and McCubbins? Also, have politics become more nationalized in the United States, as Schattschneider may have liked but critics of the influence of money have decried? For the United Kingdom, has the small local vote that Cain et al. found continued to grow? Has the growth of LDP or perhaps Scottish nationalism contributed to a larger local influence in elections?

These two countries will help elucidate the substantive issues, but also highlight a few methodological issues for studies of party nationalization. Among those concerns critical for any comparison are: the potential for weighting the statistics by the size of parties, the number of districts, or district population or magnitude; redistricting; how to deal with non-competitive districts, as I have discussed previously; and the impact of changing patterns of competition within a district.

These two countries provide a cogent comparison, because they both have two longstanding large parties (and the United Kingdom adds a smaller third party) that generally compete throughout their countries. At the same time, the parties fail to postulate candidates in a significant number of districts, thus necessitating care with methodology. Weighting the parties by district population is somewhat less of a concern in these countries, because the parties' single-member district systems yield relatively evenly sized districts. Weighting by the size of the parties does present some concerns, at least for the United Kingdom, due to the smaller LDP and regional parties. Weighting by the number of districts is not a serious concern in this comparison, since both countries have several hundred constituencies.

Next, redistricting provides a serious problem for any methodology that is concerned with over-time change. In the United States redistricting occurs every decade, but some states have had other changes, especially in the 1960s and 1980s. In the 1960s there were so many changes that analyses of the district-level swing would have to be severely limited. For the United Kingdom, "boundary commissions" redraw constituencies at irregular times. For the

TABLE 4.4 *Competed Districts: US Parties* *

	1950	1962	1970	1982	1990	2002
Democrats	419	426	422	416	402	384
Republicans	347	379	380	383	380	401

*Competed defined as winning at least 2.5%

three elections between 1997 and 2005, redistricting was limited to Scotland, but eliminating any region could bias SN in a positive direction. In this case, for example, the Conservatives won an average of about 33 percent in non-Scottish districts, but only 15 percent in Scotland.[11]

The next empirical consideration in analysis of these two countries is whether to use uncontested districts for the analysis. As I have explained, this problem is most concerning to countries that use single-member district (majoritarian) systems or those who have very small magnitude in some districts, because the parties may have little incentive to waste resources on elections where they are likely to lose. Table 4.4 uses the first midterm election of each decade to show that one or the other of the US parties have usually failed to compete in at least 10 percent of districts.

For the United Kingdom, the situation is even more complicated, because the pattern of competition changes in the different districts as third parties come and go. It is defensible to study nationalization without regard to the changing patterns, because the analysis is specifically trying to look at the consistency of support and change. But, in a manner similar to the problem with the non-competed districts, ignoring the changing participation of parties that win significant vote shares can yield misleading results. By the 1997 election this problem was much less severe, as the Conservatives, Labour, and the Liberal Democrats competed in almost all constituencies, with the exception of those in Northern Ireland. (The Conservatives did compete in Northern Ireland, but gained no more than 7 percent in any district in 1997, and less in the subsequent elections.) Table 4.5 highlights the number of districts in which the various parties competed since 1955.

These data concerns suggest, again, a need for a multi-methods approach to the study of either country or a comparison. Based on this precaution, Figures 4.5 and 4.6 show two approaches to the measurement; the first uses the M&M approach and the latter graphs the PNS versus the standard deviation of the swing for the US Democrats and the UK Conservatives. The graphs do not weight the observations, since both have hundreds of similarly sized districts. They do, however, show separate results when running the models on all

[11] As a result, I therefore exclude Scotland from most analyses.

TABLE 4.5 *Competed Districts: UK Parties**

	Conservatives	Labour	Liberals	Liberal Democrats
1955	612	617	110	
1959	613	618	216	
1964	618	618	366	
1966	617	618	311	
1970	616	618	339	
1974f	623	623	516	
1974o	622	623	616	
1979	622	623	577	
1983	633	632	320	
1987	633	633	327	
1992	644	634		631
1997	644	640		637
2001	640	640		638
2005	628	627		626

* "Competed" defined as winning at least 2.5%

districts (including districts where the party did not compete) from those where the same two or three parties competed in each year. For the United States, this means that both main parties won at least 2.5 percent in all elections in the sample, and for the United Kingdom it implies that either the Conservatives and Labour competed in the district without the third party, or that the Liberals or later the Liberal Democrats were always competing.[12] As noted, the hierarchical models also require consistent district boundaries, and thus the calculations for the United Kingdom are for four separate periods: 1955–64, 1964–70, 1983–87, and 1997–2005.[13] For the United States, this requires separate analyses for each decade, and it precludes analysis of the 1960s,

[12] The definitions of non-competition are slightly variant for the United Kingdom across the different time periods, due to the rising importance of a third party in some, but not all districts. As the third parties' support spread, it impacted the consistency in support of the traditional parties. These changes perhaps explain why Cain, Ferejohn, and Fiorina (1987) found that swings were less uniform in the 1970s than historically. My analysis does not show evidence that this trend continued. For the analysis, the number of districts where there was a consistent pattern of competition was 235 for the 1955–64 and 1964–70 periods, 551 for 1983–87, and 559 for 1997–2005. For the United States, changing the definition of "competed" to have much higher cutoff points has little bearing on the results.

[13] Boundaries are consistent for 1955–70, but I broke this into two pieces to have rough equivalents for the US time periods. There were new boundary changes for England and Wales in 2007.

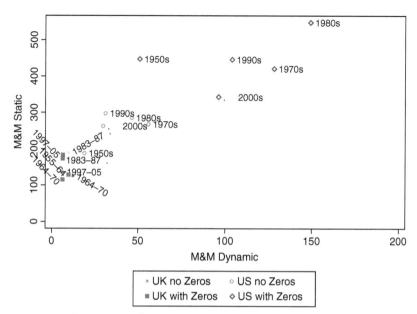

FIGURE 4.5   M&M Static and Dynamic Nationalization in the US (Democrats) and UK (Conservatives)

when there were many district changes in the middle of the decade. There has also been some redistricting in other decades, and I have adjusted the dataset accordingly.

Figure 4.5 suggests that the decision about including the non-competitive districts can determine conclusions about the comparison. When the non-competitive districts are included, then the two countries stand apart, with the US static and dynamic scores much higher (implying lower nationalization) than in the United Kingdom. When those districts are excluded, however, the differences are small. Most noteworthy, for the 1950s, the US scores look very similar to those for the United Kingdom (though in absolute terms, the US values are still significantly higher). The concerns that drove Schattschneider's research, thus, have become much worse.

Figure 4.6 substantiates this last point, especially when the analysis excludes the non-competitive districts. This graph also adds to the comparison in other ways. On the dynamic dimension the graph clearly separates the two countries, but the PNS suggests the countries are similar in terms of the distribution of support. The graph also suggests that while the change is not dramatic, the PNS scores have fallen over time for the United Kingdom, while there is no clear pattern for the United States. Third, while the difference between the two sets of data return similar scores for the UK, the decision of how to handle districts where the parties do not always compete has a large effect on the US results.

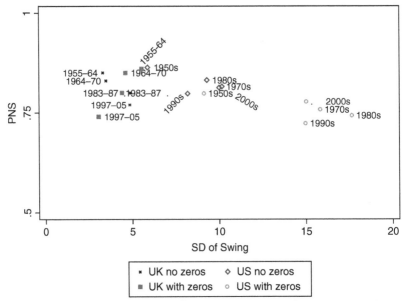

FIGURE 4.6 PNS and SD of Swing in the US (Democrats) and UK (Conservatives)

As discussed in the previous section, another methodological concern is whether to use the US congressional or presidential elections in the comparison. Interest in legislatures rationalizes a comparison of the congress and parliament, but given that the British system fuses elections of the legislature and executive, it is also reasonable to compare the US presidential election with the British parliament. Given that the models on the US presidential elections generate an "unbalanced" rather than "locally focused" categorization, the choice over levels of analysis will generate opposing conclusions.

The US–UK comparison, finally, supports the overriding conclusion that guides this book. Given that the legislative elections separate the countries much more on the dynamic than on the static scale, the generic term "nationalization" is insufficient. The data do suggest that while Stokes and Schattschneider were right in emphasizing that national issues or events translate into more consistent cross-district changes in Britain than in the United States, in neither country are elections "nationalized" by the standards applied by Caramani.[14] The British parties are "unbalanced," while the US parties – at least for legislative elections – have a "local focus."

---

[14] Stokes's work revealed a relatively large district variance component (district-time component what I have used to measure dynamic nationalization) for Britain, though he did not emphasize that finding.

Conclusion

That political parties differ in terms of organization or support bases is not a surprise. This chapter, however, has demonstrated how they differ, moving beyond general discussions and specifying how they differ in terms of two geographical aspects of their support. District-level data is messy and problematic, but armed with such data the chapter has confirmed my modeling approach by comparing the statistical results with graphical representations of numerous cases and also by describing how well the statistics fit the behavioral realities of the parties. The chapter has also furthered the methodological discussion (e.g. illuminating the importance of choosing whether or not to include uncompetitive districts in the analysis) and validated several propositions. First, it has shown that the two dimensions of nationalization are independent. Second, while there are some countries that house two or more party types, there is more variation among rather than within countries. Third, not only can there be local elements in national elections, local and regional elections can be either locally or nationally focused.

The following two chapters explain the sources of these differences, and the subsequent chapters then return to the issue of how nationalization affects political behavior.

PART II

EXPLAINING PARTY NATIONALIZATION

The first chapters in this book described the variation in party nationalization around the world and developed a statistical model to measure the two dimensions. The chapters also introduced some factors that could lead to the variation and briefly opened discussions about why nationalization is so important to politics. These two issues form the core of the current and succeeding parts of this book.

This section is broken into two parts. Chapter 4 outlines a series of hypotheses, focusing on the idea that since there are two (almost) independent dimensions of nationalization, there should be two (almost) independent sets of variables to explain them. Chapter 5 then operationalizes the variables and tests the ideas statistically. A central finding is that the electoral system, here operationalized as the number of electoral districts, drives SN, but the distinction between parliamentarism and presidentialism provides a compelling explanation for distinguishing between low and high levels of DN.

While the chapters here focus on the institutional explanations, they cannot explain intra-country variance. The chapters thus consider a number of variables that might explain why some of a country's parties are more nationalized than others. For example, do governing parties have more of a chance to extend their reach than does the opposition? Do centrist parties have more success reaching into a country's diverse regions than extremists? These types of hypotheses have strong counter arguments, and I thus conclude that intra-country variance, which is not particularly common, is explained by the lack of constrictions that the institutions create. In other words, the institutions push parties in a particular direction, but they do not determine a particular outcome.

The theoretical and statistical models discussed here are based on a paper with co-authors Stephen Swindle and Andrea Castagnola (2009). In our work we argued that "since the dimensions of nationalization are unrelated theoretically and (almost) unrelated empirically, they must reflect different causal models (p. 1323)." We argued further for the need to consider the two types of nationalization simultaneously. In these two chapters I build on that earlier work, plus literature related to one aspect or the other of nationalization (Stokes 1965, 1967; Carey and Shugart 1995; Grofman and Lijphart 1986; Morgenstern and Swindle 2005), to develop the hypothesis that different institutional variables drive the two nationalization dimensions. As in the earlier paper, I argue that "the regime type (presidentialism versus parliamentarism) – but not the electoral system – [should] drive dynamic nationalization, the reverse should be true for static nationalization," where "the electoral system – but not regime type – should take prominence in the explanation." The models here deviate from the co-authored paper, however, by focusing on the number of electoral districts in a country, rather than the distinction between proportional and plurality (single-member district) systems. Chapter 5 discusses this change and also gives more complete discussions of federalism and decentralization, ethnic heterogeneity, the influence of time, and concerns with intra-country differences. Chapter 6 then applies the new concepts to the data and finds strong support, especially for the institutional hypotheses.

5

Explaining Static and Dynamic Nationalization*

Although the term "nationalization" has two distinctive meanings, little scholarship considers the theoretical and empirical relations between them, especially in a comparative context. The objective of this chapter is to develop a set of systematic theoretical expectations that explain the two dimensions as independent phenomena. In the next chapter I will use a comparative database to test an empirical model.

The main thesis of the discussion is that since there are two (almost) independent dimensions of nationalization, there must also be two (almost) independent sets of variables to explain each. I first consider the executive system, arguing that since elections in parliamentary systems are referenda on the prime minister, DN should be higher for parties operating under parliamentarism than those in presidential systems. The electoral system is my focus for explaining the other dimension. Proportional representation gives parties incentives to compete everywhere, if district magnitudes are high enough such that small parties can compete. Proportional representation and magnitudes are correlated with the number of districts – and when that number is high, voters are squeezed into more homogeneous groups. Thus, the number of districts drives SN. Meanwhile, ethnic heterogeneity and the geographic dispersion of a country's diverse groups can affect both nationalization dimensions.

In addition to these institutional variables, the chapter also considers some party-level variables to explain intra-country variance. These include the age of

---

* Parts of this chapter are cribbed from Morgenstern, Swindle, and Castagnola (2009). There are several important differences between that paper and the current chapter. One central change is that the earlier work focuses on the difference between single-member districts and proportional representation electoral systems, while this chapter focuses on the number of electoral districts. Still, my co-authors deserve much credit in helping to develop the original ideas.

parties, the age of democracy, governing experience, and ideology. Expectations for these variables, however, are indeterminate.

Institutional Sources of Static and Dynamic Nationalization

While using different terminology and rarely distinguishing between the two types, multiple studies have focused on institutional variables to explain cross-country differences in nationalization. Three variables have taken particular prominence in these studies: the executive system, electoral systems, and federalism. First, contrasting the United States and the United Kingdom, Schattschneider argued, and Stokes (1965, 1967) and Cain et al. (1984, 1987) empirically confirmed, that the executive system – presidentialism versus parliamentarism – largely determined the level of what this book has termed DN. In addition, a multitude of studies suggest that electoral systems affect outcomes related to one or the other types of nationalization. Carey and Shugart (1995), for example, argue that closed-list proportional representation with controlled party nominations, particularly in the presence of a large district magnitude, will generate a more nationally focused policy strategy than would systems that encourage legislators to "cultivate a personal vote." And finally, an emerging literature has focused on the impacts of federalism. In their exemplary case study of four single-member district countries, Chhibber and Kollman (2004) argue that specific features of federalism explain why parties in some countries at some times develop national constituencies while others are relegated to provincial support status.

Though insightful, these studies have failed to adequately differentiate the impact of these institutional variables on the two dimensions of nationalization. However, if dynamic and static nationalization are indeed distinct dimensions, then they require separate sets of independent variables to explain them. Based on the work with my co-authors (Morgenstern, Swindle, and Castagnola 2009), I here develop the idea that the electoral system will direct movement on the static dimension, but that the dynamic dimension will be primarily driven by regime type. In addition, the chapter argues federalism should affect both types of nationalization and that the strength of its impact should be dependent on the distribution and heterogeneity of the population. The chapter also considers, but largely rejects, several other potential explanatory variables, including the age of parties, ideological positions, and governing experience.

Figure 5.1 describes the main emphases of this chapter. The main thrust of the argument is that an important electoral system variable (the number of electoral districts) has a more important impact on SN, and the executive system impacts DN. In particular, more electoral districts leads to lower SN, while parliamentarism supports higher DN. Federalism or decentralization impacts both dimensions, in a negative direction. What the figure does not clearly show is the non-linearity of the hypotheses. The rest of this chapter develops these ideas.

These hypotheses are derivatives of extant studies, but most do not consider the two dimensions at the same time. The lack of dependence in the two

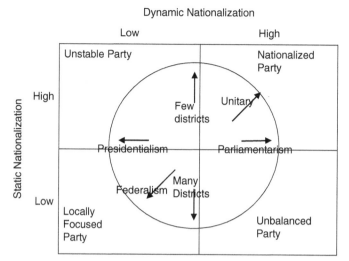

FIGURE 5.1 Institutional Hypotheses

dimensions adds complexity to this explanation; two variables that are independent of one another cannot have the same drivers. That is, if the two dimensions of nationalization are independent as I have claimed, then the prime determinants of each should also be distinct.

The Executive Systems: Impacting Dynamic, but not Static Nationalization
As argued in Morgenstern et al. (2009), the difference between presidential and parliamentary regimes should have a strong impact on DN because the electoral fates of executive and legislative candidates are so intricately intertwined in parliamentary systems. The task of selecting the executive bonds a party's legislators in parliamentary systems much more tightly than in systems where the branches are independent. Consequently, party labels tend to be much stronger in parliamentary systems, and voters, therefore, will be more likely to respond to national party appeals rather than local or candidate-specific appeals. Parties in parliamentary systems, in short, will be more nationalized on the dynamic dimension, corresponding to a rightward movement in Figure 5.1.

A similar logic tying regime type to SN, however, does not exist. Regardless of whether a system is presidential or parliamentary, parties could develop local bases, and may or may not develop national constituencies. Parties operating within both constitutional frameworks face the same challenges in spreading their support, and neither system gives parties special incentives to develop particular spatial patterns. At an inductive level, that the main parties in the United States and the United Kingdom both have variable levels of weakness and strength is supportive of this idea. Further, there are multiple countries that comingle parties with localized bases with others supported by wider (nationalized) constituencies (e.g. Canada, Argentina, Germany, Britain).

Also important to the hypothesis, parliamentarism should be more deterministic than presidentialism. In parliamentary systems, voters are necessarily influencing the executive when they choose their legislative candidate, which should lead these voters to a heightened concern with national politics. Voters in presidential systems, meanwhile, are not necessarily uninterested in national issues. The local focus should rise where executive and legislative elections are not concurrent, but factors such as the executive's sway over candidate selection or campaign finance laws could have a nationalizing impact. A refined hypothesis, then, is that while DN will be high in parliamentary systems, presidentialism may be less deterministic. That said, electoral laws, federalism, or ethnic divisions could challenge the parliamentary glue in some parliamentary systems (e.g. India and Japan).

The focus of this hypothesis is on the impact of regime type on parties in the legislature. Still, it is also useful to consider nationalization from the perspective of the support for the executive. Of course, it is not possible to separate election types in a parliamentary system. Testing nationalization in presidential systems removes one of the two potential sources of local variance – the differential qualities of the candidate – while retaining differences among the districts. Presidential elections, then, should produce higher levels of both types of nationalization in comparison with legislative elections.

Electoral Systems: The Number of Districts as a Driver of Static Nationalization

While the prime impact of the executive system should be on DN, I expect that the electoral system will have its most significant impact on the static dimension. This broad hypothesis has important implications for studies of both nationalization and electoral systems, but developing it requires delving into the many different aspects of electoral systems. An important outcome of the discussion is that a variable that is not widely discussed in the electoral-system literature, the number of electoral districts, is more important to an explanation of nationalization than other standard electoral system variables. The other conclusion is that the electoral system should have only a limited effect on DN, even though it is often invoked as a prime explanation for the cousin to DN, the personal vote.

Although I will explain that the effect of more districts on SN is partially mechanical, the impact on party behavior is still highly significant. Where there are many electoral districts, parties have to worry about many distinct constituencies. In turn, this will influence their campaign behavior as well as their priorities for government spending or other legislation.

The particular argument of this section is that a large number of electoral districts will drive down SN (vertical movements in Figure 5.1). While some countries that use proportional representation divide their electorate into a large number of constituencies (Spain, for example, has 52 districts), most countries with many districts elect a single legislator in each district. The expectation that more districts generate less SN is generated from both the direct effect of the mechanical translation of votes into seats in single-member district (SMD) or other low-magnitude systems, as well as through several indirect impacts on the nature of electoral districts when a country is divided into many parts. The hypothesis, however, is not clearly linear. While I expect that a high number of districts is a potent part of an explanation for low SN, a low number of districts is insufficient to explain high SN.

The direct effect of the district magnitude on SN is based on the idea that parties may avoid spending the necessary resources (good candidates, costs, and effort) to compete where they have little chance of winning. This is particularly pronounced in SMD systems, where a plurality of votes is required to win the seat (Duverger 1954). If the magnitude rises to even two, the number of votes necessary for winning a seat drops substantially, and more parties have a realistic chance of winning a seat. Note that the magnitude varies among districts in most countries that employ PR systems, and this creates incentives for the parties to campaign harder in the larger districts. Switzerland provides a good example. The district magnitude in its 26 districts ranges from 1 to over 30, but only 6 of the 200 seats are at stake in the SMDs. Strategic parties with limited resources, therefore, should concentrate their campaign efforts in the larger districts. Another example comes from Uruguay, where almost 50 percent of the seats are concentrated in just 1 of its 19 districts. If the parties do withhold candidates in some districts, the SN will be high, since the support levels will include some districts where the party receives zero votes. Therefore, not only should SN be lower in SMD systems, it should also decline in systems where the district magnitude varies in ways that make some districts much less important than others.

The downward pull of a high number of districts on SN would not preclude some changes over time. The main finding in Caramani's (2000, 2005) carefully documented studies is that European parties have increased their [static] nationalization over time. Likewise, Polga (n.d) focuses on cross-time changes, though he shows denationalization for parts of Latin America. These time-series analyses call attention to the limitations of institutional variables; these constants cannot explain changes. Nevertheless, my expectation is that there is more variance among cases than over time for any particular case (if the institutions do not change). Further, because Caramani focuses on state-building processes since the 1800s, his explanations for over-time change are much less relevant today, and Polga's emphasis is more on showing the patterns than on explaining why parties are not increasing their nationalization. For these reasons, my analysis will focus on the cross-country differences.

While the direct effect of the number of districts is most pronounced in SMD systems, systems that divide the country into many electoral pieces – regardless of the district magnitude – should also generate a set of indirect impacts on SN. These indirect effects work on both candidate qualities and district characteristics. First, the number of electoral districts impacts the homogeneity of districts, and the heterogeneity among them. That is, with smaller geographic regions, districts are more likely to encompass a more homogeneous group of people. This, in turn, should increase the likelihood that a district is distinct from others. It is possible that parties could try to tailor their message in different districts to the particular demands of the different electorates, but this task becomes increasingly difficult as the number of districts increases. Consequently, where districts are smaller and more numerous, the distribution of a party's support among districts should increase (or SN should decrease).

The impact on candidates supports a similar outcome. First, a reduced number of districts helps party leaders with quality control. If there are only a few districts, then party leaders have to concern themselves with a limited number of candidates, because only the top few slots on the ballots carry much electoral weight. Choosing a few good candidates is clearly easier, so the variability in the quality of candidates will increase as the number of districts increases. This should be true regardless of whether party leaders control candidate selection, it is decentralized to regional leaders, or even if the candidates can nominate themselves. Further, though the hypothesis is much stronger for closed-list systems, even open-list systems usually have a few key members, though theoretically such systems could make the coordination problem more difficult. Other systems, such as the single non-transferable vote, as in Japan pre-1993 or Colombia's pre-2003 system that allowed multiple closed lists in each party, would have a similar mitigating impact. Much would depend on the control of nominations, which is generally (but not always) less centralized in these types of systems. Still, these types of systems stand in great contrast to the task facing party leaders in other countries, who have to deal with scores or hundreds of candidates, each running an individual campaign.

It is curious that Caramani does not directly account for the mechanical aspects of proportional representation to his finding of sharply increasing [static] nationalization in Europe in the early parts of the twentieth century. He argues that PR gave incentives for parties to "expand and present candidates in all constituencies" (2000, p. 73), but he fails to recognize that the new PR systems must have necessarily shown higher (static) nationalization, even if the parties had not changed their territorial coverage. To reiterate the example from the United States, SN would appear much higher if the statistics were calculated using aggregated data from states instead of the individual electoral districts. That said, by itself the advent of PR would only produce a one-time jump in [static] nationalization, so Caramani's finding of long-term trends implies that other factors must have also been at work.

While the most general thesis is that the number of electoral districts will be negatively related with SN, other particularities of the systems can clearly drive the phenomenon. In Chile, for example, the system that has been in place since the 1990 democratic transition (but will change for 2017) virtually precludes parties from competing in all districts. It does this by dividing the country into 60 two-member districts and requiring each coalition to put forth just two candidates. Since the two coalitions usually have more than two viable players, their member parties cannot put forth candidates everywhere. Belgium provides another variant that also limits a party's participation. Since parties must put forth language-dominant slates of candidates, the parties can only participate in either the French or the Dutch speaking communities, but not both. Working in the other direction, some countries have developed requirements that their parties have significant representation across the country in order to register their parties or win representation. In Peru, for example, new parties must have committees operating in at least one-third of the provinces that are within two-thirds of the country's regions (Green and Morgenstern 2009). A law such as the one governing Nigeria's presidential elections would also support SN. There, to win in the first round, candidates must win at least 25 percent of the vote in two-thirds of the 36 states. Birnir (2008) systematizes these types of laws that restrict participation of small parties. She discusses district magnitude, financial requirements, signature requirements, and requirements related to the regional distribution of supporters. Su (2013) also considers registration requirements, theorizing about their impact on small parties. Keeping smaller parties out should increase SN for other parties.

As the maps in Chapter 2 displayed, low SN can result from concentrated support in one (or a few) parts of a country (as in Belgium or Bolivia), or from a checkerboard pattern of support (as in the United States or within England). These two patterns have different origins and thus require different explanations. The first pattern is related to historical precedents (e.g. the joining of different regions into a country), concentration of particular ethnic groups, and migration patterns. Since the groups are concentrated regionally, parties could do well by appealing to regional interests. Note that they would do well regardless of whether the regions are carved into numerous SMDs or are represented by large PR districts. The latter pattern-type, by contrast, follows a different logic. Though this support pattern might be a function of localized pockets of ethnic groups, it may also reflect urban–rural splits, as in the United States. Parties working within this context cannot make regional appeals; by definition, these parties have followers in different regions of the country, and thus their appeals must be more national. This does not preclude parties that make appeals to minorities or urban workers, for example, since such groups might have multiple concentrations. Under this pattern of voter distribution, SN would likely be much higher under PR rules than under SMDs. In a SMD system, a party that does well with a particular type of voter (ethnic groups, laborers, farmers, etc.) would win only in particular districts. Under PR, alternatively, if potential supporters were distributed in a checkerboard pattern, the party would win a similar (even if small) percent of the vote in multiple districts. For example, if US states were individual electoral constituencies, then the urban–rural divisions within the states would be masked. The Democrats, then, might still not win majorities in the Southern states, but the variance among the states would be smaller than the variance among districts within the states (which ranges from zero to one).

To summarize, the preceding discussion suggests two main testable hypotheses. First, SN will be lower when there are more electoral districts. Second, in comparison with PR rules, SMD systems should produce lower levels of SN. If ethnic groups are concentrated regionally, however, the difference between these two types of electoral systems should have less impact.

The discussion about electoral systems requires attention to several alternative hypotheses. The first is related to the impact of list type (open versus closed) on SN. The expectation is that closed lists would increase SN, since they reduce the incentive to cultivate the personal vote (assuming the district magnitude is of at least moderate size). This seems a weak alternative hypothesis, however, since the list type has no effect on the mix of voters in each district. It also seems not to matter whether or not the central party leaders or sub-national groups control the lists. The former would certainly have incentives to make efforts to appeal to provincial interests with their lists, as would the latter. Open lists should not alter these outcomes, since the candidates themselves must concern themselves with constituency-level concerns. In some sense, open systems automate the process of managing the lists. Thus, while there could be volatility among district-level factions, at the national level the party could see more consistent returns. Thus, again, open lists should not harm SN and I therefore expect that the difference between open and closed lists systems would have less of an impact than the number of districts.

It is also necessary to consider why I do not expect as strong a link between the electoral system and DN. Given the close tie between the personal and local vote, and the extensive literature tying electoral systems to the personal vote (as discussed in Chapter 1), it is necessary to delve into this hypothesis.

Earlier I argued that the most important driver of DN is the legislators' relationship with the executive. Relative to district-level concerns, campaigns in the United Kingdom, for example, place much more emphasis on the party and prime-ministerial candidate than is common in the United States (Cain, Ferejohn, and Fiorina 1987). It may be the case that when electoral systems are combined with presidentialism, the electoral system variables (ballot, pool, and vote) that Carey and Shugart (1995) hypothesize as increasing the incentives to cultivate a personal vote would harm DN. I expect, however, that while the electoral systems might have some explanatory power, the qualitative impact of the executive system will be greater. That is, the range of differences should be much larger between parliamentary and presidential systems than among countries within these regime types that have different electoral systems.

A specific piece of the argument is that the number of districts should not have a large effect on DN. This hypothesis implies that a campaign that "lifts all boats" would be equally likely where there are many districts as where there are few. As an example, Reed et al. (2012) explain a [dynamically] nationalized outcome in Japan in 2005: "[I]n words and actions, Koizumi managed to nationalize the election around a single idea (reform) and to convince voters that a vote for the LDP nominee in their district was a vote for reform" (Reed et al. 2012, p. 364). Still, once there are at least two districts, differences in sociodemographics, economics, or candidate qualities can cause disparate rates of change in the parties' electoral success for the different districts. As the number of districts increases, the likelihood of different rates of change should also increase. It seems, therefore, that DN should be low where there are many districts, but may also be low where there are few districts. It is, therefore, not necessary to have many districts to produce low DN. A question, however, is how this incentive system interacts with that created by the executive system. Under presidentialism, it seems that a high number of districts should be a reductive factor, because that executive system does not constrain DN. But, because I expect parliamentarism to work in favor of DN, there is not a clear expectation about the combined impact of these two variables. I expect, however, that parliamentarism will be the bigger force.

The electoral system variables provide several other hypotheses, when working within one of the two executive-system types. In parliamentary systems, open lists should have only limited impact on SN, as explained earlier, but they may not harm the DN, either. My earlier argument was based on the idea that parliamentary systems should produce high DN, since voters will focus on the executive election. If they concomitantly can choose among legislative candidates (i.e. lists are open), there could be some electoral variation at the candidate or factional level. But since the statistics for both types of nationalization (and legislative seat distribution) are based on aggregating intra-party choices, intra-partisan variance is immaterial. If the data were measured at the level of factions, open lists – which permit factional differentiation – would likely produce lower DN. But at the party level, it seems that open-list systems should not decrease the expected high level of DN in parliamentary systems.

The expectation of a limited impact of list type on DN is similar for presidential systems. Parallel to parliamentary systems, the number of districts should negatively impact SN, but I predicted lower DN under presidentialism. Recall, however, that in Figure 2.1 the northeast category is labeled "unstable" because low DN cannot sustain high levels of SN. Therefore, if DN is low, the expectation must be for low or moderate levels of SN. Adding the pulls toward personal votes for individual legislators that open-list systems imply would not affect this prediction. Like the predictions for parliamentary systems, while open lists allow different vote totals for individual candidates, these systems should generate relatively consistent vote percentages across electoral districts, since each list would be attuned to the particular district.

In sum, this section pointed toward a strong influence of the number of districts on SN. First, where there are fewer electoral boundaries, the parties' coordination of campaign strategies should be much easier. Relatedly, having fewer districts improves the parties' ability to choose similarly qualified candidates. Second, as the number of districts increases, so too does the distinctiveness of electoral districts, thus harming SN. An important caveat is that when ethnic groups are concentrated, the difference between large PR districts and smaller SMDs would not be as consequential as when groups are spread throughout the country. I also argued that the number of districts should have only a limited effect on DN. Its impact, however, should be more pronounced in presidential systems. The other piece of the argument in this section was that the electoral system variables typically associated with the personal vote (in particular, open versus closed lists) should not have much effect on static or dynamic nationalization.

Impacts on Both Dimensions: Federalism and Decentralization
Unlike the previous two institutional variables, federalism or political decentralization should negatively impact both dimensions of nationalization. The straightforward expectation is that decentralized political structures should increase the degree to which local politics drives elections by a) bringing extra focus on the regions, b) creating important independent political forces, and c) increasing the difficulty in coordination for the national parties.[1]

For the dynamic dimension, federalism or decentralization should generate variable responsiveness to national forces in the districts (lower nationalization), because local politicians will have interest in and capability of reacting to local events and issues. In unitary systems, national decision-makers can more easily mandate local political strategy, thus reducing local variation in response (or increasing DN).

On the static dimension, federalism should have an impact through the development and manifestation of the heterogeneity of the districts' preferences.[2] First, because federalism is often the result of divergent regional interests (based on the level of urbanization, ethnicity, or localized economic concerns), it should be correlated with SN, even if the relationship is more consequential than not causal.[3] Second, even if a country's regions were not divided by socioeconomic or sociopolitical variables, federalism should breed

---

[1] See Brancati (2008) and Harbers (2010) for an elaboration of this argument. Simón (2013) argues for a conditional relationship of decentralization and the electoral systems. He explains that federal systems are more likely to generate low levels of [static] nationalization when there is also an electoral system that promotes a personal vote. Regional parties, however, do not rely on personal-vote systems. In fact, they may be better able to form and institutionalize in closed-list PR systems where they can control nominations.

[2] As explained in footnote 1, Simón (2013) argues that electoral systems and decentralization interact such that decentralization will reduce [static] nationalization in the context of electoral systems that promote a personal vote.

[3] Agricultural regions, for example, should be expected to vote in ways distinctive from those of industrial centers where local elites have the independence to fashion regional campaigns.

politicians with ties to a region who have interests in differentiating themselves from the party. Unitary systems should reduce such independence, and by imposing more uniform campaigns, they would reduce SN.

While the association of federalism or decentralization with higher levels of one or both dimensions of nationalization is straightforward, there is a potential danger of endogeneity or reverse causality. Caramani's (2000) historical study argues that with modernization, countries overcame a regional focus – "the territoriality of political cleavages" (67) – and this naturally resulted in parties nationalizing [statically]. He explains, for example, that over time schools and the military helped created a national image, and political problems required more national attention. This led politicians to lose their positions as independent leaders of their localities and become more "representatives of the national . . . political organization." By implication, the [statically] nationalized parties would have helped to reify the countries' centralized structures.

This discussion suggests two further questions. The first regards the parties' intentional role in changing their electoral strategies. In Caramani's study, state building required that parties overcome regional foci. The base of all collective action studies, however, suggests that national needs are insufficient to drive individual parties' electoral strategies. Chhibber and Kollman (2004) and Cox (1997) provide a more complete and compelling argument that would justify Caramani's findings: that exogenous conditions created more interest in the national prizes, which in turn led regional competitors to alter their messages to embrace national themes. This story does not explain contemporary distinctions in countries or parties, but it does comport with the patterns that Caramani found of sharply increasing nationalization in Europe during the nineteenth and early twentieth centuries.

The second question is whether a reverse process would also be possible? Could countries move from a central to a regional focus, and could parties in these systems then push for decentralization? Alternatively, even within a centralized system, could parties develop a regional focus, and then perhaps lobby for decentralization?

Chhibber and Kollman answer "no." They argue that moves toward (de)centralization of government are the "consequences of larger forces that work mostly independently of the party system" (2004, p. 21). Among those forces they cite state-building efforts, wars, extension of social services, and economic necessities as the main drivers in centralization of governments. They recognize that parties can be partners in these changes, but they justify their claim of the exogenous effect by noting that the governmental changes occurred prior to the changes in the party systems. For the reverse, provincialization, they argue that provincial parties have arisen only after power was given to the local authorities, though they do accept that national parties have devolved power in response to threats from regional parties.[4]

---

[4] For a summary of this part of their argument, see pp. 227–30.

An important emphasis of Chhibber and Kollman is that federal systems are not of one kind. They provide extensive discussions of changes in the federal arrangements across time in each country, showing that changes in the federal-to-state (province) relationships correspond with the strength of regional parties. There is less emphasis on cross-country analyses, but they argue that the party system in the United States, at least since the 1930s, has been more homogeneous across the nation due to specific laws that prevent regionalization. By contrast, the Indian federalist system privileges state governments, which creates incentives for parties to form at the state level and for voters to support them. In Canada, similarly, the importance of regional governments has encouraged the maintenance of a strong regional party, at least in Quebec. Finally, although unitary, Britain's moves toward provincialization that started in the 1990s have helped smaller parties to grow there, too. For the cross-national hypothesis they offer scant data, but two pieces of evidence do suggest that India stands out, at least in the contemporary period. First, they show that the level of national taxes is lowest in India. Then, to support their claims from the voters' side, they show that Indians see state governments as having responsibility for economic matters while voters in other countries focus on the national governments.

Some parts of the analysis, however, are still incomplete. For example, in the beginning of the book the authors promote India as the clearest example of a poorly integrated party system. This is based on statistics that show an effective number of parties just above two in most districts, but many more at the national level that result from different parties competing in different states (and districts). Later in the book, however, it appears that the United States (since the 1930s) is the exceptional case, given that the same two parties compete in all districts (excepting the cases where one party runs unopposed). They are not able to explain, however, why India, Canada, and Great Britain all have important third (or more) parties, yet the United States does not. They surmise that this is a result of the weight that potentially localized parties want to have in the bargaining for a presidential candidate, but they would need a different type of analysis to test whether this is significantly different to that in countries where there is bargaining over a prime minister.

In part the authors dismiss the ability to provide inter-country explanations, saying (but not emphasizing) that federalism or decentralization will permit but does not explain whether unique parties will form at the regional level (c.f. Chhibber and Kollman 2004, p. 212). This justifies their focus on differences across time within the countries rather than on cross-country differences.[5] But for a book about federalism, it is frustrating that they cannot explain the relative differences in the systems. It seems from their analysis that Britain's devolution is comparable to the Canadian or Indian federalism, given that it has helped to produce important parties that compete in Scotland and Wales (as well as the

---

[5] They admit this in some places, saying, for example, that the analysis supports the "periodization of the nationalization of party systems" (p. 175).

Liberals who compete nationally). In their theoretical chapter, however, they argue that voters are not tempted to support local parties in unitary systems, because national governments can simply cancel local powers or override their decisions (c.f. p. 75).

Their measure of party "aggregation" is also to blame for their inability to clearly differentiate the four countries in their analysis. They measure the differences in the average number of effective parties at the district level with the effective number at the national level. As they explain, if just two parties compete in all districts (D), but each district has its own set of two parties, then the national results would suggest 2D parties competing for office. Alternatively, if the district-level candidates join national parties, then the competition at the district level could be identical to the national level. They find that Duverger's law generally holds, producing two parties per district. But in some cases, notably India, the districts do not always have the same two parties and thus the effective number of parties at the national level can be much higher than two. The implication of their theory is that regions (states) in India should be less integrated than in the other countries. This may be true, but it still fails to explain why Britain and Canada have important third parties while the United States does not. Their statistical methodology generates this categorization, and they admit that it is incomplete. The problem is that while in absolute terms the difference in the effective number of parties at the national and state levels for India (about five) is much larger than for the others, the small absolute differences between the scores for the United States (about zero) and the other countries (about one) is more consequential to describing the party systems. That is, the party system of the United States stands out because the same two parties compete everywhere, while the other systems produce important regional and non-regional parties. The fact that India produces more of them is important, but to use a game-tree model analogy, there is also a second important differentiation. At the first node, the game differentiates systems that produce two or more parties; the game then ends (at two parties) or it then differentiates among systems producing higher numbers.

Another problem with this analysis is that it is not fine-grained enough to distinguish parties that compete in specific regions from those that compete nationally, though this is an emphasis in the qualitative analysis of the book. Why, for example, is Canada's NDP successful at competing across the country, while another third-force competes only in Quebec? Importantly, if Quebec is excluded from the analysis, then the difference between effective number of parties at the district and national levels for Canada is just 0.3 (using data from 2004), a value that looks very similar to that for the United States. But, with three important parties (even excluding the BQ), Canada's elections and political system work very differently than those of the United States.

Chhibber and Kollman's (2004) focus on the integration of parties across districts is also problematic in that the concept has some relationship to both static and dynamic dimensions of nationalization, but it fails to distinguish between them. More precisely, the statistics they discuss are tied to SN, but the theory is perhaps more closely tied to DN. To generate the same number of effective parties at both the district and country levels (generating maximum integration based on their measure), SN would have to be very high. For example, assume three parties competing in all districts, two of which win about 40 percent of the vote and the third receiving 20 percent. If we denote the larger parties with capital letters and assume that each has an even chance of being the smallest party, then we can represent about one-third of districts as ABc, another third as AbC, and the final third as aBC. This would generate an effective number of parties at the district level of 2.78 and 3.0 at the national level. Under this scenario, SN would be fairly high, and the Chhibber and Kollman's measure (0.22) would indicate moderately high levels of integration. If we reduce the level of nationalization, perhaps assuming that only two of the three parties compete in each district (generating districts that would be denoted by AB, AC, or BC), then the Chhibber and Kollman statistic would indicate less integration too (with the value rising to 1.0, based on 2 effective parties at the district level, and 3 at the national level). While these examples show the direct tie of SN and Chhibber and Kollman's statistical indicator, the idea that parties aggregate by coordinating across districts suggests common platforms by the parties and responses by the voters – behaviors that define DN. In sum, the authors are convincing about the impact of federalism or decentralization on aggregation, and this has a definitional relation to SN. What is unclear is whether the mechanism apparent in their theory, which implies that (de)centralization impacts both types of nationalization in a similar way, is correct. Given, as I showed in Chapter 4, that two of the countries in their sample, Canada and the United Kingdom, have low levels of SN but high levels of DN, the theory may be incorrect or underspecified.

One final problem with the Chhibber and Kollman analysis is that they are not able to discuss which regions (or districts) will coordinate. They argue that districts within a state or province have such incentives when that level of government holds important power. But in all the cases, some parties aggregate across state or provincial boundaries. For example, in 2004 India's BJP received more than 20 percent of the vote in 19 of the country's 35 states,[6] and the Indian National Congress (INC) won as much in 30 states. Further, 2 of the 5 states where the INC failed to win an average of at least 10 percent had only a single electoral district. For the BJP, 9 of the 19 states where they won an average of less than 10 percent had 6 or fewer districts.

This discussion has several implications for my hypotheses. First, decentralization can be as consequential to either type of nationalization as formal federalism. Some countries that are formally unitary then, require a decentralized label. But, given their findings about the details of the federal arrangement, poor coding of the countries could miss the nuanced role of this

---

[6] India has 28 states plus 7 union territories.

variable. At the same time, neither federalism nor decentralization is sufficient, and may not be necessary, to lower the levels of SN or DN. Next, federalism or decentralization is a reasonable independent variable for an explanation of either dimension of nationalization, given the exogenous forces that have created it. Still, if the larger-n analysis finds a correlation, then it will be necessary to confirm which occurs first: (de)centralization or (de)nationalization. This is particularly relevant for Latin America, where many countries have moved toward decentralization in recent years. If, however, the parties in these countries showed low levels of nationalization prior to the changes, then the hypothesis would not be confirmed. Countries that have seen the levels of nationalization or federal arrangements (decentralization) changed, therefore, will provide critical cases for these hypotheses. Another implication is that while Chhibber and Kollman's theory suggest that political decentralization should impact both types of party nationalization, the analysis is most clear for the static dimension.

Summary of Institutional Variables

Table 5.1 summarizes the institutional hypotheses. The predictions are that 1) presidentialism will have limited effect on SN, but be negatively associated with DN, 2) that many districts will increase SN and have limited (but perhaps negative) impact on DN, and 3) federalism will be negatively related to both dimensions. The table captures these ideas by three indicators, +, o, and –, representing, in this same order, the hypothesized effects for the executive system, the number of districts, and whether or not a country is federal or decentralized. For example, the top left box combines a presidential system, many districts, and federalism. For SN, presidentialism is hypothesized to have no relation, so it earns a label of o. The other two variables are hypothesized to work against SN, and thus they get the negative sign. Overall, the coding of o – – should result in lower

TABLE 5.1 *Summary of Predictions* *

| | | Presidentialism | | Parliamentarism | |
| | | Many districts | Few districts | Many districts | Few districts |
		E D F	E D F	E D F	E D F
Federal	Static	o – –	o + –	o – –	o + –
	Dynamic	– o –	– o –	+ o –	+ o –
Unitary	Static	o – +	o + +	o – +	o + +
	Dynamic	– o +	– o +	+ o +	+ o +

*E, D, and F refer to executive system, the number of districts, and federalism, respectfully. Symbols (+, –, o) indicate hypothesized impact of each variable.

SN. As explained in the preceding text, these hypotheses come with caveats and nuances, including a lack of linearity and concerns of necessity and sufficiency. Further, it is unclear whether the variables might operate more as substitutes for one another, or whether summing them yields a better model. For example, will the combination from the above example of o- - produce lower SN than o+- (Presidential, Few districts, Federal)? Also, will o++ (Presidential, Few Districts, Unitary) produce a similar level of DN as +o+ (Parliamentary, Many Districts, Unitary)? Careful testing is necessary to disentangle these questions. Further, other variables also interact with the institutions, including, as the next section argues, ethnic heterogeneity.

The Interaction of Federalism and Ethnic Fractionalization

Caramani (2000, p. 102) hypothesizes that: "the factors that account for country differences today [in terms of [static] nationalization] are rather those of cultural (linguistic and religious) fragmentation … What distinguishes the European national territorial structures are the differentiated patterns of the defence of agrarian interests, regional (cultural and economic) specificity, and religious autonomy." But, Cox (1997) argues that institutions can permit or repress expression of cleavages, and thus he studies the interactive relation between electoral and sociodemographic variables. Specifically, he combines the "restrictiveness" of the electoral system with ethnic fractionalization to predict the number of parties. His suggestive study is applicable to the study of nationalization. Specifically, how does ethnic fractionalization, independently and in concert with electoral variables or federalism, impact one or the other dimensions of nationalization?

Disregarding the interaction, if there is a high level of ethnic diversity, and the groups are geographically concentrated, the electoral units will be distinctive (generating low SN), and the response of local regions to national electoral forces is not likely to follow a parallel pattern (lowering DN). The independent hypothesis, therefore, is that, as ethnic fractionalization increases, both types of nationalization should decline. This hypothesis is partially validated by Caramani's (2005, p. 311) discussion of Europe:

The multicultural countries are the most regionalized: Switzerland, Belgium, Germany and the North of Italy are in the ethnically, culturally and linguistically fragmented "city-belt" of Europe. However, Spain, Finland and Britain (the so-called "Celtic Fringe") are also characterized by cultural diversity. The homogeneous countries are the Protestant countries of the North, where Protestantism acted as an important factor for the integration of religion and language. Yet this cultural fragmentation has no impact unless it expresses territorially. There are cases in which deep cleavages are not territorial including the Netherlands, but also Austria, where the Lager constitute a functional rather than a territorial division (Lehmbruch 1967). In opposition to cultural fragmentation, the left–right dimension is a clear factor in homogenization. This dimension is everywhere homogeneously distributed.

Two sentences stand out from this paragraph. First, some of the diverse countries do not yield low [static] nationalization (high regionalization). Second, not all cleavages are regional. Further theorizing is therefore necessary.[7]

A first consideration is that the impact of ethnic diversity is dependent on the electoral system and federalism. As noted above, Chhibber and Kollman argue that regional interests arise after the devolution of power from the center. This suggests that ethnic heterogeneity will play a more prominent role in determining nationalization in federal or decentralized systems. In other words, federalism will allow for these disparate interests to be expressed in national elections.

The logic here is that a heterogeneous population constrained by strong centralizing institutions may be incapable of politically expressing those differences, and a homogeneous population with the freedom to express differences may simply have no incentive to do so. However, in all likelihood, a heterogeneous population that is given the political opportunity to express those preferences will take it.

Cox's work (1997) suggests that electoral systems should also interact with ethnic heterogeneity. In this case, however, the relationship may be less deterministic than would be a prediction for the number of parties. Here, if a group is concentrated, and relatively large *within that region*, then it is likely to compete regardless of whether the electoral system is permissive (e.g. high magnitude PR) or restrictive (e.g. single-member district/plurality systems). The number of districts would also play a role here; if groups are small, then winning representation will require either a high number of districts (regardless of the electoral system's restrictiveness), or a large magnitude PR system. Caramani discounts some of the regional parties because they garner a small percentage of the national total. But they play outsized roles in their districts, and therefore should not be discounted.

If the groups are not large enough to assure victory in restrictive systems, the permissiveness of the electoral system should play a role. In such a case, a permissive system would encourage a small group to participate, and its votes (and seats) would come at the expense of larger (more national) parties. This would also be true if the ethnic group were "pillarized" rather than regionally concentrated.[8] Thus, permissive systems should harm SN. This conjunction of forces would not necessarily impact DN.

[7] Caramani's sentence implies that he finds that regionalism is relatively unimportant (i.e. SN is high) in Spain and the United Kingdom. However, he then shows trends for individual parties that highlight the important role of regional parties in both of these countries. Overall, then, the finding of limited regionalism, which is based on averages for all the parties in the system, is misleading. Similarly, the German regionalization that his statistics produce is partially a function of dividing the CSU and CDU into separate parties. Measurement choices, again, produce different interpretations.

[8] Caramani explains that cleavages can be territorial or not. This, he argues, led to federalism in Switzerland, but "pillarization" in the Netherlands (2000; p. 81).

Differences across Time and Parties

The goal of my study is more to consider cross-country differences rather than cross time changes, but the historical focus of earlier studies (at least of SN) plus my focuses on parties rather than party systems forces consideration of intra-country differences and changes. Although I know of no studies that focus on changes in DN, the personal vote, or related topics, two studies are prominent in explaining change in SN over time. Chhibber and Kollman (2004) argue that cross-time changes have been the result of changing federalist arrangements in Canada, India, the United States, and the United Kingdom. Their study, however, is inapplicable to my broader data analysis that considers countries at a particular point in time. In the other study, Caramani argues that increasing [static] nationalization across Europe, especially through the 1800s, is an indicator of change from regional divisions to a left–right split that cut through the regions. He attributes the positive change to the socializing effects of schooling and the military, plus improvements in communication.[9]

The biggest change that Caramani shows, however, came before World War I. As noted, his broad study discusses the contribution of PR to the incentives for parties to seek broad regional support, but he fails to discuss the fact that the advent of PR, which occurred in most cases in the late nineteenth or early twentieth century, had a strong mechanical role in bringing down the parties support heterogeneity. This does not, however, detract from his interesting analysis that explains the parties' changing mobilization and organizational strategies. Further, in showing different rates by which parties (or party families) nationalized (see Figures 3.3 and 3.4, pp. 87–88), he gives weight to the non-institutional explanations. It is particularly telling that he finds that [static] nationalization reversed after World War II for Catholic and Protestant parties, while others continued in the opposite direction.

To focus on the post-World War II period, this discussion suggests that parties adapt to new structures but they need time to develop national-level structures. This seems particularly relevant for new parties, perhaps in new democracies, but Caramani's analysis of the confessional parties suggests that older parties may change their support structure as well. Mainwaring and Zoco's (2007) study of the impact of time on democratic experience might support this idea. Like Caramani (2000), they contend that over time parties should work to spread their support across the nation. The hypothesis, then, is that more mature democracies should have higher [static] nationalization. An alternative hypothesis is that the age of the party, rather than the age of the

---

[9] In his later book, Caramani (2004) does consider regional parties within the context of the general trends that he finds toward [static] nationalization. He provides a rich description of development at the party level for multiple countries, and his explanation focuses on how ethnic and religious cleavages preserve regional parties. What is still missing is why [statically] nationalizing parties were able to overcome these cleavages in some places but not others, or how both national and regional parties co-exist.

democracy, should have more impact. Still, given that some new parties gain widespread support, and some older parties consolidate their support bases in limited geographic regions, I would not expect that statistical tests would show that party age would prove to be a telling variable. For similar reasons, I do not expect democratic or party age to have a significant impact on DN.

Another important problem with the time variable is that some Latin American countries (and perhaps others) have recently experienced denationalization, at least on the static scale Polga (n.d.). Ethnic and regional parties have come to the fore, for example, in several Latin American countries, and they have gained rather than lost force in parts of Europe. Explaining the rise of ethnicity as a political force is beyond the scope of this study, but several studies do discuss the rise of ethnic parties.

Several studies show that ethnic parties have arisen due to the awakening of ethnic identities, perhaps due to the influence of international media and aid groups plus better communication. In concert with this awakening, there has been a move toward decentralization, also encouraged by international lenders and aid groups, which would encourage formation of regionally concentrated groups so that they can wield political power. Birnir (2008) adds an institutional angle, arguing that whether these new passions are converted into parties depends on the stringency of party formation rules. While acknowledging the importance of institutional reforms and other factors that have disabled the traditional parties, Madrid (2012) argues that the recent rise and success of ethnic parties in Latin America is largely the result of a change in tactics; the most successful parties, he explains, have "used a combination of inclusive and ethnic and populist appeals" (pp. 3–4). The extent to which these parties have attracted a broad range of constituents that extend beyond cultural and geographic boundaries would determine the impact on SN.

To some degree, whether parties adapt their appeals and expand their electoral take is a function of the leaders' interests. Strom (1990) defined these as a mix between votes, office, and policy. If the leaders are ensconced in their regions and are content to pursue local interests as marginal legislative players, then they may not modify their platforms. Green parties, Canada's Bloc Quebecois, and the Basque party in Spain provide examples of this type. If the parties do want to challenge for national office, then they must widen their appeals. Brazil's PT and Bolivia's MAS would provide examples of this path.[10]

These examples suggest a potential relation of SN and governing experience. At the same time, there are some ideological parties on both the left and the right, as well as parties based on dedication to the environment parties, other issues, or perhaps protest, that have national appeal but are shut out of the

---

[10] For Brazil's PT, the growth in the 1990s and 2000s was more evident at the presidential level than for the Congress. In the Congress, the party did grow, but in many states where it was very weak in 1990 it did not improve very much. Bolivia's MAS, by contrast, grew from insignificance in some provinces in 2002 to at least 38 percent support everywhere by 2009.

government. Thus, while parties with governing experience are likely to have higher SN, not all parties with high SN will gain executive office.

The preceding suggests several hypotheses. First while parties may seek to widen their appeal and thus increase their SN (and perhaps DN) by softening their stringent messages, ideologically focused parties may have small but wide appeal. Thus, ideology should have an ambiguous impact on SN (and perhaps DN). Second, age of the democracy or the party should also lack determinism, because some parties appear uninterested in pursuing votes or office over policy.

There are also two institutional hypotheses to help explain intra-country differences. The first is more mechanical than political; smaller parties that are not bounded by a specific region (which usually means that they overcome the 10 percent hurdle imposed on this analysis) will generally have higher levels of both types of nationalization. Second, where there are some small-magnitude districts, a reasonable strategy might be for a party to focus its resources on larger districts. This could generate intra-country differences, because the parties that do compete in the small districts would have higher SN scores. This could also affect DN, since the parties might forego the small districts in some but not all years. The party size variable, however, might capture the same phenomenon.

To further explore these hypotheses, it is useful to turn to the data. Building on the discussion from Chapter 4, Tables 5.2a and b detail intra-country differences, first for countries that produce variant static scores and then for the dynamic dimension. The two columns present, for each country that has important separation on the variable, the parties with the lowest (implying high values from the analysis) and highest level of each type of nationalization.

Table 5.2a highlights 17 countries with significant intra-country variance with regards to SN.[11] It is first notable that most of the parties in the top right box have moderate rather than high levels of SN. Second, of those that do have high SN, size clearly matters. The only two exceptions (with SN less than 20 and an average size greater than 15 percent) are in Germany and Portugal, where one of the parties had somewhat less consistent cross-country support than my hypotheses with regard to districting might expect.

The case of Mexico is instructive for the governmental experience variable. There the Institutional Revolutionary Party (PRI) shows more nationalization than the other parties, but its score is in the moderate category. It is unsurprising that this party, which ruled as a hegemonic force until the late 1990s (and won the presidency again in 2012), would have strong national coverage. The patterns for the other main parties are more interesting. Both the National Action Party (PAN), which held the presidency for 12 years, plus the Party of the Democratic Revolution (PRD), which has not gained executive office, have grown from their regional bases (the PAN in the north and the PRD in the south) to have national presence. Still, the PAN is very weak in some districts (it won

---

[11] As in Chapter 4, difference is defined as a difference of at least 30 on the scale, though all scores over 100 are considered similar.

TABLE 5.2A *Outlying Parties in Countries that have Variance on Static Nationalization*

Lowest SN	Highest SN
No Significant Difference on Dynamic Dimension	
Argentina	
PJ (209)	UCR (75)
Austria	
OVP (105)	FPO (14)
Brazil	
Dem (PFL) (100)	PMDB (27)
Colombia	
Liberal (89)	Conservative (33)
Finland	
Kesk (196)	Kok (34)
Germany PR	
CDU/CSU (70)	SPD (18)
Mexico	
PRD (168)	PRI (73)
Portugal	
PPD/PSD (69)	PS (18)
Romania	
SD (122)	Greater Romania (8)
South Africa	
ANC (283)	Dem Alliance (20)
Spain	
PP (144)	PSOE (43)
Countries with High Variance on Dynamic Dimension	
Bolivia	
MAS (164)	MIR (33)
Canada	
Conservatives (234)	NDP (82)
France	
PS (94)	FN (35)
Peru	
APRA (75)	Fujimorista (0)
Switzerland	
FDP (376)	SVP (89)

SN Values in ( ). Lower values imply higher levels of SN.

TABLE 5.2B *Outlying Parties in Countries that have Variance on Dynamic Nationalization*

Lowest DN (=High Score)	Highest DN (=Low Score)
No Significant Difference on Static Dimension	
Taiwan	
KMT (77)	DPP (18)
Countries with High Variance on Static Dimension	
Bolivia	
MAS (46)	MNR (15)
Canada	
NDP (51)	Conservatives (11)
France	
RPR/UMP (44)	FN (3)
Peru	
UPP (58)	APRA (18)
Switzerland	
SVP (69)	SP (5)

DN Values in ( ). Lower values imply higher levels of DN.

less than 10 percent in 18 districts), but it is present in all 300 districts and its static score improved markedly from the 1997–2003 period to the 2006–12. The PRD shows a similar pattern; it won at least 10 percent in 290 of the 300 districts, and its static score also showed increasing nationalization in those two time periods. Presence in government, therefore, would not explain these patterns.

The idea that small district magnitudes may engender different patterns among a country's parties is consistent with the Swiss experience. The Swiss have 26 districts, with magnitudes ranging from 1 (in 6 districts) to 34, and their legislature has 200 seats. Some of the parties do abstain from participating in some of the small districts. Excluding the SMDs has dramatic effects on the SN score for the Christian Democrats and the Radical Democrats (the former changes from 324 to 155, and the latter from 376 to 33). Other countries, however, do not lend much support to the idea. In Spain, for example, the two main parties both compete in the one SMD (Melilla).

The discussion suggests several conclusions. First, while most intra-country differences are of a limited nature, there are some sharp divisions. Most of these occur when there is a small party with much higher SN (i.e. low value in the table) than others. Second, the presence of small-magnitude districts is only telling in some countries, and there are ambiguous expectations about both governing experience and ideology. Thus, with the exception of average vote (or perhaps its log), this inductive view does not suggest a strong variable contending to explain intra-country differences.

Switching to the other dimension of the analysis, what variables explain intra-country differences on DN? As with the static dimension, finding that all parties in a country are similar would provide evidence for an institutional explanation. In my dataset (Table 5.2b), there are just six countries where the range of DN among the parties is large: Bolivia, Canada, France, Peru, Switzerland, and Taiwan. All of these, except for the last, also display large variance on the static dimension.

Canada, Bolivia, and Switzerland allow consideration of the explanatory variables of interest. First, the Canadian example highlights the idea that even among this small group of countries, there are more similarities among a country's parties than differences. Canada's NDP shows poorer DN than the BQ, the Liberals, or the Conservatives, but the range is only from moderate to low. The lower rate for the NDP is mostly a function of their strong advances in Quebec: while in other parts of the country the party also grew between 2006 and 2011 (from 21.2 to 27.0 percent), in Quebec the rise was dramatic (from 7.5 to 42.4 percent). As the NDP took support from each of the other three parties in Quebec, the change in the dynamic score for the NDP's was larger than for the others.

The change translated into higher values in the calculations, implying lower DN for the NDP, because the party gained on average of just 6 points in other provinces. The other parties had moderate levels of DN, owing to important, but still more consistent changes. For example, the Conservatives lost about 5 points throughout Quebec, but gained almost 5 points elsewhere. The Liberals lost about the same percentage in and out of Quebec (10 and 7 points respectively), its moderate score of 25 was the result of intra-regional changes. In Quebec, for example, the Liberals' swing ranged from a positive 1 point to a negative 18. Overall, however, this example shows more in terms of similarities among the parties than differences.

In Bolivia, the range of DN scores is only between 15 and 46, with the current president's party, the MAS, showing the least nationalization. The relatively low values (high DN) are perhaps surprising, given the volatile party system and regional divisions. The small number of districts (9), however, may help to repress the statistic. In terms of intra-country differences, it is the MAS that shows the least nationalization. That party has risen sharply since 2002, starting at just 12 percent and then gaining 20 points in each of the two succeeding elections. Given the magnitude of the swings, it is not surprising that there was some variance among the districts. What stands out from viewing the graph of district-level support (see Appendix 1), however, is more the consistency in the change for MAS. That other parties have even stronger DN, however, suggests that being in government has not been a determinant for these values.

Switzerland has multiple medium-sized parties, most of which have strong DN, and low or very low SN. Exceptions are the Free Democratic Party (FDP) and the Swiss People's Party (SVP) which fall into the low DN category. Here the variable district magnitude seems the appropriate explanation. As noted, 6 of the 200 seats are at stake in the SMDs. The parties therefore have incentives to concentrate their campaign efforts in the larger districts. The results are stark: the FDP and SVP compete only occasionally in some of the districts where there is only a single legislator at stake, thus causing high levels of volatility. Dropping the six districts from the analysis thus provides a radically different view of DN for the FDP and SVP, moving them from low to very high. The regionalism of these parties, therefore, appears more an artifact of the skewed population in the cantons combined with the electoral system than a function of the parties' limited reach in some parts of the country.

Overall, the lack of many intra-country differences provides a first bit of evidence for the role of institutional explanations in explaining DN. The exceptions do not pull strongly against this hypothesis, but they do suggest a weaker version of the expectation. Several of the countries with intra-party differences are federal or decentralized, which clearly contributes to variance in the ways the parties organize their support. But because not all decentralized countries have low levels of DN, the impact of political decentralization does not appear to be deterministic.

A final hypothesis that this intra-country analysis helps to examine regards ethnic heterogeneity. While the set of countries in Table 5.2b might suggest that decentralized political structures combined with ethnic heterogeneity may generate at least some regionally concentrated parties, the larger set of countries suggests, again, that this combination of variables is an insufficient explanation. The case of Spain, where, in spite of decentralization and ethnic heterogeneity, both parties have high DN, confirms this point.

In sum, on neither dimension are there many important intra-country differences, thus validating the variables that focus on institutions that differentiate countries. The party-level analysis is still important for distinguishing among regional parties and avoiding misleading aggregations (at least when regional parties do exist), but the consistency in intra-country results suggests that analyses will bear more fruit by investigating inter-country variance.

Necessary, Sufficiency, (Non)linearity, and Substitutability

The hypotheses I have put forth are oriented toward statistical testing, which I carry out in Chapter 6. The tests, however, are complicated because, as I have described, the expectations are not all linear, and some variables are hypothesized to be sufficient but not necessary for driving one or the other aspects of nationalization. Further, while I have discussed some interactions, I have not tried to hypothesize about whether the different independent variables should have an additive effect, or whether it is best to consider them as substitutes. In other words, if a country is pushed toward localism by decentralization, will multiple electoral districts push it further in that direction, or will it have already reached such a local focus that the other variable has no noticeable impact? Further, if the variables pull in opposite directions, does one dominate the other? The combination of multivariate tests and discussions of particular countries (including outliers) in Chapter 6 offers partial answers to these questions. They suggest: 1) the institutional variables (the number of districts, the executive system, and federalism) do have the predicted impacts, and 2) the size of the party is inversely related to the SN. With the exception of size, 3) the most other intra-country variables discussed in this chapter, including party age, ideology, and governing experience, do not show statistical significance. Finally, 4) while ethnic diversity does not work in the regressions by itself, I do find the expected relations for the degree to which ethnic groups are geographically segregated.

6

Institutions, Ethnic Heterogeneity, and Party Nationalization: A Statistical Analysis*

The chapter provides statistical evidence to explore the theories described in Chapter 5 which seek to explain parties' location on each of the two nationalization dimensions. Toward this goal, the chapter employs both bivariate probes as well as a "seemingly unrelated regression" (SUR) model in order to test the main hypothesis: that electoral systems are more important to the static nationalization, while the executive system drives dynamic nationalization. Along the way, the chapter also tests for the impact of other variables discussed in Chapter 5, including federalism, ethnic and other societal cleavages, the segregation of ethnic groups, party age, and governing experience.

Operationalizing the Independent Variables and Graphical Tests
The dependent variables in this chapter are the M&M scores derived from the hierarchical model developed in Chapter 3, for about 100 parties across 37 countries (see Chapter 2 and Appendix 2 for details).[1] As explained in Chapter 4, for most of the analysis I truncate the scores at 100 because higher values provide little added information about the level of localism.[2] I then reverse the scale such that higher values imply more nationalization. A few tables and figures use raw values, and these are noted in the respective notes.

---

* The testing strategy parts of the theory discussed in this chapter are based on Morgenstern, Swindle, and Castagnola (2009). The current chapter updates the data and refines many of the hypotheses. It also provides a more extensive review of the data, theory, and literature.
[1] Data used in some tables and in earlier chapters includes other parties and countries. The analysis in this chapter uses only those cases that meet more stringent criteria as defined later in the chapter. The two Polish cases meet all criteria, but some independent variables are undefined, thus accounting for the difference between 96 observations in some tables and 94 in the regression.
[2] Of course, there are more sophisticated methods of scaling the values, but these do not appear to have a significant influence on the result, while they do then require a more elaborate explanation of the scaling method.

While defining and measuring the dependent variables – the two dimensions of party nationalization – has required several chapters of explanation, operationalization of the explanatory variables is relatively straightforward. In this section I walk through each of the independent variables and use graphs and bivariate tests to show how each relates to the nationalization dimensions.

THE EXECUTIVE AND ELECTORAL SYSTEMS

The first explanatory variable is the form of the executive. The hypothesis is that parliamentary systems should generate higher DN, but the executive system should have little impact on SN. Most cases are clearly presidential or parliamentary, though some cases are hybrids (Finland, France, Portugal, Switzerland, and Taiwan). The dataset includes 38 parties that function in parliamentary countries, 9 semi-presidential cases, and 49 parties operating under presidentialism.

Table 6.1 shows that by itself, the executive type separates the cases not just for DN, but also for the static dimension of nationalization. Specifically, the average party in a parliamentary system has a DN score of 89, while the parties in presidential systems have scores that are about 20 points lower. This was expected. The 20-point difference on the static score, which suggests parties in parliamentary countries have more heterogeneous support, was not expected. A partial explanation is that the difference in the dynamic scores is more substantively important, since the parliamentary average approaches the maximum on that scale. The static cases, by contrast, put the average party from all executive types in the middle range. Later sections of this chapter show that a second reason for this result is that the bivariate test misses the effect of the electoral system.

A comparison of the United States and the United Kingdom – countries that both use single-member districts but differ in terms of the executive system – provides added support for this hypothesis. As I showed graphically in Chapter 4, while the parties in the two countries display similar levels of SN, DN has been was much stronger in Britain than in the United States.

TABLE 6.1 *Nationalization and Executive Systems*

Executive System	Static Avg	Dynamic Avg	n
Presidential	54.7	70.2	42
Semi-Presidential	36.7	78.4	16
Parliamentary	34.5	89.1	36
Average	44.3	79.1	96

As explained in the text, values in this and other tables (unless otherwise indicated) are based on reversed scale of the M&M hierarchical model, with transformed values truncated at 100. Higher numbers (with a maximum of 100) thus imply more nationalization, on each scale. Note that Poland is included here but not in regression analysis, due to missing data on other variables.

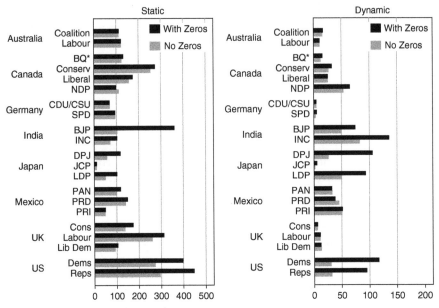

FIGURE 6.1 Nationalization, SMD Countries*
* Raw values without truncation. Higher numbers thus imply less nationalization.

While this comparison does support the importance of the executive system to the dynamic but not the static dimension of nationalization, like other low-n analyses this one is problematic. If we include other countries that use single-member districts in the analysis, we find that almost all have low SN, but there is wide variance on the dynamic dimension (Figure 6.1), suggesting that the system for choosing the executive is not determinate for DN, at least among this set of countries. Among the parliamentary countries, parties in Australia, the United Kingdom, and Germany shows very high DN, while those in India lie at the other end of the scale. The Canadian parties and the main Japanese parties are comparable to the US parties when restricting the analysis to the non-zero districts. When moving from datasets that include districts where the parties do not compete to an analysis that excludes these districts, the results show much higher, though still not high, DN for parties in the United States, Japan, and India. There are very few "zero districts" in Canada and Mexico (the other presidential case with single-member districts), however, so the results hold steady. This is an interesting result, given the high variability of the parties' support (low SN) in those two countries. A question for future research is why parties in these countries have continued to compete even in those districts where they have limited chances of victory, instead of husbanding their resources as carefully as those in the United States, India, or Japan.

One more piece of evidence also supports the idea that presidential systems generate more locally focused *legislative* elections than do parliamentary systems. While most of the data in this book focus on legislative elections, if we test data from presidential contests a much more nationalized picture emerges. As an example, DN for Chile's Concertación coalition at the legislative level yields a very low raw value (42; where higher numbers indicate more variance and thus lower nationalization), while the results for the presidential elections yield a value (13) that would indicate a party with high DN. Results for the United States are even more dramatic: for the 2000s, the statistics measuring DN using legislative elections are about 100, while results for the presidential contests are rock bottom (about 10).[3]

In sum, while parties in most parliamentary systems do have high levels of DN, and most presidential systems have moderate or low levels, there are a few exceptions. Among the exceptional parliamentary cases it appears that the use of single-member districts – or other systems that use many electoral constituencies – may be a countering force.

THE NUMBER OF DISTRICTS

The main hypothesis that I developed in the previous chapter regarding the electoral system focused on the number of districts. This variable ranges from just 7 (in Costa Rica) to over 500 (in the UK and India). There are two main parts of the electoral system hypothesis: 1) electoral systems explain SN more than DN, and 2) a low number of districts would not determine the level of SN, but it would necessarily be high if there were many districts.

Table 6.2 details the evidence for these hypotheses. When there are many electoral districts, SN is weak, and it goes up as the number of districts increases. Interestingly, there are a few parties (in Chile, France, and Spain) that do have relatively strong SN even in the face of a large number of districts. The table also provides support for the second hypothesis, because there is

TABLE 6.2 *Nationalization and the Number of Districts*

Number of Districts	Static Avg	Dynamic Avg	N
<25	57.9	84.0	42
25 to 50	47.5	73.9	29
>50	17.9	77.0	25
Average	44.3	79.1	96

See note, Table 6.1.

---

[3] Excluding the zero districts does sharply reduce the values for the US parties (to under 50).

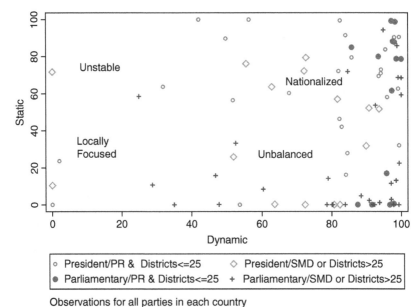

FIGURE 6.2 Nationalization by Executive Systems and Number of Districts

only a weak correlation between the number of electoral districts and DN. Dynamic nationalization is a bit higher when there are few districts, but the substantive difference between a party that scores 74 rather than 84 on that scale is marginal. Note that if we restrict the analysis to those countries where there are fewer than 10 districts (Bolivia, Costa Rica, and South Africa), the range on DN is still very wide (from about 50 to 100).[4]

INTERACTING THE EXECUTIVE SYSTEM AND THE NUMBER OF DISTRICTS

Figure 6.2 codes the data for the executive type and the number of districts to empirically validate the hypotheses regarding the interaction of the executive and electoral systems.[5] While not explaining all the variance (I address some additional variables in later sections of this chapter), the figure shows that 1) parties in parliamentary systems that have few districts have high levels of DN,

---

[4] In the regressions at the end of this chapter, I find a linear relation between the number of districts and SN, but a curvilinear (logarithmic) relation also returns significance for the variable. This specification shows that adding a few more districts is relatively unimportant once a threshold is passed.

[5] The five semi-presidential cases – Finland, France, Portugal, Romania, and Taiwan – are coded as parliamentary in this graph.

2) only parties operating in presidential systems are at the extreme low end of the dynamic scale, and 3) the only cases where parliamentary parties score on the low end of DN are those where there are many districts involved (but most in this situation still have high DN scores).

The first test is whether a small number of districts is associated with placement in the top part of the graph, and, of these, whether parliamentarism pushes the cases to the right. Among the parliamentary cases that have a small number of districts this is borne out, with two exceptions: three parties from Belgium and one from South Africa defy the prediction and land in the *unbalanced* (southeast) corner of the graph. The results for Belgium, of course, are owed to the arrangement that requires parties to participate in either the French or the Dutch speaking communities, but not both. The low SN, therefore, is the result of parties receiving zero votes in about one-half of the constituencies. For the African National Congress (ANC), the results do not fit the prediction as well, but the weak SN is perhaps a bit misleading. South Africa has only 9 electoral districts, and the ANC support ranges from dominant (over 80 percent in 4 regions in 2009) to strong (a bit under 50 percent in 1 region). The low SN thus fails to capture the idea that the ANC does compete well everywhere. Meanwhile, the other main party, the Democratic Alliance, obtains a high SN score, because while it is strong where the ANC is weakest, its low support elsewhere constrains the SN value.[6]

For parties in the parliamentary or semi-presidential countries that utilize at least 100 electoral districts – Australia, Canada, France, Germany (SMD tier), India, Japan (SMD tier), and the United Kingdom – almost all land in the lower right part of the graph, with low SN and high DN. The only exceptions fall into ambiguous areas of the graph. The French Gaulists, for example, are in the middle range on both variables and the Indian parties have low SN but only moderate DN.

The next expectation is that parties in presidential cases with many districts will tend toward the *localized* (southwest) part of the figure. Those parties that land in that quadrant – the two Argentina parties, the United States (usually, and especially when including uncompetitive districts in the analysis), and the Colombian Liberals – are all presidential and have at least 24 districts.[7] Many other cases with these characteristics, however, are not confirmatory. The graph confirms that presidentialism pushes cases to the left part of the graph, but the association between parliamentarism and high DN is stronger. Further, the number of districts does not seem to predict the Cartesian placement for the parties in presidential systems.

---

[6] For Finland (which is not a pure parliamentary case), most parties do fall in the nationalized box, but the Centre Party (Kesk) has wide variance in its support. In particular, it receives very low support (less than 10 percent) in the Swedish-speaking region of Ostrobothnia and the region that houses Helsinki (Uusimaa), and very high support in the some of the rural regions.

[7] The two open circles in that quadrant are for Argentina, which has 24 (provincial) districts. The US parties have had higher DN in the 2000s, at least when using just districts where both parties won at least 10 percent.

Two-level Systems

Three countries in my database – Germany, Mexico, and Japan – use two-tiered electoral systems,[8] which divide their countries two ways: a large number of single-member districts (the SMD tier), and a smaller number for proportional representation elections (the PR tier) (see Shugart and Wattenberg 1993; Moser and Scheiner 2012).[9] As such, these systems provide a bit more evidence about the importance of the number of districts to static (or dynamic) nationalization, though a few caveats are important. First, in Germany the tiers are linked, such that votes in one tier affect outcomes in the other. The end result is that since seats are determined by the PR tier, the SMD tier is less important. In Mexico the problem is more severe, since voters just have one vote which counts toward both tiers.

This leaves Japan, where voters make separate selections for each tier. The differences in the results are stark; using the 11 PR districts (which they use to distribute 180 seats) yields remarkably high SN for the country's parties, while running the analysis on the returns from the 300 SMD districts (even when excluding zeros) puts the parties in the very low category.[10] Part of this is a mechanical effect, since aggregating the single-member districts into larger regions masks the heterogeneity in the parties' support.[11] The Japanese parties vary in the types of districts where they have strength (the LDP is stronger in rural districts), but because the small number of PR districts conjoins the different types, the parties appear to have homogenous support. This is not a necessary result; if the parties' strength varied by geographic regions that correlated with the PR boundaries, then there would be a smaller mechanical effect. The mechanical effect, however, does not fully explain the different results. The correlation between votes in the two tiers for Japan is not very high.[12] This suggests that a significant number of Japanese voters do split their tickets, and, as such, it could mean that the incentive systems inherent at the two different tiers do play a role in the electoral outcomes. This is confirmed

---

[8] Panama and Hungary also have two-tiered systems, but I only have data on one tier.

[9] Korea (which I cut from the analysis due to data problems) and Taiwan also have a proportional representation tier, but they have only one PR district. Nationalization is necessarily undefined where there is only one district.

[10] Analysis was run on the 2000, 2003, and 2005 elections, because I lack the data for 2009 for the PR tier at the district level. The SMD tier yields similar values for the elections of 2003, 2005, and 2009.

[11] The tests for the mechanical effect are straightforward: compress the SMD districts into the PR boundaries and then calculate the static (or dynamic) statistics using the average vote within each PR-level district. Districts within states or provinces (as in the United States or Canada) would provide a similar test.

[12] For the LDP in 2003 it was about 0.67 in 2003, and only 0.42 in 2005. These values eliminate districts where the LDP did not contest a single-member district. There were 24 of these in 2003 and 10 in 2005. As a comparison, the correlation for Germany's CDU/CSU was almost perfect, at least 0.94, for each electoral year 1990–2009 (calculated at the level of the single-member districts).

in looking at the standard deviation of the LDP's vote. Using the 300 districts (and excluding those where the LDP failed to compete), the standard deviation is about twice as high for the SMD vote (9.4 in 2005) than for the PR vote (4.4 in 2005).[13] Thus, PR seems to promote a more nationalized distribution of the vote.

At first glance these results partially counter the hypothesis that expects that the electoral system would affect SN but have less impact on DN. The more nuanced hypothesis, however, must include the observation that while low levels of SN would be compatible with any level of DN, where a party had homogeneous voter support (high SN), votes would have to move in similar ways (high DN) to maintain the consistent across-district support.

Putting the Japanese results back into a comparative context helps to reconfirm the idea that the single-member district (or personal-vote-supporting) systems do not necessarily yield low DN. As noted, in several other parliamentary countries that use single-member districts – including Canada, Germany, and the United Kingdom – the parties have high DN, even though SN is low. India's parties, however, are low on both scales. Again, it seems that a large number of districts allows sharp differences in the support for parties across districts, but does not prescribe that type of pattern.

FEDERALISM/DECENTRALIZATION AND ETHNIC HETEROGENEITY/
SEGREGATION

To account for some of the unexplained variance, Chapter 5 argued for adding federalism and ethnic heterogeneity to the mix. The main hypothesis there is that political decentralization, especially in the context of minority groups that are geographically concentrated, should decrease nationalization on both dimensions. I begin with a simple dichotomous discussion of federalism or decentralization, then add a more sophisticated measure that also accounts for the ethnic makeup of a country. Each variable clearly helps explain some of the variance.

Coding a country's federalism is not always straightforward, but only a few countries (e.g. Spain) are controversial. Based on standard measures plus a review of regional tax collection or expenditure, about one-half of the countries in my database are federal or decentralized.[14] Figure 6.3 clearly shows this effect by labeling all federal countries and those like Spain and Peru that have undertaken extensive decentralization with an "F." Very few parliamentary cases in the upper right corner are federal (and none are at the extremes of the *nationalized* quadrant), and almost all parliamentary systems that are not in that corner are federal or decentralized. There are five parties in the lower right corner from non-

---

[13] The PR vote is reported for the 300 districts, but it is aggregated into the 11 PR districts for allocation of seats. I lack that data for 2009, and thus cannot run the model.
[14] See also Hooghe et al. (2010).

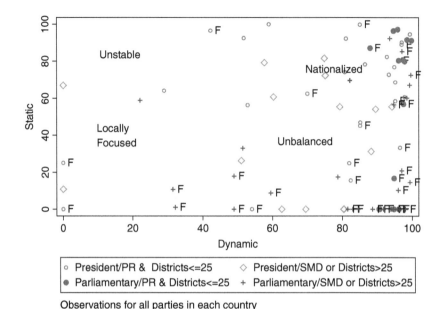

FIGURE 6.3 Nationalization by Executive and Number of Districts, plus Federalism

federal parliamentary systems, but three are from the United Kingdom, which arguably should win a decentralized label (as applied by Chhibber and Kollman). Further, the large number of districts there provides a good explanation for its low value on SN. The others are one party in Romania (42 districts) and the DPJ in Japan (300 districts). It is important to note that in spite of political decentralization, many of the parliamentary cases still score very high on the dynamic scale. This perhaps supports the idea that federalism permits, but does not determine DN. Further, among the parliamentary cases it appears that while centralized systems are almost assuredly nationalized on both dimensions, decentralization is a poor predictor of either dimension of nationalization. Adding the number of districts to this mix adds more explanatory power, but primarily where that number is low. In particular, parliamentarism plus centralization and a small number of electoral districts lands parties in the upper right box. But, while moving to either a decentralized system and/or more electoral districts produces no cases in the extreme upper right corner and many cases in the lower right, the correlation of SN or DN with decentralization is weaker than with centralization.

The political decentralization variable also works with the presidential cases, though there are fewer that are not well explained by the combination of the executive and electoral systems. First, of the presidential cases in the *nationalized* corner of the graph, all have few districts and most (including three observations from El Salvador and one from Paraguay) are unitary. The one case that is listed as federal, presidential, and having few districts is in Uruguay. It is formally unitary, but has experienced some decentralization. This supports the theory. The other cases that are not well explained by the executive and electoral system variables are the two open circles in the bottom left of the graph, both of which represent parties in Argentina. Argentina is a federal state whose governors have large sway over politics. It is no surprise, then, that the low number of districts (24) does not prevent the localism from dominating legislative elections.

While the degree of centralization is a straightforward and relatively powerful explanation for the level of both SN and DN, as explained in Chapter 5 these types of correlations might confuse the direction of the causal arrow. Caramani (2000) argued that centralizing the governmental structure led to higher levels of party [static] nationalization. But do nationalized parties continue to centralize the government? And if they do decentralize, might that reduce the SN? Changes in the federal structures and levels of nationalization can help disentangle these questions.

Chhibber and Kollman (2004) reject the reverse causality thesis. Their strongest evidence comes from the United Kingdom, where they show that devolution preceded the rise of the regional parties. The Belgian parties, as discussed by Caramani (2000), provide a similar example. The division of the country into two linguistic parts, Caramani explains, led to two different party systems: one Flemish and the other Walloon. Thus, SN decreased sharply, as the parties competed in only one of the two parts of the country. Among the countries in my dataset, the Bolivian case provides another natural experiment to test the theory, and the evidence again supports the idea that decentralization preceded the lower levels of nationalization (Table 6.3). Bolivia began a move toward decentralization in the 1990s, and the process accelerated through 2009 when a new constitution recognized a "plurinational" state and autonomous departments (Centellas 2010). The country has only nine electoral districts, which should produce a high level of SN. Only one party, the MNR, competed in each of the elections from 1985 to 2005 (and it failed to compete in 2009). That party provides particularly good evidence, since its leader was in the presidential office during the first moves toward decentralization (in 1994). Running the model on the three elections from 1985 to 1993 for that party produces SN values about twice as high as it does for the period 1997–2005. This is consistent with the evolution in the standard deviation of the party's support. In 1993 that value was just 4.9, which was much lower than in previous elections. In spite of that consistency, the party's president pursued decentralization. The result was much lower SN (yielding a higher standard deviation in support) in the succeeding elections. The values for the ADN, the other party that competed both before and after the decentralization, show a similar trend: lower SN after the policy change. The standard deviation of support for the parties that did not exist prior to the decentralization but have competed in the last few elections is also large, at least relative to others competing with so few electoral districts. In sum, decentralization preceded the drop in SN.

TABLE 6.3 *Bolivia: Cross-District Variation in Support for the MNR*

Year	Average Support across Districts	Standard Deviation in Support across Districts
1985	35.3	10.6
1989	29.5	7.8
1993	36.1	4.9
1997	21.3	7.0
2002	27.8	8.3
2005	11.0	10.9

Refined Measures of Federalism and Decentralization, plus Ethnic Segregation

The multifaceted nature of federalism and decentralization adds another layer to the analysis. The World Bank gathers data in ways that allow a coding according fiscal federalism.[15] Specifically, they use IMF Government Finance Statistics to provide sub-national revenues and expenditures, which they compare against national government data. In countries where sub-national governments raise and/or spend more money, they should be more pertinent to politics. If local or regional issues are more important, both dimensions of party nationalization should be lower.

The World Bank data ends in 2000, and I took the value closest to that date. For a few (mostly Central American) countries, there is no recent data, so I estimated them based on their neighboring countries.[16] Overall, the expenditure data in my set of countries run from about 2.8 percent (in Panama) to almost 60 percent (in Canada). The revenue data is even lower in Panama (0.8 percent), but Canada is also the highest on this dimension (52 percent).

For societal fragmentation and segregation, I rely on data published by Alesina and two sets of co-authors. First, Alesina et al. (2003) provide data on fragmentation based on ethnic, linguistic, and religious segments. From this dataset, I captured the maximum and average values for the three types of societal fragmentation. Portugal and South Africa are at the extremes for both the averages and maximums; the average of the cleavages in Portugal is 0.07, compared to 0.83 in South Africa.

---

[15] www1.worldbank.org/publicsector/decentralization/fiscalindicators.htm

[16] The three Central American countries with no data on federalism were all unitary: El Salvador, Guatemala, and Nicaragua. Research confirmed similarities in their very low level of decentralization, and I thus estimated these based on an average value from Costa Rica and Panama. There is also no data for Taiwan; it too is unitary, and I estimated it based on other unitary countries with similar levels of population and GDP.

The nationalization hypotheses, however, require a further step, since the important question is whether the ethnic groups are segregated regionally rather than integrated throughout multiple electoral divisions. The Alesina and Zhuravskaya (2011) study provides the requisite data. Taking into account the number and size of each group, they provide comparative indicators for "segregation," again for language, ethnicity, and religious groups. Table 6.4 highlights the countries that score particularly high or low on the three scales, and Figure 6.4 displays the country-level results for the ethnic segregation variable.

These data are an important advance on previous works (such as Cox 1997, but also including Morgenstern et al. 2009) that use ethnic fractionalization indices which do not account for geographic segregation. Like other indicators, however, they are not without weaknesses. Colombia, for example, is among the countries with a very high value on the ethnic segregation index. The result, however, is driven by the high concentration of Afro-Colombians in one small department (Choco). At the other extreme, Canada has a very low value of separatism, in spite of a clear religious and linguistic divide at the Quebec borders.[17] Another problem is that the regions from their analysis are not always coterminous with electoral districts. This is most problematic in the single-member district countries (the United States has 52 regions and the United Kingdom has 13), but it is also a concern in several other countries. Nonetheless, these data provide a significant advance over previous alternatives. As such, it helps to capture some distinctive patterns. The outlying district in Colombia, for example, has a distinctive pattern in the vote, with the Liberal party winning over 90 percent of the vote in that department in 2002, while in most districts it won well under 50 percent.[18]

In order to capture the idea of ethnic segregation plus the impact of federalism, I multiplied together the variables measuring federalism and ethnic segregation (using the maximum for ethnic, linguistic, and language segregation and the value for sub-national revenue share). This generated a variable that ranges from about 0.07 to 0.83, with a mean of 0.33. The results for each country are shown in the bar chart in Figure 6.5.

The graphs in Figure 6.6 integrate the ethnic segregation and federalism results into the analysis. To emphasize their impact, the left panel of Figure 6.6 considers the highest quartile of cases for this variable, and the right panel takes the lowest quartile. Where segregation*federalism is very high, almost all cases

---

[17] Using the authors' data, I reproduced the scores for several countries, and most were replicable. The values I produced for Canada, however, are inconsistent with what the authors display in their table. Either way, Canada still scores very low in this index. I use the higher value in my tests.

[18] There was one other district, Arauca, where the Liberals also won about 90 percent of the vote in 2002. This district is not distinct in terms of ethnicity, however.

TABLE 6.4 *Ethnic Segregation: Sample Cases* *

	<= 0.01	> 0.1
Ethnic	Argentina (0.012)	Belgium (0.203)
	Austria (0.011)	Colombia (0.280)
	Czech Rep (0.004)	Ghana (0.112)
	Germany (0.001)	Guatemala (0.384)
	Hungary (0.003)	Honduras (0.215)
	Japan (0.002)	Mexico (0.160)
	Netherlands (0.001)	Panama (0.186)
	Peru (0.002)	S. Africa (0.247)
	Sweden (0.001)	Spain (0.244)
	US (0.011)	
	Korea (0.002)	
	Italy (0.006)	
Linguistic	Brazil (0.006)	Belgium (0.203)
	Czech Rep (0.004)	Colombia (0.280)
	Japan (0.002)	Guatemala (0.495)
		Honduras (0.215)
		India (0.146)
		Italy (0.141)
		Mexico (0.142)
		Nicaragua (0.116)
		Panama (0.186)
		S. Africa (0.247)
		Spain (0.244)
		UK (0.170)
Religious	Australia (0.003)	India (0.186)
	Austria (0.006)	
	Chile (0.000)	
	Peru (0.001)	
	Portugal (00.)	
	S. Africa (0.009)	
	Switzerland (0.007)	

*Not all variables are defined for all countries.

in the graph are at the bottom, indicating low SN. Where it is low, there is more diversity in the outcomes. A first finding is low segregation*federalism seems to push up DN, even among the presidential cases. There are a few presidential cases, still, with low SN (namely, the Frente Amplio in Uruguay and APRA in

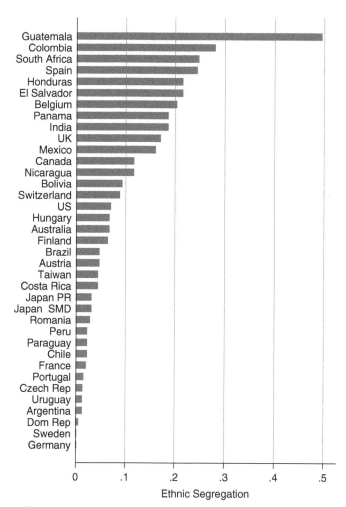

FIGURE 6.4 Ethnic Segregation, by Country

Peru). As expected, the cases with parliamentary systems and few districts are mostly in the upper right corner, indicating high nationalization on both dimensions. There are two exceptions in terms of SN, both from the PR tier in Germany. The most glaring exception is with the Linke (Left) party, which formed from a merger with two other parties in 2007. Its cross-state (*land*) support is highly variable, ranging from about 3 to 25 percent. Where it is weak the Green party does a bit better, but there is not a clear tradeoff in the votes, as the Linke also seems to hurt the CDU/CSU more in some *land* than others. The other party that does not fully meet the expectations is the CDU/CSU. For the 2005–13 period its static score is around 60, and it was even lower

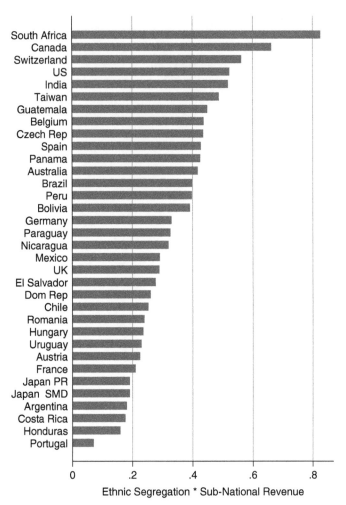

FIGURE 6.5 Ethnic Segregation and Federalism

in earlier time periods. Its support, however, has always been relatively consistent; in 2013 it won a minimum of 29 percent in all 16 *land*, and a maximum of 49 percent. There has been some fanning in, as its support where it had been weak in 2005 and 2009 (especially Berlin, Brandenburg, and Bremen) rose sharply without big changes in other areas. The other major party in the analysis, the Social Democratic Party (SPD), has maintained consistent support around the country (a high SN). In 2009 the party broke from the ruling coalition, and it lost 10 points nationwide. This loss was evenly distributed, and the new range of support was between 15 and 30 percent, with a standard deviation of just 5.2.

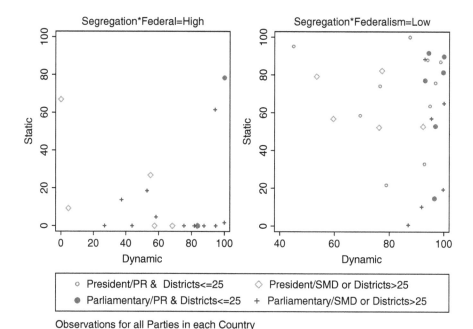

FIGURE 6.6 Nationalization: By Federalism, Ethnic Segregation, and Institutions

Alternative Variables and Further Bi- and Tri-Variate Tests on Executive and Electoral Systems

In arguing for the importance of the number of electoral districts, I discounted the hypothesis, based in part on my own work with Swindle and Castagnola (2009), that the electoral system, when coded based on Carey and Shugart's (1995) model that was intended to capture incentives to cultivate a personal vote, would affect DN. Here I test this alternative hypothesis. In that previous work, we focused first on the separating out of single-member district systems; in my current data set that is the case for about one-fourth of the parties in my dataset. I also test several means for operationalizing the personal vote.

Hallerberg and Marier (2004) provide the most systematic method to operationalize the incentives to cultivate a personal vote.[19] Their model sums the ballot, pool, and vote codes as defined by Carey and Shugart (1995), and

---

[19] I also experimented with several other systems, and relied on multiple datasets to code my data. Chang and Golden (2007) (who trace their work to Beck et al. [2001]) code open versus closed list systems, and also district magnitude. Their system, however, does not fit single-member district systems into the continuum. Golder (2005) provides a very useful database and helps to code the two-tier systems. His data, however, does not capture a key personal vote characteristic, whether a list system is open or closed. Still, this database was invaluable in helping to code countries for placement in the Hallerberg and Marier (2004) model.

then transforms the sum (plus 1) by adding the natural log of the district magnitude for open list systems or dividing by that figure for closed list system.[20] The authors then divide the result by 10. This produces an upward sloping curve (indicating higher levels of incentives to seek the personal vote) for open list system and the reverse for closed list systems. Hallerberg and Marier's work focuses on Latin America, and Hallerberg (2004) then extends the empirical analysis to Europe. In Figure 6.7 I portray the figures for the cases in my dataset, using updated (and sometimes corrected) information about the electoral systems (see Appendix 3 for details about the coding). Some of the systems do not lend themselves to easy coding; Austria and the Czech Republic, for example, are "semi-open" systems in which personal votes do not alter the party's list unless enough voters choose to reorder the list. These types of systems, perhaps, require a more fine-grained coding system than suggested by Carey and Shugart.

While the H&M method is useful in attempting to operationalize Carey and Shugart's (1995) insight that district magnitude has opposing effects for open and closed list systems, the results are problematic for a statistical study. First, summing the ballot, pool, and vote categories is arbitrary, and assumes an even weight among the categories. Further, it assumes independence among the categories, which is incorrect. As an example, if leaders provide voters with a fixed ballot (ballot= 0) then there cannot be pooling at the sub-party level (pool must equal 0), and a vote must also be 0 (voters cannot cast votes for multiple candidates or below the party level). Another concern is that the model uses average district magnitude. This is problematic for those countries where the magnitude is highly variable. In Peru, for example, the averages are skewed by one district that has a magnitude of 35, which is five times greater than the next largest district.

Also problematic to the H&M model is the arbitrary degree of separation that the two formulas create. Necessarily (and perhaps logically), this creates very small values for the closed list systems; empirically, it generates a value of 0.1 for single-member district systems (except the United States, which gets scored commensurate with open lists due to the primary system), and it would fall to 0.02 for a system with an average district magnitude of 100. In my sample, most closed-list cases have scores around 0.05. By contrast, open list systems with a district magnitude of only 2 must have scores greater than 0.14, which is three times the value for open lists. Empirically the difference is much greater, with all open list system scoring at least 0.5. This may be a reasonable difference, but there is no empirical basis for it. The slope of the curve that defines the impact of the district magnitude is similarly arbitrary.

---

[20] The first of these variables refers to whether the ballot is fixed, pooling refers to whether votes are pooled at the party or sub-party level, and the last variable indicates whether voters cast votes for the party or individual candidates.

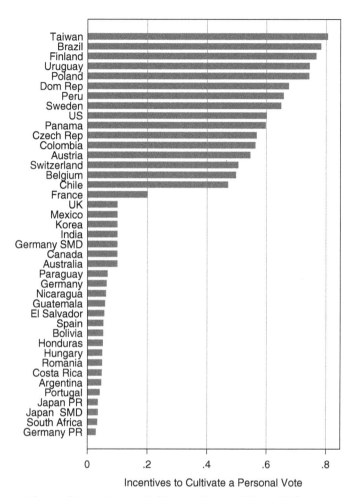

FIGURE 6.7 Electoral Incentives to Cultivate a Personal Vote (Hallerberg and Marier Method)

Figure 6.8 shows some of the problems with this approach. In the graph, each different symbol represents a different combination of electoral system types, with the three numbers indicated in the legend representing the codes for ballot, pool, and vote. Following Carey and Shugart, each variable is coded from 0 to 2, with higher numbers indicating less partisan control (or toward a personal vote). Empirically there are just seven combinations of these variables. As indicated in the graph (with x's), the closed list systems (0,0,0), regardless of district magnitude, are all along the bottom of the graph with scores less that 0.1. H&M code single-member districts like the closed list systems, except for the United States, which, owing to its primaries, earns a score of 0.6 based on coding the

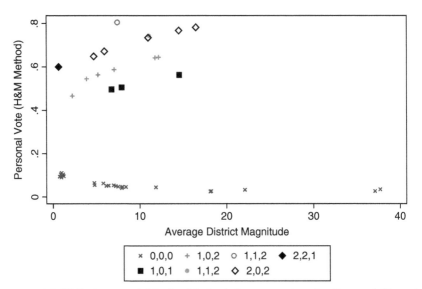

FIGURE 6.8 Hallerberg and Marier Method for measuring the Personal Vote, by District Magnitude*
* Numbers in legend refer, respectively, to scores for ballot, pool, and vote, as defined in text.

system as (2,2,1). All other countries that do not use single-member districts or closed lists earn scores between about 0.45 and 0.8. Graphing the results reveals, in sum, that the H&M method a) puts almost no importance on the district magnitude for the closed list systems (since all the scores are very low), and b) there are very large difference between open and closed list systems. These may be reasonable conclusions, but there is not a solid theoretical basis to justify the magnitudes of the differences. Is the tendency toward personalism five times as high in the open list systems as in those with closed lists?[21]

Overall, the empirical implication of the H&M system is less a continuous scale than a rough grouping of countries into three categories: closed list systems at the bottom (average score of 0.05), single-member systems with a value of twice that the first category (average 0.1), and open list systems five times higher than the middle category. Grouping the cases and then letting a regression determine the relative distances between them, therefore, seems a better strategy.

---

[21] The H&M system does not account for the semi-open systems, where voters can affect the order of the list if candidates meet a threshold of support. Modifying the calculations for these systems by dividing by the natural log of the average magnitude, instead of adding it, would move the Colombian and Austrian cases into a more middling category.

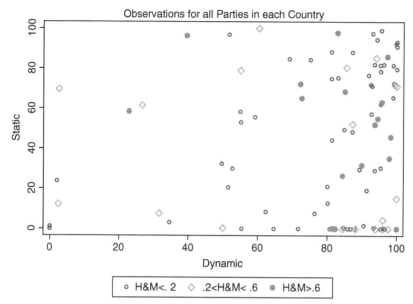

FIGURE 6.9 Nationalization by Personal Vote-Seeking Incentives

Still, to demonstrate that the sophisticated method does not strongly correlate with nationalization, Figure 6.9 uses the revised H&M model to categorize the countries, and then applies those categories to the nationalization results. No strong patterns appear; each of the three populated corners has examples from all three categories of personal-vote-seeking systems. Using the un-revised model does not aid the correlation.

As with the tests on the number of districts, a better test conditions the personal-vote-seeking incentives with the executive system. The left portion of Figure 6.10 focuses on the parliamentary systems, and still no significant relationships appear. Most parliamentary systems fit into the first category (low personal vote incentives) and thus the graph is dominated by cases under a single electoral system. Noteworthy is that the black dots appear, still, in all three inhabited corners. Adding a code for federalism ("F" in the figure) does not help distinguish the impact of the H&M-based coding. The right side of the figure provides the same analysis for the presidential cases. Again, the patterns are not strong, but perhaps the graph could justify the necessity (though not the sufficiency) of low incentives to cultivate a personal vote for a party to land in the upper right corner (nationalized) of the graph. However, there are two exceptions: one case from Uruguay (not surprisingly) and one from Peru (surprisingly) also land in the top right quadrant. The "federalized" label may be misleading for these countries, because (as noted earlier for Uruguay) while both are decentralized, they are formally unitary. Their

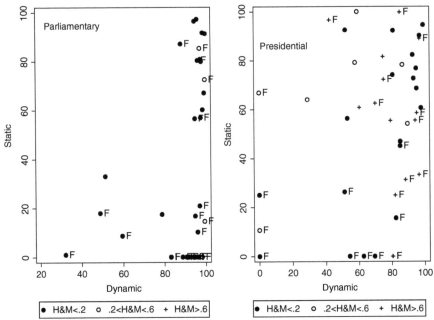

FIGURE 6.10 Nationalization and Electoral Systems by Executive Systems*
* US values are averages for 1990s and 2000s.

electoral systems could both favor a personal vote. Peru has a straightforward open-list system, which should reduce their DN, but Uruguay has a unique "double-simultaneous vote" that ties legislative elections to the presidential elections. Finally, Uruguay is a homogenous society, while Peru has ethnic and geographic divisions. Perhaps the best explanation for the Peruvian exception is the size of the Peruvian Fujimorista party; it had just an average vote of 11 percent, just above the cutoff for these graphs. As noted in earlier chapters, small parties are likely to show low levels of variance in their vote (and thus appear highly nationalized). Further, in the first year of the data series, the Fujimoristas had an average vote of under 2 percent. The variance of the party's returns in 2006 and 2011 suggests its nationalization (on both dimensions) has decreased.

Based on the useful idea of quantifying the personal-vote-seeking incentives, while recognizing the method's weaknesses, in the regression analyses that follow I test several alternative measures of the electoral system. I first show the utility of the number of districts in my model. I then use the H&M method directly and also test a series of dummy variables that distinguishes the groups of systems. To preview the results, I find that the multivariate tests substantiate the theoretical discussion: the number of districts is a better variable than are the models of the incentives to cultivate the personal vote.

The finding about measuring the electoral system, still, is preliminary to the theoretical issue of how the electoral system has a more substantial effect on SN than the other dimension. That too is substantiated in the regressions. One other electoral system hypothesis I discussed in Chapter 5, based on Duverger (1954), suggested that parties have an incentive to put more effort into districts that are rich in seats than those where few seats are in play. The testable hypothesis, then, is that countries that have some or all districts with low district magnitude will have lower SN than those where all districts have a high enough magnitude to support a multitude of parties. All single-member district countries, then, should have low SN, and there is a potential for an impact in Belgium, Finland, Greece, Italy, Spain, Sweden, Switzerland, several Central American countries, Uruguay, and Chile, all of which have one or more districts with magnitude of one or two.

It is not fully possible to test this in the same multivariate cross-national model that other hypotheses suggest, since it focuses on where parties compete within countries.[22] An intra-country analysis of those countries that do use a mix of single-member districts and districts with a larger magnitude, however, can elucidate the validity of the hypothesis.

A first case where a country includes multi- and small-magnitude (M) districts is Uruguay. The country has 99 electoral seats, and over half of those are in Montevideo (M=45) and Canelones (M=12). Of the 17 other districts (known as departments), several have a magnitude of just two. In the earlier part of the post-dictatorship period (which ended in 1985), the upstart Frente Amplio was much stronger in the capital than elsewhere. By the time it won the presidency in 2004, however, its support outside the capital had grown. The growth was relatively consistent across the country, however, which does not support the idea that parties ignore small-magnitude districts. It may be a special case, however, since their unique electoral system ties legislators, senators, and presidential candidates.[23] Therefore, while it is an example of a party that built from a regional stronghold, its subsequent growth did not solely focus on the larger districts; as it grew in Canelones, it grew everywhere else, too.

In Switzerland, the 26 cantons serve as electoral districts. While Bern and Zurich have 26 and 34 seats available respectively, 5 cantons elect a single legislator and 2 others elect just 2. Clearly, then, parties have an incentive to focus their efforts in Bern and Zurich, and in general it seems the parties there do respond to this incentive. In 2007, neither the SP nor the SVP, for

---

[22] A possible test would be to add a variable indicating that a country had at least some small-magnitude districts. This would not be adequate, however, to capture the nuance of where a party competes.
[23] Votes for these three levels are fused. After a primary (and ignoring the possibility of a runoff for the presidency), voters choose the president, a set of senators, and another set of lower house representatives on the same ballot (see Moraes 2008).

example, competed in 3 of the 5 single-member districts. The FDP skipped four of those districts and dominated the fifth (with 72 percent of the vote). The Christian Democrats (CVP) did not have candidates in 4 of the 6 districts that return 1 or 2 legislators, but it ran uncontested in another and won 84 percent of the last of these.

INSTITUTIONAL HYPOTHESES, SUMMARY

To summarize the institutional hypotheses, Table 6.5 refers to the predictive tables of Chapter 5 and fill in the boxes based on the analysis for the largest party in each country. As discussed in Chapter 5, the predictions for the executive and the number of districts can be negative, zero, or positive, while the federalism variable is only negative or positive. Further, the prediction is that the executive and electoral systems work on only one dimension, while federalism affects both. The symbols (+, –, o) refer, in order, to the prediction for the executive, the number of districts, and federalism, and the overall prediction is based on the idea that the combination of the variables can reinforce the predictions or can work in opposite ways.[24] Using the average score for included parties as the cutoff, the table thus indicates, for example, a positive expectation when there are two +s.[25] It then evaluates each hypothesis for the largest party in each country, highlighting the cases that are not consistent with the predictions.

The results of the table provide strong support for the hypotheses. Of the 41 cases where there is a prediction, only 7 estimates are not as expected. Of those that do not meet expectations, 2 use semi-presidentialism, for which I do not have strong expectations. Another exception is the US case, but it is right at the dividing line and it would meet the expectations for other time periods. Uruguay's Frente Amplio was expected to have a higher SN, but its value has risen in recent years and the country's other parties do follow the predictions. The biggest exceptions, then, are Japan's LDP (single-member district tier) and the PT in Brazil.

Party-Level Variables

While Chapter 5 was not sanguine about the intra-country explanations, it suggested tests on party (and democratic) age, governing experience, ideological differences, and size. First, Caramani (2000) and Mainwaring and Zoco (2007) theorize that the age of democracy should be related to [static] nationalization, and I suggested using the parties rather than a country-level

---

[24] The data suggest other counting systems could be appropriate. The high values for all cases in the southeast box of the lower table, for example, could suggest that parliamentarism pulls more strongly toward high dynamic scores than federalism pulls in the opposite way.

[25] An alternative could weight the 3 variables, but the summation meets most expectations.

TABLE 6.5 *Summary of Institutional Predictions*

	Presidentialism					
	Many districts				**Few districts**	
Federal/ Decentralized		**Static o−−** (<45)	**Dynamic −o−** (<79)		**Static o+−** (?)	**Dynamic −o−** (<79)
	Brazil	55.5	94.2	Argentina	0	0
	Colomb.	10.7	0	Bolivia	0	54.1
	Mexico	0	69.5	Peru	62.5	70.0
	US**	0	80.5			
Unitary		**Static o−+** (?)	**Dynamic −o+** (?)		**Static o++** (>45)	**Dynamic −o+** (?)
	Chile	50.4	79.2	Costa Rica	90.2	97.0
	D. Republic	81.6	74.9	El Salvador	60.7	97.8
	Honduras	82.3	92.8	Guatemala	92.5	51.8
				Nicaragua	46.9	85.2
				Panama	78.3	86.5
				Paraguay	74.2	80.7
				Uruguay	33.3	96.5

TABLE 6.5 *(continued)*

Parliamentary & Hybrid

	Many districts			Few districts	

Federal/Decentralized

	Static o-- (<45)	Dynamic +o- (?)		Static o+- (?)	Dynamic +o- (?)
Australia	o	83.1	Belgium	o	94.7
Austria	o	98.1	Germany PR	56.9	97.5
Canada	o	88.7	South Africa	o	90.7
Ger smd	10.2	96.0			
India	8.7	59.5			
Spain	o	91.8			
Switzerland	o	48.9			

Unitary

	Static -o+ (?)	Dynamic +o+ (>79)		Static o++ (>45)	Dynamic +o+ (>79)
Japan SMD	33.0	51.5	Czech Republic	91.5	98.5
UK	o	94.0	Finland*	o	99.0
Poland*	51.2	87.1	Japan PR	97.2	98.6
Roma*	o	84.5	Portugal*	82.0	93.7
France*	50.9	56.1	Sweden	60.2	98.5
Taiwan*	58.9	22.1			

Cutoffs for the high and low are based on mean scores of parties included in regression analysis (see Table 6.6), but values in table refer to largest party for each country.

Static expected relation: Presidential o; Many Districts –; Federal –

Dynamic expected relation: Presidential –; Many Districts o; Federal –

Cases not meeting predictions are highlighted.

*Countries are semi-presidential; Predictions are thus valid for districts and federalism, but there is no expectation regarding the executive system.

**US values are averages for 1990s and 2000s.

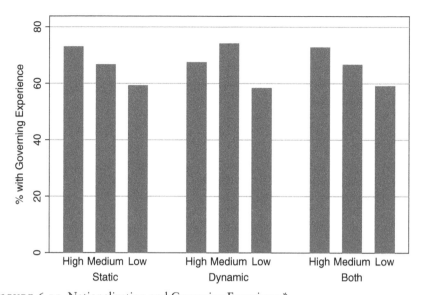

FIGURE 6.11 Nationalization and Governing Experience*
* Categories defined by the mean +/1 one-half of a standard deviation

variable. Party age is not always easy to code due to parties sometimes changing names or merging with other parties, and in some cases the parties are older than the democracy. In tests, I considered both the raw age and its log. Bivariate tests (not shown), however, show little promise for these variables.

The second party-level variable discussed in Chapter 5 as potentially impacting one or the other dimension of party nationalization was governing experience. Here I used a dummy variable for parties that had controlled the presidency or, for parliamentary systems, the prime minister's office at least once during the period under investigation.[26] I also considered coding for cabinet membership, but this is ambiguous for presidential systems and I lack information for some countries and some time periods. Figure 6.11, which graphs the level of the two types of nationalization versus governing experience, gives a bit of evidence for a relationship. It shows that those with governing experience score somewhat higher on both scales than those without experience, but the relationship is not linear for DN. Especially since these data largely neglect regional parties, this finding is significant because it implies a correlation between a party's ability to broaden its geographic coverage and likelihood of participating in government.

---

[26] Because there are just two competitors and hence just one party in the analysis, I coded governing experience with a 1 for the United States and Chile.

Then, to test for whether a party was centrist or ideologically extreme, I followed MSC (2009) and used a combination of legislator surveys (Alcantara Sáez n.d.) and a survey of country experts (Huber and Inglehart 1995). As before, I scored parties based on their ideological distance from the country's mean score after combining the two data sources based on the countries where the coverage overlapped.

Bivariate tests on these variables generally fail. The parties' age or the log of that variable have correlation coefficients between -0.05 and -0.20 with the two dimensions of nationalization. The log of the age of democracy is a bit larger (in absolute terms), but is still just -0.4. The ideology variable also fares poorly, and no specification of experience shows a strong relationship.

A final party-level variable discussed in Chapter 5 was size, which I measure as the average vote total across districts for the three years in the analysis. As explained, the analysis only includes parties that won an average of at least 10 percent of the vote, but even with this subset the size variable is important because the impact of the other variables should be magnified in small parties. These variables have only minimal correlations with the dependent variables: -0.23 for SN and -0.03 for DN.

In sum, while a multivariate model is still necessary to fully test these intra-country variables, the eyeball analysis does not suggest a strong possibility of uncovering explanations for intra-country differences, with the possible exception of governing experience. This is less than optimal, but perhaps not unexpected given that there are few countries where parties are of different types. Still, there are some differences, which implies that the institutional variables circumscribe without prescribing a party's level of nationalization.

Multivariate Tests

As a means to test the different hypotheses in a multivariate environment, I build on the SUR model[27] my colleagues Swindle and Castagnola and I developed (Morgenstern, Swindle, and Castagnola 2009). In the current project, I have extended and updated the data set and improved the measurement of both the dependent and the independent variables. Operationalization of the variables plus the relevant data for the regression are provided in Appendices 2, 3, and 4, and a more comprehensive dataset is available on my website. The new results support the conclusions of the earlier paper: different institutional variables drive the two dimensions of nationalization.

---

[27] The structure of the data also suggests that regression should cluster the observations by country. The standard seemingly unrelated regression (sureg) command in Stata does not permit clustering, and thus we used "mysureg," a maximum-likelihood estimator, available at www.stata-press.com/data/ml2.html. The results are substantively the same as the standard "sureg" command but the former does not provide the full range of summary statistics. The tables that follow, therefore, report on the standard "sureg" package available in Stata.

As explained in the referenced paper (Morgenstern, Swindle, and Castagnola 2009), generalized least squares models such as SUR have two important virtues: they allow us to test both dimensions simultaneously with a similar set of independent variables, and they take advantage of a possible tie between the two dependent variables to improve efficiency (see Zellner 1962; Greene 1997). In our case, though our two dependent variables are presumed independent of one another, since they measure two dimensions of electoral dynamics and we are interested in testing the impact of many of the same explanatory variables on both dependents, we must consider the possibility of correlation among the error terms that would be derived from separate regressions.

As in the earlier paper, I also ran separate OLS models (with robust standard errors due to heteroskedastic errors) and found correlated residuals. This justifies use of a SUR model.

The general form of the regressions that I tested is as follows:

Party nationalization (static or dynamic)= f(

  regime type
  federalism or decentralization
  electoral system
  ethnic heterogeneity and segregation
  federalism*segregation
  party age
  ideology
  party size
  governing experience)

As noted, I have taken care with several data concerns. First, it was necessary to eliminate small parties, since they will necessarily have small variance in their nationalization. As explained in Chapter 3, this is a preferable alternative to the various weighting schemes. As also discussed in that chapter, for the countries that have single-member districts (Canada, India, the United States, and the United Kingdom) plus the country that exclusively uses two member districts (Chile), I have used only the districts in which the party under investigation competed.[28] Strictly regional parties are also excluded, but their impact is implicit as they affect the nationalization (at least static) of other parties. Third, I ran LR tests, and used the results for the restricted models where the tests suggested that "fanning" was significant (see Chapter 3). I have also

---

[28] As explained, using all districts exaggerates the static and dynamic values (at least for parties that win significant votes in some districts). In Germany and Mexico, countries with two levels of systems, the included parties competed in almost all districts, so dropping the uncompetitive districts has no significant impact on the analysis. In Japan, however, the main parties do fail to compete in a significant number of districts (observations in the analysis fall from 900 to 825 and 823 for the LDP and DPJ respectively). Removing the zeros (vote<10 percent) does significantly affect these results and I therefore use only the competitive districts.

restricted the model to one observation per party, except where there are two-level electoral systems. Fourth, as in other parts of this chapter, the regressions use a truncated version of the dependent variable, limiting the top value at 100. This is theoretically valid, since values beyond some threshold are meaningless in defining the relative weight of local versus national politics. Truncation also provides a better test by limiting the impact of outliers. Still, running the data with either the un-truncated or logged data still supports the main conclusions.

Table 6.6 reports three sets of regressions.[29] The first two regressions differ in how the electoral system is measured, and the last drops the (insignificant) ideology variable, thus increasing the number of observation because that variable is unidentified for several parties. Further, I have again reversed the scales, such that higher values imply less variance or more nationalization. Finally, Appendix 5 shows the results for regressions similar to models 1 and 3 that use just one observation per country. In spite of reducing the number of observations, those results confirm other findings and allay concerns about bias.

Overall, the regressions give solid support for the hypotheses. Most clearly, the tests on the institutional hypotheses perform as expected, and there is also evidence that the social geography matters, too. Regarding the intra-party explanations, the log of party age and party size were both significant in explaining SN. Ideology and governing experience do not gain statistical significance.

The Executive and Electoral Systems

The first row of the table indicates that presidentialism reduces DN from both statistical and substantive perspectives, while it has no significant impact on SN. The coefficient implies that presidentialism reduces DN by more than 20 points – a substantively large value, given that the average party in the sample has a DN value of about 70.

The regressions also include a dummy for semi-parliamentary systems. Because they are hybrids, I have not theorized about these types. The regressions suggest that these systems reduce both types of nationalization.

The next independent variable tests the impact of the electoral system. The first and last sets of regressions (columns 1, 2, 5, and 6) operationalize this variable as the number of electoral districts. As forecast, this variable has no statistical impact on the dynamic dimension, but does drive SN. I also tested for the impact of the log of the variable, and it works in a similar way. In columns 3–4 I use the modified personal vote index, as discussed earlier. Consistent with the discussion about the problems with such indices, the variable does not

---

[29] Tests without the countries with small population (Costa Rica, Uruguay, and Panama), which account for ten observations, return essentially identical results.

TABLE 6.6 *SUR Model Results, Dependent Variables: Static/Distributional and Dynamic Nationalization Scores*

	Model 1		Model 2		Model 3	
	Static	Dynamic	Static	Dynamic	Static	Dynamic
	(1)	(2)	(3)	(4)	(5)	(6)
Presidential	4.28	−23.84**	10.35	−23.87**	5.78	−23.64**
Semi-presidential	−18.27**	−16.34**	−18.62**	−18.66**	−19.25**	−16.80**
Number of Districts	−0.07**	−0.02			−0.07**	−0.17
Personal Vote			−0.52	9.18		
Federal or Decentral	−35.79**	0.15	−34.29**	0.33	−34.05**	−1.45
Max Segregation	−25.57	−11.52	−29.41	−6.89	−27.41	−5.42
Federal* Segregation	−53.83	−124.63**	−74.25	−133.63**	−64.81	−124.16**
Extremism	2.88	0.81	2.07	1.02		
Governing exper	10.71	1.82	17.22**	3.48	5.90	1.65
Ln (Party age)	2.43	−1.81	−0.64	−2.27	1.92	−1.25
Average Vote	−0.83**	−0.20	−1.11**	−0.23	−0.87**	−0.17
Constant	78.00**	109.64**	79.86**	106.94**	88.86**	108.96**
N	85	85	85	85	94	94
R^2 adj	.55	.30	.45	.30	.51	.29

** $p \leq .05$ * $p \leq .1$

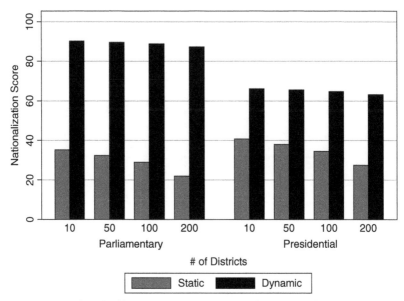

FIGURE 6.12 Predicted Effects: Executive System and Number of Electoral Districts

perform well, yielding insignificant results for both the static and dynamic dimensions.[30]

Figure 6.12 provides a graphical view of these results (using the third regression model). In that figure, bars representing DN for the parliamentary cases are sharply higher than those of the presidential cases, while the SN bars are of similar height when comparing the two groups. The lighter SN bars, however, decrease as the number of districts increases, while the dark DN ones show no significant change as the number of districts moves from 10 to 200. In short, the executive system drives DN while the number of districts drives SN.

The description above suggested that the interaction of the electoral and executive systems could also drive one or the other dimensions of nationalization. To test this, I first created a series of dummies that segmented the number of districts at 25 and interacted those dummies with the regime variable. These models did not give evidence that the interaction added much explanatory power. I then considered whether the electoral systems might have different levels of impact within presidential or parliamentary systems. Running the regressions on just the presidential systems, the general result is upheld: the number

_____

[30] While most other measures of the personal vote failed to find significant results, I did confirm, consistent with Morgenstern, Swindle, and Castagnola (2009), that differentiating single-member districts from multi-member systems did signify that the electoral system affects static but not dynamic nationalization. The variable is correlated with the number of districts, however.

of districts only affects SN. For parliamentary systems, the variable proves to be statistically significant for both nationalization dimensions. The substantive effect, however, is very small; moving from 0 to 100 districts only reduces the predicted value of the SN from 33 to 28 under these conditions.

These extra tests, in sum, confirm two ideas. First, electoral systems affect SN but not DN. Second, the results raise issues related to the study of the personal vote. On the one hand, they help to substantiate the central relationship that grounds the work that has followed Carey and Shugart's classic article (1995) on the personal vote. As I argued earlier, however, too much of that work relies on the purported incentives within the electoral system as a proxy for the actual behavior. DN, by contrast, directly measures the behavior, thus allowing a test of the incentive system. With this measure, I have been able to show that while the electoral system does impact voting behavior, some well-known measures of the electoral system do not work well in explaining the degree of localism in elections. There is another side of the issue, however. The personal vote concept is theoretically close to DN, but my analysis shows the electoral system only explains SN. This could disqualify the common use of electoral system traits as a proxy for the personal vote.

Federalism, Decentralization, and Ethnic Divisions

The next variables in the regressions are the dummies measuring federalism or decentralization, the maximum of ethnic segregation, and the interaction between these variables. The interaction term is significant for both types of nationalization, in all but one regression, and federalism by itself is significant for each of the tests on SN. The segregation variable is always insignificant, but if the interaction is left out of the regression, then that variable does turn significant. Without the interaction, federalism is also significant for DN.

The effects are substantively very strong. Based on the Model 3 (and using CLARIFY), moving from low (0.02) to high (0.2) segregation in a presidential and federal system reduces SN from 39 to 23, and DN from 72 to 49, and the changes are of a similar magnitude for parliamentary systems. Holding other variables constant but changing from a unitary to a federal system also shows sharp reductions in both types of nationalization. In sum, social geography, reinforced by federalism, is strongly related to voting patterns.

Intra-country Explanations

The next series of variables, which measure party age, governing experience, and ideology, attempt to explain intra-country variance. As in the bivariate tests, the regression produced null findings with regards to ideology and gave only minimal credence to the idea that governing experience is associated with higher SN. In part, the weakness of these variables reflects the strong explanatory power of the inter-country (institutional) variables and the limited intra-country variance within most countries, especially with regards to DN.

As in the bivariate analyses, the log of a party's age was insignificant. The logged age of democracy did show such a relationship for SN, but the results suggest that older democracies have *lower* SN (and are unrelated to DN). This does not necessarily contradict Caramani's (2000, 2005) work on nineteenth-century Europe, but it does call into question the findings of Mainwaring and Zoco (2007), who find that current party systems working in older democracies have higher [static] nationalization.[31] If anything, my regressions suggest that parties are de-nationalizing on the static scale as democracy matures, and there is no evidence that the age of parties themselves affects the degree of either type of nationalization. The sample only includes those parties that are relatively large (average vote of 10 percent) and have survived at least three elections.[32] The finding about democratic age working against SN and not supporting DN, even with this biased sample, suggests a reversal of the trends that other authors encountered.

The final variable in the model is party size. While it is a potential intra-country variable, it is more useful as a control. Regardless, it has the predictable (negative) impact on SN and is insignificant for DN.

Conclusion

In earlier chapters I argued theoretically and empirically that the two dimensions of nationalization are (almost) independent. Given that independence, there must be distinct causes for each phenomenon. The statistical tests in this chapter confirm that idea. In particular, electoral systems are related to SN, but the regime variable drives DN.

There are other variables that affect both types of nationalization, namely federalism and ethnic heterogeneity, at least when groups are geographically concentrated. However, neither the maturation of democracy nor of the parties themselves seems to lead to higher levels of either type of nationalization.

This chapter was motivated by an attempt to explain nationalization. In the following chapters I move nationalization to the right side of the equation, showing how it affects different aspects of the political world.

---

[31] Further calling that result into question, the variable does not gain significance (Models 5–6) when the data include the several Latin American countries for which I lack ideological data.

[32] Dropping Central America does not affect the results; dropping all of Central and Latin America yields a positive impact of logged party age on DN, but the variable is insignificant for SN.

PART III

IMPLICATIONS: NATIONALIZATION AS AN EXPLANATORY VARIABLE

On its face, finding implications of party nationalization should not be a difficult task, since it is uncontroversial that geography affects politics. But in turning to the effects of party nationalization in this part of the book, it is necessary to underscore the difference between operational definitions and the concept of party nationalization. The measurement of nationalization is based on consistency in distribution and change of electoral support of parties. That, however, is simply a means of operationalizing the distribution of voters, and the degree to which local factors influence their voting decisions. The three chapters that comprise this part the book continue to measure voting distributions, but the broader goal is to examine how geography affects politics. Chapters 7 and 8 consider the relation of nationalization and accountability and representation, and Chapter 9 examines how electoral ties among distinct geographic areas affects legislators' behaviors. Before moving to those chapters, this introductory note explores the literature on the effects of nationalization and the problems with considering just one of the two dimensions.

Exploring the Impacts of Nationalization
There is significant scholarship that seeks to explain the effects of party nationalization. Calvo and Lleiras (2012), for example, hypothesize about the relation of the nationalization of electoral competition to the nationalization of legislators' efforts with respect to policy. Citizens and analysts of the United States have long discussed the merits of pork directed to impact individual districts by re-election–seeking politicians. In other countries the effects of geography have had more dramatic impacts, as politicians spur irredentist movements, support economically distorting tax or subsidy programs, and build their version of bridges to nowhere.

Previous chapters highlighted factors that lead to nationalization; institutions were important there, and thus we can trace the role of institutions on politics through their impact on nationalization. As an example, PR elections generally have fewer and wider constituencies, and thus higher static nationalization. Persson and Tabellini (2003, 2004) show that PR elections lead politicians away from just targeting small groups of supporters, and conclude (2004, p. 25) that: "With proportional elections, legislators are elected in large – often national – districts, giving parties strong incentives to seek support from broad coalitions in the population. Majoritarian elections are conducted in smaller districts, inducing politicians to target smaller, but pivotal, geographical constituencies."

Distributional implications are critical, and take many significant forms. Jurado (2014) finds a positive relation of nationalization and social spending, and Hicken et al. (2010) find that poorly nationalized countries even distort the provision of immunizations. In a startling article, Steele (2011) finds that distributional politics led to "political cleansing" in Colombia. The violent displacement of citizens creates a vicious cycle, since it concentrates and distorts the distribution of voters.

Impacts of forces related to the dynamic dimension are evident in discussions that catch legislators acting for their personal electoral gains or advancement, rather than as faceless agents of their parties. Argentina has closed-list proportional representation, but the static and dynamic nationalization are low. In interviews, legislators consistently emphasized their "home style" (Fenno 1978). One, for example, told me about how she constantly knocks on doors and speaks at neighborhood meetings. She was clear that she had to emphasize her own work and policy positions, rather than discussing partisan issues. She talked, for example, about her work on a bill about bullying and helping voters with personal problems (such as a tree falling on their house). One UCR house member described the legislators' role as "local representation ... while the parties are national." A legislator who left the Peronists to join a small party confirmed this view, arguing that "there are now two types of representation: party and local representation." She said this as part of a complaint about the party trying to impose decisions on the legislators, but gave several examples where regional interests were of critical importance to the decisions.

There are many other studies that highlight the role of provinces in policy making in Argentina. Llanos (1998) provides several clear examples, focusing on the period when there was a very dominant president, Menem, who was infamous for using decrees to make policy. Even in that period Llanos describes how legislators forced consideration of provincial interests during privatization processes, such as transferring public lands that were important to the hydrocarbon industry to the provinces.[1]

---

[1] I thank Agustin Vallejo for pointing me to this work. See also his study (unpublished) on the Menem period.

The Argentine examples are useful for two reasons. First, they illustrate how the local vote (the inverse of DN) drives politics, which contrasts with the many studies that highlight regionalism, which is a concept closer to static nationalization. Second, the Argentine example shows that the local vote is important, even within the context of an electoral system that should not support a personal vote.

Policy makers are acutely aware of these themes and design institutions in response. Most prominently, Lijphart's (1969, 1977) central concern with consociationalism involved a search for institutions that would build accommodation among regional groups. A clear (but largely unsuccessful) attempt to reduce regionally divisive candidates was the requirement in Nigeria that presidential candidates gain at least 25 percent of the vote from two-thirds of the country's states.

USAID is also concerned with regionally focused politics and the role of institutions. In Peru, national parties can compete at the local level, but the reverse is not true. "Parties" that only compete in sub-national elections, termed political "movements" and "organizations," are prohibited from competing for national office. This limits the ability of the national groups to organize at the local level or institutionalize regional–national links. Other pieces of their institutional framework, including the ease by which new parties can form, the open list proportional representation system, the non-concurrent timing of national and regional elections, and party finance laws, also contribute to a chaotic system. Politicians and international aid groups recognize the problem, but forces are aligned against fixing it. First, a seemingly supportive policy of USAID prevents the agency (or its contractors) from directly working on needed institutional reforms. Their "party strengthening" program has a stated goal of building linkages between parties' politicians, supporters, and administrative offices at the national and peripheral levels. Their training programs, however, are limited in that they are prohibited from suggesting solutions to Peru's political fragmentation, because this would imply harming some of the competitors. This odd policy is the result of the legal requirement that USAID and its contractors support all non-violent political parties, in combination with the idea that a policy that reduced the number of parties would imply advantaging some parties over others (Green and Morgenstern 2009).

Even without USAID support, politicians in Peru, of course, understand the problems of political fragmentation. The fragmentation, however, serves the interests of some politicians and thus they block reforms. The political groups, first, enjoy their autonomy. Second, in the era of antipathy toward parties, personalist politicians see building their own machines as a better investment than political parties.

In sum, politicians, activists, citizens, and even academics recognize the impact of region on electoral politics. It is therefore not a challenge to find examples where aspects of party nationalization work as an independent variable. Still, most analyses focus on just one of the two nationalization dimensions or their facsimiles. Given the importance of region but the one-dimensional nature of most studies, the chapters in this part of the book are a call for extending the analyses to explicitly include both static and dynamic nationalization in a wide variety of studies. Before moving to those chapters, I briefly review several studies that focus on just one dimension of the nationalization, and explain what they miss.

One-Dimensional Analyses

The chapters that follow emphasize the two dimensions of nationalization as distinct but sometimes interacting variables. This is a turn from the majority of analyses that study just one aspect of nationalization or themes that are close to those subjects. Before entering into the analyses in the following chapters, here I review some of those one-sided analyses.

Studies That Use Static Nationalization (or Its Facsimiles)
In their study of Western Europe, Lago-Peñas and Lago-Peñas (2009) explicitly link [static] nationalization to political outcomes. Their concern is with "rigidity" of spending options. They argue that where party systems are not nationalized, local politicians play a greater role, and thus there are more veto players in the system. As a result, national leaders have less ability to respond to economic or other crises. They then conduct tests about the relationship of nationalization and what they term "transfer payments" – which they define as public-goods spending. They do not find that the share of transfer payments is higher in nationalized systems, but they do find that a smaller percentage of spending persists across years in systems with more nationalization. That is, when systems are not nationalized, the spending is rigid.

This is a provocative argument, but I have a few quibbles and a theoretical concern about their ignoring dynamic nationalization. First, the measure of [static] nationalization that Lago-Peñas and Lago-Peñas use may not be adequate to test their theory. First, the theory is about government spending, but the measure they use, the inflation rate (see Chapter 2), gives a system-level rather than a party-level score. In the authors' home country of Spain, for example, the PSOE (Spanish Socialist Workers' Party) has wider and more homogeneous coverage than other parties. Are they as constrained as others? Further, how much pull do the regional parties have in countries such as Spain or Canada to lock in spending (especially at the cost of national public goods)? An alternative hypothesis might be that national parties can ignore the regional competitors since the latter cannot win national office. Finally, in ignoring DN, the authors have missed the opportunity to develop a variant of the hypothesis. If DN is high, then parties should worry about spending on public goods since it will affect their vote in all regions. But if dynamic nationalization is low, the parties in power might want to use the purse in variable ways. The hypothesis, then, might be that public goods are better provided by parties with high DN. This would suggest the thesis would be more successful in explaining outcomes in the United Kingdom than in, for example, Argentina.

In a recent paper, Castañeda (2013) follows a similar path, but applies his analysis to Latin America rather than Europe. He too explores how [static] nationalization affects the patterns of government spending, hypothesizing that more nationalized systems will bring a higher percentage of spending on public goods. The relation, he argues, is also conditioned by the size of the president's coalition. In addition to using a different region, Castañeda operationalizes his variables in a different way. For targeted spending, he looks at transfers to sub-national governments. He also adds a proxy for central government non-targeted spending: public employment expenses. To measure [static] nationalization, he generates a Morgenstern and Potthoff score for each party and then calculates the average to provide a score for the system.

While Castañeda's findings are intriguing, he too could gain by also considering DN. If presidents have a dynamically nationalized coalition, they can fend off demands from regions with national programs. Transfer payments to regions, by contrast, might be a cause and/or consequence of countries whose governing parties seek opportunities to make differential appeals. If static but not dynamic nationalization is low, the government might see incentives to target the transfers to particular regions. If this happened, low static nationalization might not raise the overall level of transfers.

Crisp et al. (2013) also focus on the role of nationalization in the distribution of government spending. Their innovation is to consider the distribution of the public, as well as the distribution of party support. This is an important addition to the literature, since it considers Katz's warnings that parties can have similar vote support due to similar policies or distinct appeals to distinct constituencies.

Next, Simmons et al. (2011) argue that foreign investors take [static] nationalization into account in choosing among potential sites for their investments. When [static] nationalization is low, they argue, investments are at risk, since parties may appropriate returns for redistribution. In one regard, this hypothesis is opposite that of Lago-Peñas and Lago-Peñas, who presume that regional powers can freeze policies. And, of course, it too could benefit from considering DN. If DN is low, then new governments can operate without concern about some regions; taking resources in one region might help them in one region and hurt in another. If DN is high, then the parties' support should move in similar ways, regardless of how they move resources.

Highlighting the rising interest in the theme, a recent dissertation also examines the impacts of nationalization. In "The Impact of Localism on Public Goods and Services Provision," Canavan (2014) explores several areas where political geography affects government spending patterns. He too focuses more on a concept close to static nationalization, and finds (among other things) that [statically] nationalized parties engage in less pork-barrel spending and that coalitions with broader geographic coverage help to minimize targeted spending.

Studies That Use Dynamic Nationalization (or Its Facsimiles)

Looking from the side of dynamic nationalization, there is also a problem with one-dimensional analyses. Few studies directly address this dimension, but it plays a central role in Cox and McCubbins's (1993) prominent study, and there are an almost uncountable number of studies in which the explanatory variable is the personal vote – which I have argued is a related but narrower concept. Personal vote studies take the form of arguing that legislators who have electoral incentives to make non-partisan appeals to constituents will use their influence to target pork or other types of resources to their voters, conduct personalized campaigns, conduct extensive constituency service, or sponsor legislation favored by their supporters. In almost all cases, there is room to add a SN dimension to this analysis. For example, legislators from safe districts have different levels of motivation to conduct one more town hall meeting than do legislators who have more serious concerns about winning the next election. In theoretical terms, given that election outcomes are a function of both partisan and personal characteristics, candidates have greater incentives to build their personal appeal where partisanship is insufficient to win. Thus, empirical tests that search for the relation between personal-vote-seeking incentives and candidate behavior could gain from considering the varying level of partisanship across a country. For Cox and McCubbins, as I detail in Chapter 9, this means that the analysis is underspecified, in that it suggests that all legislators are equally concerned with building the party label. Adding the static dimension would generate hypotheses about differences among legislators, such that legislators in safe seats, for example, might be less inclined to delegate powers to the central leadership. From a comparative perspective, a hypothesis could contend that countries where a party's legislators have similar support among regions might be more willing to solve collective action problems than where regional support is diverse. There are multiple examples in the comparative literature that similarly focus on just the personal vote or DN, and could gain from adding the other SN to their models.

One prominent example that uses a personal vote index as an independent variable is Hallerberg and Marier's (2004) "Executive Authority, The Personal Vote, and Budget Discipline in Latin American and Caribbean Countries." In addition to updating and modifying the Carey and Shugart system (as discussed in Chapter 6), they hypothesize that the personal vote should drive up budget deficits. Simplifying their argument, the idea is that legislators with incentives to pursue a personal vote will be profligate spenders, thus driving up budget deficits.

They are also interested in the strength of the president, and thus their regression, which tests the relations for 20 presidential cases across multiple years (n=179), interacts the presidents' powers with the personal vote index. Their model suggests that the personal vote has a strong negative impact on budget deficits, and that "centralization of the budgetary process is especially effective where incentives toward the personal vote are high" (p. 580).

As I have argued since Chapter 1, using DN instead of the personal vote index would give a direct measure of the degree to which voters are responding to locally based politics. Here, however, my interest is in noting that this interesting paper could still be improved by adding the static dimension of nationalization. The paper is predicated on the idea that presidents are concerned with national spending and public goods, while legislators are locally focused. As such, if the parties have disparate support around the nation, then the parties (including the president's party) would have different spending concerns than where the parties have consistent support. The logic here is that where support is consistent, both presidents and parties should be more concerned with maintaining a balance in the spending.

There are several studies that use the personal vote to explain other aspects of economic growth or reform. Bagashka (2012), for example, argues that the personal vote harms economic reform, again because higher personal voting incentives lead legislators to focus on local rather than national concerns. Her study focuses on Eastern Europe; she operationalizes the personal vote by interacting Carey and Shugart's ballot, pool, and vote variables with district magnitude, as set out by Wallack et al. (2003).[2] Her dependent variable is the European Bank for Reconstruction and Development's index of economic reform.

Her panel data (with 279 observations) shows clear effects of the personal vote, but here again SN could improve the analysis. Clearly reformers must be concerned with and contend with different regional economic orientations and interests. If the reformers' parties have much stronger support in rural areas, for example, then they might be encouraged to promote very different policy reforms than parties that have similar levels of reform across the country.

Another paper, by Crisp et al. (2004), explains that personal-vote-seeking incentives encourage legislators to promote locally oriented bills. In their words, "we expect more legislation targeting national issues when legislators do not face copartisans (or personal vote-seeking incentives are lowest) and more legislation to deliver local pork-barrel projects and particularistic services when personalizing effects are introduced by the party's candidates election procedures or by electoral laws at the house level" (p. 831). Here the authors code each country for the role of the party in controlling access to the ballot, plus the district magnitude, to generate a proxy for the personal vote. To construct their dependent variable, they coded 19,000 bills in ten countries for whether they were "targetable" to local constituencies. Their results show

[2] Her system also accounts for potential contaminating incentive systems in two-level systems.

that personal-vote-seeking incentives lead legislators to initiate many more targetable bills, and that where those incentives are high, targetable bills are more likely to win approval.

This is another paper where using the two dimensions of nationalization could strengthen the models. As in the other examples, the local vote would give a direct measure of legislators focus on their individual constituencies, while their independent variable looks at implied incentive. For our purposes here, the concern is that the authors could improve their analysis by including a measure of SN. Clearly where all of a party's legislators have consistent levels of support, they would have different incentives regarding whether they would initiate or approve targetable legislation.

As a final example, Nielson (2003) tests for the impact of electoral systems on trade policy, based on the theory that personal vote electoral systems lead legislators to fight for protectionist tariffs. As in the other examples, DN would improve the proxy for the personal-vote-seeking incentives, and the static dimension of nationalization would strengthen the analysis by pointing to the legislators' different regional concerns.

Nielson graciously provided his data, and, after reproducing his results, I re-analyzed his models using DN in place of his coding for the personal vote. He tests several different dependent variables with different sets of countries, and I lacked the requisite electoral data for two of his three analyses. I do have the necessary data for his model that focuses on "Tariff Dispersion." My results did not give strong support for his conclusions. Why? In looking at the data, the personal vote has a reasonable correlation with DN, but there are some important outliers (Argentina and Guatemala have low personal vote scores and poor DN, and Uruguay has the opposite relationship). Uruguay is perhaps very influential in his models, as it is the source of the two extreme outliers in the data; while no other country has a score for Tariff Dispersion of mor than 63, Uruguay is listed with values over 200 for 1971 and 1972. If I drop Uruguay from the analysis, I then do find a significant result (p= 0.06) for DN in the model. The implication of this tinkering is that the results are sensitive, in part because of the nominal nature of the data. The personal vote scales based on electoral rules are problematic, in that they provide (perhaps) ordinal rather than cardinal values. As such, while we might agree that closed-list rules provide fewer incentives to cultivate a personal vote than do single-member districts, the extent of the difference is not clear. Using DN, by contrast, gives a precise quantification of the importance of local politics, and it looks at the results of elections rather than perceived influences.

Roadmap

In sum, one-dimensional analyses of party nationalization leave numerous analytical holes. In an attempt to patch a few of those, Chapter 7 addresses broad questions of accountability and national integration, arguing that the responsible party model requires at least moderate levels of each dimension. Chapter 8 provides more detail for this question by looking at retrospective and prospective voting. It shows that voters' choices over incumbents (retrospective voting) are sometimes more nationalized (on both dimensions) than their choices over the challenges (prospective voting). Put differently, national factors can drive retrospective choices even where there is a high role for localism in prospective choices. Chapter 9, finally, asks how DN affects cooperation among legislators.

7

Regionalism, Accountability, and Party Nationalization

The core idea in a representative democracy is that voters hold political parties accountable for their decisions and pick alternatives based on the competitors' policy positions. These ideas, which form the base of the "responsible party model," are challenged when not all voters react in similar ways to an incumbent's decisions or a challenger's positions. If voters in different regions act in disparate ways, then the parties might be more responsive to some regions than others. In such a case, the parties might not work toward building a national constituency, an outcome that would hamper a country's integration. Party nationalization allows a window into these themes, facilitating analysis of the degree to which parties work to develop a national constituency and are then held accountable for policies and outcomes that have national reach.

The responsible party model runs afoul when parties have low levels of one or the other dimensions of nationalization, because that would imply that voters are driven by regional or local issues and context. In addition to the theoretical problems about accountability, low party nationalization implies normative problems for national integration. The theoretical concern with regional parties is that since their support is based at least partly on their identities rather than retrospective judgments of the accomplishments of the incumbent, accountability suffers. There may be value in terms of representation in having voters choose on identities, but accountability requires that voters consider changing conditions in evaluating the incumbent's performance. On the normative side, a country's integration requires that voters in all sectors reflect on the incumbent's performance; where voters ignore performance and act solely based on regional identities, irredentism is a threat.

This chapter shows how static and dynamic nationalization can help to evaluate the tension between identity voting and the responsible party model. It concludes that accountability requires that parties have significant penetration into all regions, which is related to SN. Accountability also requires high DN, however, because this indicates that voters everywhere evaluate incumbent performance in a similar way. A further requirement is that there are enough marginal voters willing to shift their votes such that changes in votes can transfer into shifts in legislative seats.

These ideas emanate from several sources. As first articulated by Ranney (1954), under the "responsible party model" if voters "approve[d] of the general direction the party in power ha[d] been taking ... they [would] return that party to power." If, however, the voters judged otherwise, they would vote for the opposition. While simple and attractive, the ability of voters and parties to live up to this ideal has generated much discussion. Key (1966) was among the first to show the utility of the model for US presidential races, but others have expressed doubts about its applicability to legislative elections. Schattschneider (1960 and American Political Science Association 1950), for example, was worried about voters judging, and US parties thus emphasizing, local (or "sectional") rather than national issues. Others questioned how well citizens were able to assign blame. In this vein, Manin, Przeworski, and Stokes (1990) questioned the role of institutions in inducing politicians to act in the interests of the citizenry, and Powell and Whitten (1993), as well as Powell (2000), argued that accountability requires "clarity of responsibility." Similarly, Jones and McDermott (2004) show that divided government can confuse voters' judgments. Here, I will argue that nationalization indicates whether voters are clear in their judgments.

Another piece of the discussion is based on Caramani (2000, p. 67), who argued that the spread of parties' support signaled an increase in national integration because it meant a growing focus on ideological concerns over territorial cleavages. As the [static] nationalization process proceeds, he explains, "political and electoral beliefs attitudes, and behavior are diffused through national territories ... [and] local candidates are no longer independent figures and lose their character of representing the local community. Rather they become representatives of the national centre of the political organization" (p. 68). The message, then, is that when parties are [statically] nationalized, there is a reduced tendency toward regionalism.

Static nationalization therefore provides a measure of national integration. Where parties are shut out from some areas – or, stated in reverse, maintain bailiwicks or a regional focus – voters from those constituencies will face different choices in their attempts to reward or punish politicians based on the national context. The disconnect among those voters, which would be evident in a low SN score, implies a limit on national integration. Stronger SN would not imply a lack of conflict among or within regions, but it would imply a nationally integrated system of accountability, since voters everywhere would face similar choices.

Dynamic nationalization is also necessary to show national integration, because it shows that there is a similarly sized set of marginal voters in each area who are willing to be persuaded by national issues or events. When DN is low, voters in different regions are moving in different directions, and this would indicate that they are responding differently to similar stimuli, or they are responding to different stimuli (and/or candidates) altogether. This scenario would challenge the notion that the electoral process is a good means for holding incumbents accountable.

This chapter uses these ideas to evaluate the role that regional parties play in hindering accountability of incumbents. There are two main issues. First, are the regional parties so dominant that they prevent parties that seek wide support from penetrating the regions? Second, are there sufficient voters who are willing to move between the incumbent and regional alternatives – marginal voters – to threaten and reward the incumbent in a manner consistent with notions of accountability? Relatedly, does a shift in votes generate a sufficient shift in seats in all of a country's regions such that parties cannot ignore any of them? An incumbent party's inability to gain votes and seats in particular regions based on its performance in government would signal limited integration and accountability.

While the two dimensions of party nationalization can help identify the degree to which regions and their different voting groups are integrated into national politics, they can also misrepresent parties that participate in just one or a few electoral districts. Statistics will clearly indicate that some parties in Bolivia, Belgium, India, or Spain lack static or dynamic nationalization, but this is an incomplete story. In part it is incomplete because it does not signify the lines on which there is competition within the regions where these parties compete. Not all competitors in Quebec, for example, are foremost regional parties. Further, the static story does not show the degree to which voters in those regions are influenced by national politics and circumstances.

Second, by themselves, nationalization statistics would fail to differentiate regional parties such as the Bloc Quebecois (BQ) in Canada from parties in countries such as Chile and the United States, the latter of which owe their low nationalization (on both scales) to a failure to compete in multiple or non-regionally concentrated areas. In this and the following chapter I argue that the dimensions of nationalization, when taking special account of and even working within the regions that have regional parties, provide an important indicator of the role of local identities to voting and have important implications for the responsible party model.

The methodologies for studying the two dimensions of nationalization can help to answer several questions about accountability and integration. First, SN *within* the regions where the non-national parties compete will show the degree to which these parties have support throughout the region. Is the party fully regional – or localized? The size of the regional parties is of course a second concern; stated in reverse, for the parties that compete nationally, how strong are they within each of a country's diverse regions? Have the national parties been able to penetrate the regions, and thus move the country toward integration?

The DN of the *national* parties provides a view of whether those parties can sway marginal voters in the *regions* based on *national* themes. If change in support for parties that compete nationally varies across regions, then regional issues and identity must be particularly prominent in the voters' minds, and accountability would suffer. This chapter examines DN of parties where there is regionalism – that is where SN is low – and evaluates the degree to which the regions contribute to low levels of DN. It focuses on parties that head or have headed their respective governments, in order to emphasize accountability of those responsible for national conditions.

Unlike earlier chapters that emphasized analysis of parties over party systems, this chapter is concerned with the interactions among parties and those parties' sizes. These factors, plus nationalization, can define a party system. Still, I do not follow conventions and provide a summary value for the party system, because, as I argued in Chapter 4, averages, even if weighted, are misleading if the component parts of the system are very different from one another. Instead, the discussion considers the relationship between parties that compete nationally and those that compete in one or a limited number of a country's regions. A key concern is whether the parties with a broader reach penetrate and thus help to integrate all of a country's regions. The two dimensions of nationalization provide the requisite information to address these questions.

This chapter first develops the argument about the role of nationalization in discussions of representation and accountability. That discussion suggests that national integration and the responsible party model require three criterion: that SN be at least moderately high, that DN be high, and that seats transfer when sufficient voters change from one party preference to another. The chapter discusses each of these in turn, adding caution about the raw nationalization scores, since they can result from different voting patterns.

Representation and the Responsible Party Model

This section develops the argument about the relation between nationalization and the responsible party model. The thesis is that accountability requires that ruling parties have a reasonable level of support in a country's different regions (at least moderate SN) and that support everywhere should be related to the incumbent's performance (a high level of DN). It also requires that the regions own enough legislative seats such that when there are electoral shifts, there are also changes in the number of seats that the incumbent party wins.

Both SN and DN play roles in showing whether a party fits the responsible party model. A low SN suggests some regions' voters are generally much less receptive to a party's message than others. A party without receptivity is incompatible with one that is responsible. A low DN also symbolizes a deficit of responsibility, because it means that the party is a) unable to attract additional voters in some regions even in good times or b) its support does not fall even in bad times. The one caveat to this idea is that if a party's support "fans in" by gaining more support where it had been weak without losing it where it was strong, the responsible party model could be undamaged.

On a normative level, it may be the case that lower DN is sometimes favorable. It might be desirable, for example, that a government pass policies favoring a poor region over a rich one, and this could lead to different reactions (low DN) across the country. This notion, however, is incompatible with the responsible party model, which requires that the government will be held accountable for the national context. Passing policies that are more favorable to some areas than others could signal responsiveness to constituents, but regional divisions in how constituents respond to the party also suggest a lack of national unity and thus a problem for the responsible party model.

Regional parties are a threat to the responsible party model because where they are strong, voters must be moved by identity more than economics or policy performance, thus breaking the accountability link between incumbent parties and the state of the nation. Even if the regions have particular economic concerns, strong regional parties signify a problem for accountability because they indicate that voters privilege issues of identity or that they do not see the national parties as protectors of regional interests. Regional parties are useful for representation, and votes shifting from a more national incumbent to a regional party in bad times would be consistent with accountability. Accountability is not working, however, if voters support particular parties regardless of the incumbent's performance. Voting based on identity may be useful for representation, but it works against accountability.

The concern about the distinction between representation and accountability became clear after the 2016 vote in Spain. The Partido Popular (People's Party; PP) gained the most votes and, after an arduous process, formed a government. The party's support was very limited in two of the country's regions, Catalonia and the Basque Country, where national identities have led to discussions of separatism or at least pressing for a Quebec-like special status. With barely 10 percent of the seats in each of these regions (which overall account for 63 of the county's 350 seats), a prominent political scientist in Spain, Manuel Alcántara, asks in his newspaper column, "Is the PP capable of governing Spain with a minimally integrative vision?".[1]

SN and DN can help assess whether voters from different areas respond in kind to an incumbent's performance. The magnitude of shifts is also important, but there are two sides to the issue. If there are a limited number of marginal voters – that is those who are swayed by policies and conditions rather than non-moveable identities – then incumbents may be able to discount the regions. The incentives to ignore the regions in such circumstances, however, are a function of the number of seats available in the region and whether small vote shifts will affect the number of seats the party can win.

---

[1] My translation; Salamanca RTV Al Dia, 7/1/16; *La Perplejidad Electoral*.

There is another side of this equation, however. If there are too many marginal voters, then volatility is a threat. While Bartolini and Mair (1990) caution that electoral volatility is not the same as regime instability, Roberts (2014, p. 20) says that "large scale iterative vote shifts" indicate "detachment and alienation" for voters, and others worry that if too many voters move in response to policy or contextual changes, parties might not institutionalize, outsiders would likely be prominent, and policy gyrations would be excessive (Mainwaring and Scully 1995; Carreras 2014).

For accountability, the question is whether regional parties, by capturing voters based on identity, limit the potential for shifts in votes. In this book I have focused on party-level analysis, since the nationalization of one party does not determine that of another (except in the case of systems with just two parties). The existence of regional parties, however, must limit SN for at least some parties.[2] This is harmful to the ability of parties to integrate a nation in the sense described by Caramani (2000, 2005). Low SN, however, does not prescribe low DN, and thus a question for accountability is whether the regional parties limit not just SN but also DN. Where regional parties have a strong grip, there would be few marginal voters who are willing to switch to or away from the incumbent based on changing conditions. A low DN score could capture this idea by showing distinct regional patterns in the vote. Where regions drive down the DN for national parties, accountability is challenged since voters in the regions must be responding to different stimuli or differently to a similar incitement. In contrast, where the change in the national parties' support is consistent across the country – that is DN is high – in spite of the presence of regional parties, accountability is clearer and the regions are more integrated into the national framework.

Figure 7.1 provide a hypothetical illustration. Seven of the ten districts move in perfect rhythm, while the party wins less support in the other three. In the district represented by the heavy gray line, the party's support is lower, but it still moves in tandem with the seven districts where the party is stronger. The tandem movements suggest that national conditions drive electoral outcomes, at least for those eight districts. The direction of changes in the district represented by the dotted line oppose those in most of the rest of the country, suggesting that a single policy or outcome produces variable responses. Taxing farm exports to support urban development, for example, could divide rural and urban voters. This is problematic in terms of integration, but it is a form of accountability given that voters are responsive to national conditions or policy.[3] Finally, in the exceptional district represented by the dashed line, voters sometimes move with and sometimes move against the pattern of the

---

[2] Even in the presence of regional parties, any given party that competes nationally could win a relatively consistent percentage of the vote everywhere, thus keeping a high level of SN. Some parties that compete nationally, however, must have lower support in districts where regional parties are strong.

[3] Note that the direction of the change is more important than its magnitude for this argument.

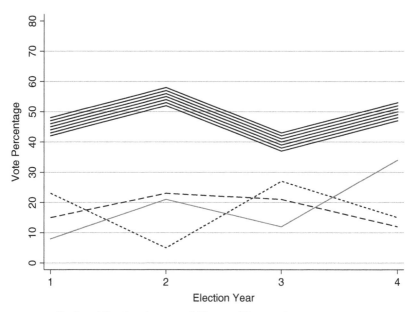

FIGURE 7.1 Regional Parties, Accountability, and Integration

other districts. There the party can expect a moderate level of support, but marginal voters are irresponsive to national conditions. If they are motivated, instead, by local factors, accountability is a concern.

This discussion suggests three criteria for evaluating the responsible party model. First, SN must be at least moderate, such that governing parties have support in all regions. An important caveat is that the low SN could be the result of pillarized or regional patterns. These both pose potential problems for accountability, but they have different meanings for integration.

The second criterion is that the governing party maintains a high degree of DN, regardless of SN or whether the low SN is the result of pillarization or not. High DN implies that a similarly sized proportion of marginal voters in each area are willing to be persuaded by national issues, events, or context. If those proportions vary (i.e. DN is low), then the party would have strong incentives to be more responsive to some areas than others. This could still be consistent with a notion of accountability, but it would be a regionalized version of the concept.

The clearest case of regionalized politics, which here represents the opposing pole from the responsible (national) party model, would be one where a party has low levels of both SN and DN, because this would imply the party is unable to make inroads into some areas, and that marginal voters are unswayed by factors influencing voters in other parts of the country. In pillarized systems, low DN could signify one of two types of politics. First, it could suggest that local factors drive elections, as I argued in Chapter 2. A second possibility, however is that the pillars move together, perhaps based on similarities in sociodemographics. If, for example, cities are spread throughout a country and urban voters act differently from those in rural districts, there would be two sets of non-regionally concentrated districts moving in distinct ways. This would yield low DN, but it would not indicate the same type of localism as in cases that focus attention on candidates or particular characteristics of the districts.

When pillars are not tied, the responsible party model is clearly troubled because it implies that even good performance by a party will not necessarily bring new support. Tied pillars do not present the reverse situation, because they foretell societal divisions. Politicians in these systems could act strategically to attract one or the other sets of pillars, but the cost could be acrimony from the other part of the country.

There are two caveats to this second criterion. The first is that there must be a significant number of marginal voters (i.e. those open to changing their partisan choices) across the country. DN could be high if few voters change their stripes, but the responsible party model would lack a necessary element if a governing party has limited hopes of gaining votes in some districts or regions in spite of an uptick in national conditions. The second caveat, as noted earlier, is that if the party gains more votes in places where it had been weak (or vice versa), then DN could be low while accountability would be functioning.

The third criterion for the responsible party model is that when an incumbent party experiences a shift in votes due to its actions in government, it should also feel a change in terms of the number of seats. This book has focused on shifts in votes, but an analysis on seats – and data at the district level are now becoming available – would provide another valid view of nationalization and would be particularly relevant for accountability.

Criterion 1: The Level of SN and the Patterns That Produce Low SN

A country's integration is clearly troubled if an incumbent party is unable to garner votes in some regions and thus earns a low SN label. But parties with low SN are not of a single type, and some are more concerning than others. This section thus analyzes the types of patterns that produce low SN and discusses the different meanings and implications of each.

Concerns about integration and accountability arise when low SN results from smaller parties shutting out (or strongly limiting) incumbents in one or more regions of the country. This is the case in countries such as Belgium, Canada, Spain, and the United Kingdom. Each of those countries has regional parties that compete only (or mostly) in a geographically confined region. The existence of these regional parties, however, does not always imply that other parties are shut out. In Canada, the BQ competes in all 75 districts in Quebec, but none outside of that province. It does not, however, consume all the votes in the province. Further, its support is highly variable. For 2006–2011, that support ranged from 4 to 56 percent in Quebec's 75 ridings, yielding a very high M&M static score (130.8) when applied just within the region. The Conservatives, meanwhile, averaged about one-fourth of the Quebec vote in 2006, and won more than 50 percent in a few districts. Given the country's plurality-based electoral system, these vote totals translate into many wins for the Liberals and Conservatives, and the BQ has never won more than 54 of the 75 seats available in Quebec (and it has won far fewer in recent elections). In sum, the BQ's low intra-province SN means that the party has strong but localized support and, by implication, the national parties are central players in Quebec. That they have less success in some parts of the region, however, will also influence the parties' strategies in dealing with policies that affect the province. The strategies could change sharply if Canada were to adopt a PR electoral system – which the new prime minister, Justin Trudeau, has proposed – because while the BQ could remain a regional power, the pillarization would be less evident. Competition, further, would then revolve around the search for votes throughout the province, without concern about trying to win particular localities. Where now the parties' best strategies might be to focus on districts where competition is close, in a PR system it would not matter where the party wins votes. A strategic party under the proposed system, then, would develop policies and focus resources in ways to earn the most votes possible, regardless of where marginal votes are located.

Regionalism is not the only voting pattern that produces low SN scores among parties that compete nationally. Such scores can also result when parties fail to compete (or compete well) in a set of scattered districts.[4] As described in Chapter 2, the ideal-type here is a "pillarized" support pattern, but there could also be an intermediate variant, where support varies sharply among states (where "state" is shorthand for what some countries call departments, provinces, etc.). Of course, if the states are grouped geographically the system could look regional, and in some cases there would not be a meaningful distinction between concerns focused on states rather than regions. I am conceiving state-oriented parties as systems where the involved states (or provinces or departments) do not attract the parties based on a regional identity. Parties may base their strength in these states on particular policy issues or ties to state governors. This is a gray area, but in federal countries like Brazil and Mexico parties use ties to state politicians to build their support, though that support is not based on state identities. This allows them to expand and develop bases in multiple states, regardless of geography.

Argentina's Radical Civic Union party (UCR) provides an imperfect example of a state-oriented party. It garnered a high M&M value (74.9) for 2003–2007 because it won less than 10 percent in Buenos Aires, the federal district, and several other provinces, while winning above 40 percent elsewhere. The example is imperfect since there is variability in the patterns, with the

---

[4] If the average level of support is small, a large number of zeros in the data can generate low variance and thus a high SN value.

UCR scoring well in those same provinces in other years. Another imperfect example is Colombia, where in the three elections of 1994, 1998, and 2002 the Liberals consistently won more than 50 percent of the vote in a number of departments, in spite of the fragmented party system and proportional representation. Those departments are regionally concentrated in the coffee-growing area and other parts of the south, but the party also had support in other parts of the country. In 2006 and 2010, the system moved more toward the regional category, as the president's party (PSUN/LaU) did very poorly in the southern departments (where the guerrilla movements have been strongest).

While a low level of SN that results from highly disparate support at the state or regional levels generates clear concerns for national politics, when it results from pillarized patterns of support the concerns would be about local politics and local-level accountability. To analyze the parties with pillarized support, Table 7.1 lists the major parties (here defined as those having headed the government) that have failed to put forth legislative candidates in at least some of their countries' districts, but still win a large percentage of the vote where they do compete. That list, which also incorporates parties that fail to compete in one or more states or regions, includes parties in Argentina, Belgium, Canada, Chile, Colombia, Finland, France, India, Japan, Korea, Peru, Switzerland Taiwan, the United Kingdom, and the United States. For each, the table lists the percent of districts in which the party competed and the party's SN raw score (M&M value); as expected, SN is weak for these parties. The pillarized category is most pertinent to countries that have many electoral districts (that number is indicated in the table), because these allow variable support levels – perhaps ranging to zero – within as well as among a country's states or regions. The table focuses on parties that fail to win any votes in one or more districts, but if we relax the criterion to consider parties that win under 20 percent of the vote in some districts but much more elsewhere, the set of countries grows to include parties in Mexico and the Dominican Republic, among others.

The relation among pillarization, SN scores, and accountability or integration requires a more detailed look at the voting patterns. First, are the low SN scores the result of a just a few districts where the parties fail to compete, and is that absence in one year sui generis or a consistent problem? The number of districts in which the pillarized parties fail to compete varies in and among countries, but most of the parties that I have labeled pillarized compete in most districts. Some, however, have particularly unstable support in some districts, and in many cases a lack of participation (or very low support) in one year does not foretell support in another. For example, the French center-right party Union for a Popular Movement (UPM) failed to compete in 24 of the country's 577 districts in 1997; the pillarized label is appropriate because these districts were spread across 13 departments. Its SN level is in the moderate category, but even that level is somewhat deceiving given that it is present and viable in most areas, and

TABLE 7.1 *Parties Failing to Compete in All Districts*

	PRS'/1	# Dists / % competed	SN		PRS	# Dists / % competed	SN
Argent. (2011)		24		Japan (2009)		300	
PJ	S	95.8	108.3	LDP	P	97.0	93.1
				DPJ	P	90.3	105.7
Belgium (2010)		11		Korea (2012)		289	
CD&V	R	54.5	120.8	Democratic		72.0	195.0
MR	R	63.6	252.4				
PS	R	63.6	233.5	Peru (2011)		25	
				APRA	S	96.0	28.1
Canada (2011)		308					
Conserv.	P	99.7	232.2	Switz. (1999–07)		26	
				CVP	S	80.8	323.7
Chile (2009)		60		FDP	S	85.2	376.3
DC	P	65.0	63.7	SP	S	81.5	181.7
PPD	P	45.0	183.1	SVP	S	81.5	89.3
PS	P	40.0	115.5				
RN	P	85.0	144.2				

TABLE 7.1 (*continued*)

	PRS/1	# Dists / % competed	SN
Colombia			
Cons. (2002)	S/R	33 / 70	33.0
Lib. (2010)	S/R	90.9	89.2
PSUN(2006)	S/R	87.8	16.8
Finland (2011)			
SFP/RKP	R	19 / 47.4	135.9
France (1997)			
Socialists	P	577 / 99.3	102.9
RPR/UMP	P	95.8	68.0
India (2004)			
INC	S/P	543 / 76.6	472.3
BJP	S/P	64.7	102.6
Taiwan (2004)			
KMT	P	29 / 89.7	156.3
UK (2005)			
Conserv.	R/P	646 / 97.5	152.8
Labour	R/P	97.1	373.6
USA (2010)			
Democrats	P	435 / 96.1	403.4
Republican	P	96.1	450.4

/1 P=Pillarized, R=Regional S=State

where the party was absent in 1997 it did compete in other years (it was present in all districts in 2007), sometimes doing very well.

The Japanese LDP also competes in almost all of its country's 300 districts (skipping just 10 in 2009). Its SN (M&M value 93.1) indicates even more of a local focus than in France, but cutting out the districts where it failed to compete cuts that value in half. Analysis of integration and accountability, then, relies on a closer look at those districts. In 3 of the 10 zero-districts for 2009 the party scored a majority of the vote in 2005, but in the other 7 the LDP did not compete that year either. Four of these 7 are in Osaka, but the party won an average of 34 percent in the other 13 districts of that prefecture. Though this is lower than in some other prefectures, the data do not suggest that the problem has moved beyond one of localism to the prefecture level. Noting that the Koumei party was strong in the Osaka districts where the LDP was absent leads to a discussion of the relation of these two parties, which has evolved and changed.[5]

While these examples show pillarized parties competing in almost all districts, there are examples of parties that skip more districts that also fit this category. In most districts the Japanese Communists earn under 10 percent, and in 2009 they failed to compete at all in about one-half of the districts. In a few places, however, they won more than 20 percent. In Chile, several parties show a similar pattern, but for that case integration and accountability do not only rely on the parties; each party pertains to a coalition and the coalitions are present in all 60 districts. Thus, even though some the individual coalition partners compete in less than one-half of the districts, voters can respond to the coalition.[6]

Parties frequently have traits from two or more of these categories. India's National Congress merits the pillarized and state labels, for example. The country has 35 states,[7] and while there are clear state-level differences in support for the two main parties, there are also many pillars of that strength within most states. In Uttar Pradesh, for example, the Indian National Congress won more than 50 percent in 2 of the state's 80 districts in 2004, but did not compete in 7 others. Overall, the party failed to compete in 69 of 543 districts in 1998, and these districts were spread across 13 of the country's 35 states. But, 24 of the zero-districts were in Bihar, and in other election years it also failed to compete in dozens of Bihar districts. The state of Tamil Nadu shows a similar pattern. The INC did not participate in almost three-quarters of the state's 39 districts in 2004, but where it did participate, it won *a minimum* of 50 percent. Table 7.2 emphasizes this variety by providing a state-by-state breakdown of the number of districts where the Bharatiya Janata Party (BJP) or India National Congress (INC) failed to win any

---

[5] See, for example, chapters by Reed and his collaborations in his edited volume (2003).
[6] Chile will implement a new electoral system for 2017 that will not constrict the parties as has been the case since 1990. The change will show if the pillarization is a reflection of electoral support or system restrictions.
[7] Several of these "states" are termed "union territories," but as a shorthand I will refer to all of these as states.

TABLE 7.2 *Districts Competed by State in India 2004*

States	Total Districts	INC Competed	BJP Competed
Andhra Pradesh	42	34	9
Arunachal Pradesh	2	1	2
Assam	14	14	12
Bihar	40	4	16
Chandigarh	1	1	1
Chhattisgarh	11	11	11
Daman & Diu	1	1	1
Goa	2	1	2
Gujarat	26	25	26
Haryana	10	10	10
Himachal Pradesh	4	3	4
Jammu & Kashmir	6	3	6
Jharkhand	14	9	14
Karnataka	28	28	24
Kerala	20	17	19
Lakshadweep	1	1	0
Madhya Pradesh	29	29	29
Maharashtra	48	26	26
Manipur	2	1	2
Meghalaya	2	2	1
Mizoram	1	0	0
Nagaland	1	1	0
Nagar Haveli	1	1	1
Nicobar Islands	1	1	1
Orissa	21	21	9
Pondicherry	1	0	1
Punjab	13	11	3
Rajasthan	25	25	25
Sikkim	1	1	0
Tamil Nadu	39	10	6
Territory Of Delhi	7	7	7
Tripura	2	2	1
Uttar Pradesh	80	73	77
Uttaranchal	5	5	5
West Bengal	42	37	13
Total	543	416	364

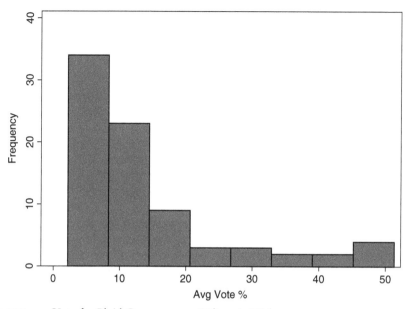

FIGURE 7.2 Vote for Plaid Cymru across Ridings in Wales 2001–5

votes. These values certainly suggest much wider concerns than for the cases discussed above, where pillarization was localized and inconsistent.

I also applied both the regional and pillarized labels to the British Labour and Conservative parties (and the Liberal Democrats; LDP), because they have variable levels of support across and with the country's component regions, except in Northern Ireland, where these "national" parties are almost completely absent.[8] Pillarization is evident, because there are dozens of ridings, which are spread throughout the country, where these parties fail to win even 10 percent of the vote.[9] Elsewhere, the SN values show varying success within the regions. Within Wales, Plaid Cymru has an M&M static score of over 140 (for 1997–2005), which reflects the fact that its support ranged from about 2 percent to over 50 percent (Figure 7.2). That variation is also indicative of the inconsistent level of support for other parties in this component country of the United Kingdom. Similarly, in Scotland both the national and "regional" parties – in this case the Scottish Nationalists (SNP) – compete among one

[8] In 17 districts (of 528) the Conservatives won less than 10 percent of the vote in at least one of the three elections between 1997 and 2005. The Conservatives have had candidates in several Northern Ireland districts, but only once between 1997 and 2005 did one of their candidates win more than 5 percent of the vote, and that candidate only won 6.8 percent.

[9] There appears to be more consistency in these parties' pillars than in some of the other countries displayed. Still, since they are spread throughout the country, the pillarized label is most appropriate.

another for votes. Scotland (for 2005) had 59 districts for the Westminster elections, and the SNP only has a strong following in a few, winning just 5 or 6 seats in the 1990s and 2000s. There, the Conservatives won more than 10 percent in 41 of the 59 districts in 2005, and the LDP reached that level in 57 districts and reached 10 percent in every Scottish district.

Analysis of the geography of the vote *within* Northern Ireland also contributes to the discussion of integration. Northern Ireland has two parties that dominate the vote there, neither of which competes in the rest of the United Kingdom. The first of these, Sinn Fein, has its votes concentrated in a subset of Northern Ireland's districts, such that it received between 55 and 70 percent of the vote in the 3 elections under study in Belfast West, but won less than 10 percent in about one-half of Northern Ireland's 18 districts. As a result, its static score within Northern Ireland was very high (287). The Ulster Unionists, the other party that is only present in Northern Ireland, had a static score of 94.5, based on an average (but falling) support of 27.5 percent. Both parties thus rely on pockets of support. The strong support for Sinn Fein in parts of Northern Ireland has created a long-term crisis for the UK, but the low SN also reflects the concentration of the conflict within Belfast rather than throughout Northern Ireland. Still, without competition from Labour, the Conservatives,[10] or the Liberal Democrats, the status of the region will remain as the primary electoral issue. Note that while the Good Friday Agreement of 1998 did shake up competition within Northern Ireland, even that landmark did not lead to an integration of the region's parties into the national political process. Perhaps a system of proportional representation would help, as it would give the national parties a chance to win support and an incentive to seek support throughout the country. Under the current single-member district system, the national parties are shut out, thus leaving Westminster without parliamentarians who both represent Northern Ireland and seek support based on the broad national agenda. From the Northern Irish voters' vantage point, they cannot praise or punish national parties based on their performance, which creates an incentive to focus on local issues.

Some countries have parties that merit all three labels: a state focus, regionalism, and pillarization. In addition to the pillarization noted earlier with respect to the French UPM, the parties there also exhibit traits of state orientation and pillarization. The country's 577 districts are distributed among the 113 departments, and for a few departments (notably the islands of Guadaloupe, Reunion, and Martinique) the National Front fails to compete in any of the districts each year. The National Front, while not having been a governing party, thus provides an imperfect example of a state-oriented party. Regionalism is also evident, because the Socialists are stronger in the east (or southeast) and the UPM and Nationalists are stronger in the West.

---

[10] The Conservatives do put up a few candidates, but seldom win more than 1 percent.

The US parties also exhibit traits of the three types. Especially in the 1980s and 1990s, and in some cases after that date, the Democrats failed to compete in many southern districts. Of course, prior to the civil rights movement the Republicans were shut out of much of the South. There are still some other states where one of the parties does not always compete, too. In California, Ohio, Pennsylvania, and Wisconsin, for example, the Democrats consistently fail to put forward a candidate in several districts, and in 2010 the party won less than 20 percent in 34 districts. The US case, therefore, has traits of regionalism, state orientation, and pillarization.

These traits reflect the concerns about politics and accountability raised by Schattschneider (American Political Science Association 1950) more than half a century ago. Given the single-member district system, plus the incumbency advantage and gerrymandering, the link between the parties' accountability and the national mood is not as strong as it could be. Of course, consideration of the other dimension of nationalization, which is the subject of the next section, will add to this discussion.

These examples suggest cautions for the comparative study of SN. There are valid concerns about parties with low SN, but the political processes depend on whether the parties' support is pillarized or regional. This yields an electoral system argument about politics. Pillarization requires many electoral districts, and perhaps high barriers to representation (plurality elections or other quirks). Proportional representation, by contrast, should minimize the SN (as seen in Chapters 5 and 6). In Bolivia, large electoral districts and proportional representation have allowed or encouraged the Movement Towards Socialism (MAS), which grew from its support among the indigenous populations to compete even in regions that have traditionally been dominated by more conservative parties. One of those regions, Santa Cruz, provides an illustration. Santa Cruz is not monoethnic, and its multiple ethnic groups live both in the large capital city and in many rural areas. With multiple seats available through the PR system, the MAS has an incentive to mobilize potential supports, even if it cannot expect to be the largest party in that province. When the party first appeared in 2002, it won less than 7 percent in Santa Cruz and the other three "half-moon" (*media-luna*) provinces, while winning more than 25 percent elsewhere. By expanding everywhere – it won over 20 percent in three of the four half-moon provinces in 2009 – the party has arguably improved the integration of the country.

To conclude this section, it is useful to provide a statistical mechanism for measuring the relative impacts of states, regions, and pillars to the SN scores. By adding another random effect to the statistical model (see Mustillo and Jung 2016)[11] that I have been using in this book, it is possible to measure the role of states or regions statistically. As an example that focuses on states, Table 7.3 portrays values for Mexico in the elections 2006–12. The first three rows show

---

[11] The new stata command is: mixed vote year year^2 ‖statecode: ‖district: if country=="X" & party=="Y," mle variance

TABLE 7.3 *Nationalization Accounting for States: Mexico 2006–12*

| | Static | | Dynamic |
	State	District	
PRI		49.5	51.3
PAN		117.7	32.1
PRD		148.5	38.0
PRI	39.1		54.6
PAN	93.5		61.6
PRD	122.9		54.9
PRI	38.7	3.5	51.3
PAN	90.6	31.8	32.1
PRD	121.2	18.2	38.0

the values in the original model, which ignores states and thus only evaluates the variance in the 300 districts. The second three rows change the analysis to consider states (but not districts), and the last three rows include states and districts as random effects in the model. Note that the dynamic levels are identical for the first and last models, because both estimate SN at the lower geographical level. The middle model tries to distribute that variance within a much smaller number of states, and thus it puts more variance into the residual. In the case of the PRI, there is little attributed to the districts when both states and districts are in the model, and thus the residual (capturing DN) changes little.

The last model allows interpretation of the relative importance of states and districts to each party's static support. It indicates that the PRD is the most variant among the states, which comports with its stronger showing in southern states. The PAN also has variable support, and its stronger showing in the north generates a high score on its static-state value. The PRI competes everywhere, and thus states are less important as foci of their support. However, the model also suggests that what variance the PRI does experience is at the state rather than the district level. Overall, the electoral support is dominated by between-state differences, rather than by variability between districts within states.

Other cases would show the opposite. Table 7.4 provides three more examples. For Canada, the provinces and districts provide equally large impacts on the variation, for the United States the districts are much more important, and for India's National Congress Party the states are more important. Note, however, that again these are party-specific results. India's BJP has high values (much variance) both across and within the states.

While these examples focus on states, the analysis is equally applicable to regions, or a three-level model that includes region, states, and districts. This would be appropriate for countries that have variance at each of these levels, such

TABLE 7.4 *Static Nationalization Scores Accounting for States*

	State	District
Canada Conservatives	129.2	117.3
India INC	131.0	68.1
India BJP	196.4	178.0
US Dems (2000s)	28.0	303.8

as the United States and perhaps France. This type of methodology could also be applied to other groups of districts, perhaps helping to measure the relative impact of urbanism or diverse pockets of minority populations.

The idea that the states, regions, and districts have relative weights suggests a value in turning the raw data into percentages of total variance explained. Stokes (1965, 1967) did this in his original work in order to compare the weight of what I have termed static and dynamic nationalization. I have refrained from doing so because it would be misleading to talk about a high contribution from any factor if the total the total variance is small.[12] But, for a given party whose electoral returns produce cross-district and/or time variability, ratios of these different variance components could be a valuable analytical tool.

In sum, different geographic support patterns can generate low SN and each implies different interpretations for the responsible party model. Regional parties do not always shut out parties with a national reach, but the lower the support for otherwise national parties in a particular region (in comparison to those parties' support elsewhere), the lower the level of integration. Further, low SN that results from this voting pattern must also signify a regional rather than a national view of the political context, which would be inconsistent with the notion of a responsible party. Low SN that results from pillarization rather than regionalism is probably less of a concern to integration, but like regionalism, stable pillars (which are not common in many of the countries) would imply polarization, poor accountability, and extreme forms of local politicking. Finally, the examples suggested that regions are not themselves necessarily internally unified in their voting patterns. This complicates discussions about integration, concerns with irredentism, and accountability. The electoral system thus matters, because internal variation is only evident (or politically relevant) if the regions are divided into multiple districts. Furthering these discussions, however, requires adding the second dimension of nationalization, because it is not only the spread of support that matters for

[12] Ratios would allow a clear ranking of the cases, but they could be misleading if the total of the two values is low. If we were to run the analysis on Germany's CDU/CSU, for example, since the total of the two values would be only about 50, it would be misleading to rank the relative importance of one type of variance with those of the cases from the table that have total variance of 200 or more.

accountability and integration, but also the degree to which those votes move in response to national context or parties' actions.

Criterion 2: Accountability Requires High DN

There are almost no cases where SN is high and DN is low, because maintaining an equitable distribution of votes requires consistency in movement. As I have shown theoretically and empirically, however, low SN can accommodate any level of DN. Of particular concern for this chapter is whether when SN is low, DN parties are successful in attracting marginal voters throughout the country. Similar levels of success everywhere – a high level of DN – accords better with the responsible party model. The discussion of cases suggests, however, that while the responsible party model is under threat where DN is low, perhaps it is not fully broken.

There is one voting pattern that could yield low DN without harming the responsible party model. Following Mustillo and Mustillo (2012), I described a situation of "fanning in" when a party gains more votes in places where it had been weak relative to where it had been strong (or vice versa) such that the result is a lower spread in the party's cross-district vote. Poland's Civic Platform, for example, has a moderate DN level if fanning is unaccounted for, but including the extra term in the analytical model drops the DN by one-half. If it is the case that the party made greater gains where it had been weak, then DN would be low but the responsible party model would not necessarily be harmed. There could be damage to the model, however, if the low DN was the result of the party losing votes where it had been strong.

Among other parties with governing experience that have low SN, DN is particularly strong for the German CDU/CSU, the Finish Kesk, the Australian Labour Party, the Austrian Socialists and People's Party, Uruguay's Frente Amplio, the South African ANC, the Socialists (PS) and Social Democrats (PPD/PSD) in Portugal, and sometimes for the People's Party (PP) and Socialists (PSOE) in Spain. As an example, in Portugal, the Socialists' decline in 2011 was felt everywhere; across the country's 20 districts the party lost an average of 8 percent, and that loss ranged between 5 and 10 points for 19 of the districts (it lost 14 points in the Azores). The vote was even more tightly wound around a 10 point swing in favor of the Social Democrats – except, again, for one district, Madeira, where it gained only 1 point. It is notable that these two exceptions, the Azores and Madeira, are both series of islands, considered as special autonomous regions under the Portuguese constitution. In sum, even though the parties' support ranges broadly, the consistency in the direction and magnitude of responses from around the country implies that the governing Portuguese Socialists were held accountable for the difficult economic situation at the end of the first decade of the twenty-first century and voters also coordinated on an alternative future.

Portugal's neighbor provides a mutation of this pattern. Voters in three semi-autonomous regions – the Basque Country, Galicia, and Catalonia – typically give less support to the PP (and to a lesser extent the PSOE) than in other regions, opting instead for regional parties. But as in Portugal, the DN has been strong, at least in terms of voting against the incumbents. In 2015, the similarity in the swings away from both the governing PP (an average swing of –16.3 with a standard deviation of just 4.6 points) and their traditional competitor, the PSOE (average swing –6.2, standard deviation 3.4), was remarkable, especially given the stark changes to the party system. Voters that year granted more than one-third of the vote to a new party plus one that had been small and based in one region (Podemos, and the Citizen's Party). In short, voter frustrations had a national character in 2015.

This is somewhat different than the pattern of previous years. As I describe in more detail in Chapter 8, voters everywhere turned against the governing PSOE in 2011, owing to the economic collapse; DN was strong. At the same time, regionalism had a clear effect on prospective votes, such that many voters who fled the PSOE in Catalonia and the Basque Country chose the (regional) nationalist or separatist parties rather than the conservative but anti-separatist party with national reach, the PP. DN is stronger for the incumbents, then, than for the challengers. This suggests that while local issues (identity and autonomy) are important to voters in Spain's regions, they weigh those interests against the national economy when making their vote choices. Accountability, thus, is intact, even if national unity is threatened.

One way to analyze the relation of regions and accountability is to consider how important the regions are to DN scores. Low DN always signals the importance of localism and is thus a threat to national-level accountability, but only in some cases do the regions themselves drive down the level of DN. There are several ways to test this relation.

For Canada, excluding Quebec from analyses changes the statistics for DN sharply. Using all districts, the data suggest that localism is very important to the New Democratic Party (NDP) and to a lesser extent the Conservatives. Quebec drives these conclusions, however. Excluding that province from the analysis drops the DN value by about two-thirds (from 65 to 20) for the NDP and one-third (from 32 to 20) for the Conservatives.[13]

India is a more complicated case, since the parties' level of competition varies among and within the country's 35 states. The low DN reflects both the within- and among-state variances in how marginal voters move. Dropping individual states from the analysis, therefore, has limited impact (in part because no state has more than 15 percent of the districts).[14] But the DN within the states does

[13] Given the lower overall DN value on the Liberals, excluding Quebec has little impact.
[14] Dropping Uttar Predesh (with 80 districts) from the analysis actually increases the DN by a small amount.

show a high level of inconsistency in how the states contribute to the national DN. For the 80 districts in Uttar Predesh, for example, the DN score for the INC is less than one-half of its national total (40 versus 94) and the BJP score also falls sharply (from 64 to 47). In Maharashtra, the state with the next highest number of districts, the DN score for the INC is close to the national total of 98, but in West Bengal (42 districts) the DN score is just 14. If more states had statistics that looked like West Bengal or Tamil Nadu, where the INC and BJP only compete in a few districts, we could conclude that the low DN is high due to inter-state differences. But, other states suggest that the statistics reflect inconsistent reactions among voters within and among the states.

The United States generates similar results to those in India. Analysis within the most populous states does not yield high levels of DN, perhaps due to incumbency advantages and because all states suffer from rural–urban splits and other sources of diversity. Thus, while there are clearly some state and regional differences in the vote for the US parties, the high level of localism has clear district-level roots. Those roots clearly hinder the idea of a national mandate. To give an example of the problem, consider the 2004 election, when George Bush ran for re-election. The presidential election was controversial, but overall there was a very slight decline (0.2 percent) in the average vote for the president's Republican legislators. Those legislators, however, should not have considered their elections to provide a national mandate, because while 90 districts gave the Republicans at least 5 more points than they had 2 years earlier, 107 districts gave that much more to the Democrats. In 2008 the swing to the new president's Democrats averaged 2.3 points in the house, but President Obama's idea of a national mandate had to contemplate the 174 districts that swung against his party.

In sum, while inter-regional factors are not unimportant in these cases, the particularly low levels of DN are the result of inconsistent electoral changes within the regions. On the positive side this implies that the national parties do have opportunities to present their cases and win votes in regions/states where they have previously been weak. But, the high degree of localism, signaled by the combination of low SN and DN, works against a model of the ideal-typical party responsible for national conditions.

The next piece of the analysis is whether the pillars within these countries move together. I analyze this possibility by eliminating districts where the party of interest wins only a limited number of votes. Doing so will (almost) necessarily raise the SN, but DN could still be variable if the pillars are not tied.

Argentina provides a first example. Eliminating two districts where the PJ won less than 20 percent raises the SN by about 15 percent, but has only a very small effect on the DN.[15] Mexico's DN is only of middling height (32 for the

[15] The analysis deletes the two districts where the PJ won less than 20 percent in the first year of the analysis. The M&M value drops from 208 to 175, while the DN value rises, from 108 to 117. In this and the following analyses on the United States and India, I use the basic M&M model.

PAN), and eliminating the places it scored less than 20 percent does not impact DN. The Indian parties, finally, show a similar pattern. Dropping the 229 districts where the National Congress party did not win at least 20 percent in 1998 changes its SN score from over 250 to just 31, but the DN score, again, changes little (from 136 to 122). Running the analysis where the INC won at least 40 percent in the first year of the analysis returns very similar results, suggesting that there is still volatility even where the party has shown strength.

Other cases do show some commonality in the movement of the pillars. While both US parties have recently competed in most districts, one party or the other consistently dominates many districts, which is congruent to noting the high (and perhaps growing) level of polarization among red and blue areas. This is evident in the 192 districts where the Democrats won at least 60 percent of the vote in 2008 plus the 121 districts where Republicans did that well. Further, much of the variance in the parties' vote is accounted for in the districts where one of the parties fails to run serious campaigns in some years. Eliminating the 73 districts where one of the parties failed to win at least 20 percent of the vote in 2006 only moves the SN for the Democrats for the 2006–10 elections a bit, but it moves the DN value by almost one-fourth (from 84 to 65). There is thus still a high level of volatility in the competitive districts (which I tested by re-running the analysis on the districts where the Democrats won at least 55 percent of the vote), but the sharpest pillars are also the most unstable; of the 12 districts where the Democrats failed to compete in 2006, they did put forth candidates in all but one of them in 2008 and/or 2010, and usually won more than 30 percent of the vote.

In sum, the low levels of DN in these countries seems to be a function of local-level politicking, rather than parties winning groups of districts that are tied by common interests or characteristics. A more detailed analysis could uncover correlates of districts that do move together (and I use those subsets in the next chapter) but this analysis confirms that these parties cannot count on parallel responses from districts that for a given year produce particularly high or low support. Other factors may still point toward a working responsible party model (e.g. a correlation of the average swing and economic changes or, as Jacobson and Kernell [1983] found, patterns of retirement), but the strong role of local politics challenges the basic version of the model.

Criterion 3: Electoral Volatility and Seat Shifts

A high level of DN (plus at least moderate SN) is insufficient to define accountability, because if too few votes change to affect seat tallies, then voters are not responding to contextual or governmental changes. Few democratic countries, however, show such stability in the vote as to make this a serious concern – and probably most parties "run scared" (Jacobson 1987) even if there is stability during some electoral periods. At least in the countries in my database and with the important exceptions of the two regions in Belgium and the UK's

Northern Ireland, the national parties have the opportunity to win (or lose) marginal voters and seats in the countries that have electorally distinct regions. Still, the geography of the vote – in terms of seats, votes, and the changes thereto – leads to different conclusions about accountability and potential party strategies. A review of the cases shows that by reducing proportionality, districts with low district magnitude are less able to reward or punish incumbents as the responsible party model requires.

While it is beyond the scope of this project to measure the degree of responsiveness of voters to changes in national context, the statistical model does provide a useful variable for such an analysis. A question for such a study would relate, for example, how votes change in response to an increase in economic growth. The fixed effects from the statistical model measure those trends, while also accounting for the nationalization components (c.f. Mustillo and Jung, 2016).

For my purposes here, such tools are superfluous, as it is only necessary to indicate that there is significant volatility in the "special" regions. As an example, in Canada, the Conservatives and Liberals exchanged about three points in the average vote in Quebec between 2006 and 2008, before both experiencing sharp falls in support in 2011 when the average vote for the NDP rose from 12 to 42 percent. In Catalonia, Spain (and elsewhere), as I detail in the following chapter, the Socialists experienced a sharp drop in 2011, even though the alternative national party, the PP, gained very little. Recent elections have shown the PP vote to be unstable in Catalonia. After growing to over 20 percent in 2000, the party shrank back to 13.4 percent in 2016, in spite of nationally winning the most legislative seats of any party (and the prime minister's office).

Regionalism plays out differently in the United States. While there are enough swing states and districts to make elections meaningful on a national level, there are clearly districts where the opposition has little chance, even if there is a national mood shift. As an example, regardless of national shifts in opinion, in three of Alabama's seven districts the Democrats never closed within 20 points of the victorious Republicans in (at least) the first decade of the 2000s, and in one of those districts the Republican candidate won 90 percent or more in each election.

Moving further down the scale of limited votes shifts are the cases of Northern Ireland in the United Kingdom and both the French and Walloon regions of Belgium. Votes do shift among parties in these cases, but the parties that compete in other parts of the United Kingdom are not present in Northern Ireland, and Belgian parties only compete in one but not the other of that country's two regions. This cannot be consistent with the ideal of the responsible party model.

This book has focused much more on votes than seats, but the issue of accountability requires that at least the incumbent party is vulnerable to shifts in its take of legislative seats. The electoral system comes into play here, because it influences where parties compete and win seats, which, in turn, impacts SN and notions of accountability. The main concern here is with the district magnitude, and whether that magnitude varies across the country.

As Duverger (1954) explained, parties do not always have incentives to compete in low magnitude districts because they require a large percentage of the vote to win a seat. For this reason, it is more common in countries with single-member districts for parties to skip the contest in some districts. Most countries that use proportional representation vary the district magnitudes, based on regional or state populations. As a result, some parties may find costs outweigh benefits to compete where there are few seats available. Accountability clearly suffers if a governing party ignores some districts, or if large vote shifts do not affect the distribution of seats.

The United States provides a simple example of how vote shifts do not always produce changes in seats. The 30-point gain for the Republicans in Alabama's District 1 meant nothing in 2008, since they already owned the single seat in that district. Of course, a tiny change in the vote in a close single-member district race could also change distribution of 100 percent of the seats.

Turning to the effect of varying district magnitudes, the two largest Swiss parties – the Christian Democrats (CVP) and Social Democrats – each skipped the 2007 contest in four of the six single-member districts. They both competed in all the other 20 districts, with one exception: the CVP skipped one two-member district. Taiwan provides another example. Its magnitude ranges from 1 to 16, and again parties refrain from putting forth candidates in some of the single-member districts.

Finally, in Uruguay the Broad Front (FA) has much greater support in Montevideo than in most outlying departments. If it had a straightforward department-based electoral system, its incentive to expand outside of Montevideo would be limited, because more than 40 of the 99 house seats are distributed based on support in capital, while the district magnitude is just two or three in most other departments.[16] In spite of the varying magnitudes and perhaps socioeconomic factors that lower SN for the Uruguayan parties, DN is high, perhaps owing to the double-simultaneous vote, which fuses legislative and executive elections. The cross-department consistency in vote change, however, is not matched in the change in seats. While the FA party grew by around 10 percent or more in all but one department between 2004 and 2009, it gained three seats in Montevideo, one in Canelones (where the district magnitude is 14), and none in the remaining 17 departments. Even the 17-point uptick for the FA in Rocha produced the same outcome as before: one seat for the FA and one for the

---

[16] As explained by Daniel Buquet (personal communication), two factors should counter the focus on Montevideo. First, voter lists for the president, senate, and house are tied, and there is a single national district for the first two of these offices. Second, while seats for the lower house are distributed in the departments, votes are first aggregated nationally. This means that even if a party does not win sufficient votes in the interior to deserve a seat in a particular department, those votes do affect its overall seat distribution.

National Party. Surely this challenges the notion that the party has been rewarded for its positive national campaign or performance in government.

Discussion

This chapter has inaugurated the discussion of how nationalization affects politics and what the nationalization statistics signal in terms of accountability and integration. On a theoretical level, the chapter argued that low SN or DN challenge notions of a responsible party model. Methodologically, the chapter cautioned against a blind view of nationalization scores, in part because the scores cannot differentiate pillarized and regional support patterns; either of these patterns will lower SN, but they signal different concerns for politics. Similarly, the source of low DN can be a function of inter-regional differences, intra-regional politicking, or both of these patterns. There is also the issue of seat transfers; if changes in electoral support do not produce changes in seats, then parties will lack incentives to respond to voter concerns.

The presence of regional parties is problematic for integration, and notions of accountability require that voters choose based on policy and context rather than identity. Still, unless regional parties shut out parties that compete nationally and gain control of the national government, voters can still hold incumbents accountable. There is thus a distinction between systems with regional parties and regionalized systems. While the latter implies a model where different parties dominate different regions, in the former national parties compete alongside regional parties and voters can turn to or away from them based on retrospective evaluations. When voters everywhere do this in similar proportions, there would be evidence of a national response. Voters could also respond in dissimilar ways to a common treatment (Katz 1973a), but a situation where some parts of the country vote differently than others – whether in terms of levels of support or consistency in changes therein – must signal problems for governance, integration, and accountability.

8

The Role of Party Nationalization on Party Unity and Retrospective Voting*

In this and the following chapter I continue the discussion wherein nationalization of parties and party systems is on the right side of the equation, considering how the two dimensions of nationalization affect, condition, or put into context different political outcomes. As such, the discussion is meant as a query into how national events (here with a focus on economic changes) are channeled through the distribution of voters in static and dynamic terms. In even broader terms, it is a query into the relation of national context and political geography.

The chapter is built around analyses of several cases to show how party and party-system nationalization condition voters' responses to economic change. High DN implies that voters act collectively, and accountability is clear. But if DN is low, especially for an incumbent party, accountability for national conditions is not straightforward. These points are almost definitional, but my case studies suggest two new twists. First, the level of DN is not a constant, and can grow sharply, especially in particularly hard (or perhaps good) times. This pattern is only pertinent to incumbent parties, however. Where there are multiple challengers, voters who all agree to throw out the bums will not necessarily agree on the best alternatives. This is because all voters can witness and judge the incumbent, but not all have the same choices over alternatives. Further, they may be more likely to divide on proposed solutions, perhaps based on the concerns of their particular locale. The result is unity – high DN – on retrospective voting, but a local focus – low DN – for prospective voting.

To pursue this line of thought, this chapter focuses on several countries where the incumbent party suffered dramatic drops in support: Spain, Argentina, and Canada. These cases are useful because while the pre-crisis levels of both types of nationalization were distinct for the incumbents in these countries, the crisis generated high levels of the nationalization – especially dynamic – for each. The

* Some ideas in this chapter appear in Morgenstern, Smith, and Trelles (2017).

effect on their opponents, however, does not have a consistent story. I also look at Bolivia, where in 2009 the incumbent Movement Towards Socialism (MAS) party experienced a significant gain. That gain was also experienced nationally, in spite of the traditional regionalism that divides the Bolivian voters. As in the other countries where there was more consistency in response to the incumbents than the challengers, the opponents of the MAS did not suffer in an equal manner across all the countries' regions. Again, then, retrospective voting was more dynamically (and statically) nationalized than was prospective voting.

Accountability and Economic/Retrospective Voting
This part of the book could be summarized as arguing that the two dimensions of nationalization – generally working in tandem – define party politics in terms of local versus national orientations. In turn, the relative balance of national and local politics implies different types of relationships between voters and legislators, which defines accountability and influences legislator behavior.[1] The remainder of this chapter and the succeeding one look at the effect of nationalization on two parts of these broad issues. This chapter focuses on accountability in terms of the voters' abilities to coordinate in response to economic changes. The second, which I hold for Chapter 9, is the degree to which there is inter-regional cooperation within parties. I look at this in terms of voting unity and bill co-sponsorship, with a particular focus on the United States, but also in three Latin American countries.

To provide several specific examples, this section evaluates how the effect of the economy on electoral outcomes is processed through party and party-system nationalization. If party nationalization is conceptualized as the distribution of voters and the consistency in their responses, then the previous statement is tantamount to saying that party nationalization conditions the effect of the economy. Voters' responses to economic change provide a window on the representative process. But, how do voters display their (dis)pleasure with ruling parties when politics has a strong local element? In such situations, to what degree do voters consider economics rather than regional identities, nationalist appeals, or other campaign promises that parties use to attract voters?

Studies of retrospective voting fail to consider the conditional effect of localism, but, as I argued in Chapter 7 and will show here, the two dimensions of nationalization have a necessary impact on how closely voting behavior and economic conditions (or other environmental conditions that presumably affect voting) are tied. I also argue that economic voting is complicated by differential considerations for retrospective and prospective

---

[1] There is still more to do on this topic, because as Kitschelt and Wilkinson (2007) emphasize, there are different forms of accountability mechanisms, some of which have a non-programmatic or local focus. Clientelism – their focus – does not mean a lack of accountability, but it produces a distinctive type of represented-to-representative relations.

voting. Even among voters who agree on where the blame lies for a poor economic situation, there is not necessarily agreement on the remedy. As a result, the party system, the distribution of voters (SN), and the degree to which local factors generally impact on voters' decisions (DN) condition how voters reconfigure themselves after losing faith in an incumbent party.

The central argument of Chapter 7 was that the consistency in voter movements, and to a lesser degree the range in a party's support levels, provides a window into the degree to which voters hold a party, as a whole, accountable. Where DN is high, the party falls (or rises) as a unit, presumably in response to its overall performance.[2] In contrast, where DN is low, the party's support moves in different directions in different districts, presumably as a result of variable performance in the districts or the attractiveness of its district-level candidates. If the district-level factors are strong, accountability for national conditions is harmed because the incumbent party's candidates may be able to avoid retribution against strong anti-party shocks. In such a circumstance, the party would also have trouble gaining support for good behavior.

To study how economic voting is conditioned by party nationalization, I focus on three cases where the incumbent party collapsed – Spain, Argentina, and Canada – plus Bolivia, where the incumbent saw a sharp rise in support. The first three of these cases have some parties that are nationalized on one or both dimensions, but the systems are not. The national crises, therefore, could not yield consistent (nationalized) partisan responses. Instead, the analysis shows that voters respond to crises in disparate ways: they are dynamically nationalized with regards to the incumbent party, but their prospective choices are tinged by local factors. In other words, retrospective voting is dynamically nationalized, but prospective voting is not. For Bolivia, the party system is decidedly regional, but the ruling MAS has grown in all areas. The growth, therefore, has suggested a more nationalized electorate.

The following discussion begins by comparing Spain and Argentina, cases with different types of party nationalization (one has a strong regional parties, and in the other the "national" parties have low DN) but similar electoral systems. I then add Bolivia, where survey evidence elucidates the relation between ethnicity, region, and government support. The subsequent section adds Canada, another case with a strong regional party, in order to highlight patterns of voter shifts under conditions of single-member districts. There too I find a clear difference between retrospective and prospective patterns, but the electoral system context allows an extra analysis into whether parties are more vulnerable to losses in areas where they are strong or weak.

---

[2] As noted earlier, Katz's (1973a) criticism suggests that national movements could imply regional strategies. Consistent movement, however, would be unlikely if a party had different strategies or campaigns in the different districts.

NATIONALIZATION AND ECONOMIC/RETROSPECTIVE VOTING IN
ARGENTINA AND SPAIN

Traditional studies of retrospective voting focus on the link between voting preferences and objective measures of the economy or voters' evaluations of their personal economic situation. Such studies are also careful to control for other influences, such as partisanship, ideology, and sociodemographics. In their cross-national study that emphasizes context, Powell and Whitten (1993), for example, add that the clarity of governing responsibility, "ideological image," and the governing parties political base explain which countries generate the clearest links between economic conditions and vote choice. Like most other studies, however, their dependent variable is the vote (or change in the vote) for the incumbent party, with little consideration of the array of alternatives open to voters. Another recent example of such a model is that of Fraile and Lewis-Beck (2012), who focus on the Spanish case. These authors begin their study by noting that most studies of Spain do not find solid evidence of retrospective voting, arguing that ideology is a more important determinant. Using survey responses to a subjective measure of the economy, however, these authors do find a clear link between economic evaluations and vote choice.

The results of these types of studies are not necessarily surprising; if there is a representative link, then voters will throw out the bums when the economy declines. Who, however, do the voters exchange for the bums? Further, how do voters in different regions, given different propensities to support national or regional parties, direct their hopes when they lose faith in the incumbent?

The severe economic crises in Argentina and Spain provide opportunities to address these themes. Argentina suffered its economic collapse between 1999 and 2001, while Spain's came in 2011. Not surprisingly, the incumbent parties suffered at the polls in both countries. But, the response by voters was conditioned by the strong relevance of local factors in the vote (which yields low levels of static and dynamic nationalization). Specifically, as I will describe, the number of parties and the two dimensions of nationalization translated into consistent losses for the incumbents across both countries, but variable opposition gains. In other words, there was high DN with respect to the incumbent loser, but low DN with respect to the challengers. This suggests that voters use economic clues for retrospective voting, but perhaps because it is harder to foretell the future than read the past, other factors influence prospective voting.

Spain. Spain's crisis officially began with a contraction in the economy in the latter part of 2008. The depths of the crisis were most signified by the exceedingly high unemployment, which reached 24 percent in 2012. Youth unemployment has been double that rate. In 2011, at the peak of their economic crisis, Spain held elections. The voters punished the incumbent PSOE, costing them an average of 14 points in the country's 52 districts.

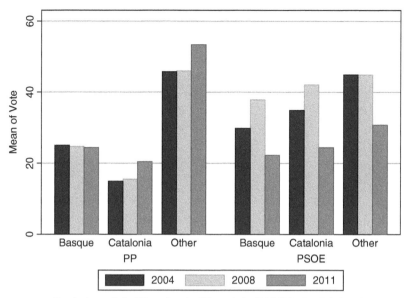

FIGURE 8.1 Evolution of the Vote for the PP and the PSOE in Spain's Regions

The national economic crisis drove the incumbent PSOE from power, but the effects on elections were uneven across Spain's districts and provinces.[3] Further, the effects were different for the parties, and thus the context of nationalization, at both system and party level, adds nuance to the analysis of the voters' responses. Moving from the district to the regional level, Figure 8.1 compares the two main parties' support in the Basque Country and Catalonia with the rest of the country. Most clearly, the PSOE has more consistent support across the regions (high SN). The PSOE's higher DN is also evident; note that the size and direction of the "steps" between the more bars is uneven for the PP (People's Party). Figure 8.2 details the district-level vote for the PSOE and PP across several elections, including the crisis periods.

The vertical range among the lines suggests that the PSOE has moderate SN, since the difference in support where the party is strongest is at least 20 points from where it is weakest in any given year. It is notable that support for the PSOE is only moderately lower in the three autonomous communities than in the rest of the country.[4] At the same time, the PSOE demonstrates a case of relatively high DN, since the vote across the country's 52 districts follows a

---

[3] Recall from Chapter 1 that the districts are grouped into 17 provinces, several of which have special status that recognize their nationalities and languages.

[4] The graph includes Navarra with the Basque Country provinces, but it is not formally a part of that autonomous community (see footnote 8 for more discussion). Vote for the PP is higher in Navarra than in the other three provinces.

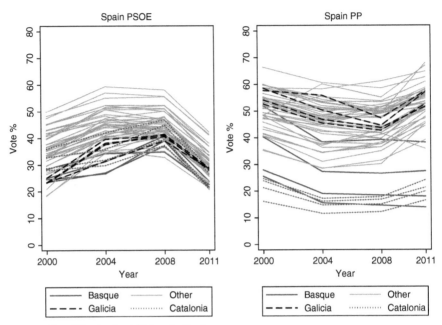

FIGURE 8.2 District-Level Vote in Spain

roughly parallel pattern. This is most clear for the change between 2008 and 2011, which shows the party suffering a similar level of change across all districts. Specifically, in its best showing in 2011, the PSOE lost 10 points, while in the worst the swing was a negative 22 percent. There is also some evidence for fanning-in, as the range of support narrows in the last two elections.

Owing to the country's regional party system, which generated less-than-high level of SN and DN for some parties, the PSOE's losses did not directly translate into PP gains.[5] Overall, the PP saw its vote increase by about 7.5 percent – only about one-half of what the PSOE lost – and the variance was such that the party actually lost votes in four of the provinces. On the static dimension, the graph shows that the range in support for the PP is large, since it does poorly in Catalonia and three of the four Basque Country constituencies.[6] In short, while the PSOE is a nationalized party, the party system is not.

Including the other parties reveals the rest of the story. In addition to the PP and PSOE, which are relatively large parties that have support across the nation, Spain's system has several parties that only win votes in one of three semi-autonomous regions, plus a few small parties that compete either regionally or

[5] On the Spanish party system, see, for example, Linz and Montero (2001).
[6] Again, the graph counts Navarra among the Basque Country provinces. See footnote 7.

TABLE 8.1 *Vote for Regional Parties in Spain*

	Catalonia		Basque	Galicia
Year	CIU	ERC	BNP*	BNG
2004	24.6	19.8	37.6	11.3
2008	24.1	10.5	34.1	11.3
2011	35.3	8.5	47.1	10.7

*Calculated as all parties less the PP, PSOE, IU, and Upyd. For 2011, this is effectively EAJ_PNV plus AMAIUR. For earlier years it includes some smaller parties. See text for party names.

nationally. Together, these parties absorbed the PSOE's losses that did not go to the PP. Table 8.1 shows the evolution in support for these parties.

In Catalonia, which has four electoral districts, the Convergence and Union (CIU) and the Republican Left of Catalonia (ERC) together win about one-half of the vote, but neither competes outside of that region. There is a similar story for the Basque Country; there the regional parties have divided and recombined themselves at times, under the names Amaiur, the Basque Nationalist Party (EAJ/PNV), and Navarre Yes.[7] Together they won about 35 percent of the vote in 2004 and 2008, but then jumped to 47 percent in 2011. Galicia also has a regional party: the Galician Nationalist Bloc (BNG).

The complex pattern of support and vote interchanges among the parties suggests low nationalization for the system. In interviews, analysts and politicians in Spain explained that Amaiur's rise and the PSOE's fall were not mirror images of one another. Instead, the change was a result of different voters who stayed away from the polls. As partially confirmed in survey data, Amaiur, which was an outgrowth of a less-than-democratic and outlawed Batasuna Party, was able to attract voters who abstained in the past.[8] Few residents who had previously voted for the PSOE, then, would likely switch to that party.

A final issue in the analysis is how the votes translated into seat changes in Spain. Spain employs a proportional representation electoral system, but many of the electoral districts return only a few legislators (i.e. they have a small district magnitude). But the size of the districts is large enough that the system is not "majoritarian in disguise," and the system does generate a high level of proportionality. That is, given the average district magnitude of about 5, a

---

[7] Navarra is recognized as an autonomous community (and separate province) in the Spanish constitution. The population of Navarra includes, however, a large number of Basque nationalists.

[8] In the Centro de Investigaciones Sociólogicas MD2655 survey, a very high number of PSOE voters said they abstained in the regional election, or would not indicate their preference. On the other hand, those who said they planned to vote for the PSOE in the 2012 regional elections consistently stated that they voted for the PSOE in the 2011 national elections.

small change in votes may not show up with a similar change in the number of seats in all districts, but the average of 52 distinct shifts in the vote should generate a proportionate effect on seats. For 2011, the electoral system converted the PSOE's 15 point drop in votes to a loss of 17 percent of its parliamentary seats (falling from 169 to 110 of the 350 seats). The PP's eight-point bounce led to a nine-point increase in its seat share (rising from 154 to 186).

In sum, strong DN yielded a consistent and dramatic decline for the PSOE in 2011, but multipartism and the regional nature of the party system limited the electoral shift toward the PP. Further, given the electoral system, the PSOE remained an important player in the legislature; if Spain had had a majoritarian system, such a strong vote shift would have decimated the party, as discussed below with the example of Canada.

Argentina.   In the face of a declining economy, the end of the second (and final) term of their president's time in office, and a split in the party, Argentina's Peronists lost the 1999 presidential contest to the Radicals. The recession soon worsened, and president Fernando de la Rúa faced midterm elections in 2001. His party lost ground in 23 of the country's 24 districts, with an average loss of about 16 points, though the losses were much higher in some provinces. Later that year angry riots led him and several interim presidents to resign.

Argentina provides an example with less party nationalization than in Spain, but like that case, the crisis produced a nationalized reaction against the incumbent party. As Figure 8.3 shows, Argentina's parties score low on the static dimension, and much lower in terms of DN than the Spanish parties. Most clearly, the helter-skelter pattern in the lines on the graph suggests that a good year in one district does not imply the party will gain everywhere, so DN is very low. This low DN is matched with a wide range in the parties' cross-district support, so SN is low for both parties.

Because DN is lower in Argentina, when the incumbent Radicals (UCR) faced the voters during the economic crisis of 2001 they suffered variable levels of punishment and the Peronists did not always gain from their rival's lost votes. The Peronists (Justicialistas; PJ) did gain in 16 provinces, but they lost ground in the other eight (Table 8.2). Further, even among the provinces where they did gain, the degree of change was uneven.

These patterns are the result of a different type of complexity in Argentina's party system than in Spain. The Peronists' and their traditional rival, the Radicals (UCR), have similar static and dynamic nationalization patterns. The complexity of this system, however, is based more on factionalism than on regional parties. There are provincial parties, and the existing parties sometimes form electoral coalitions with others, but only in some of the regions. In many districts the Peronists run under different labels, but join the party when their candidates get to the capital city. Further, the UCR has run in coalition with

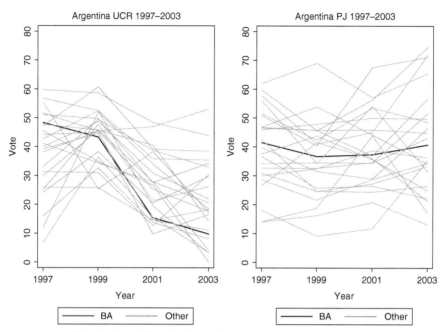

FIGURE 8.3 District-Level Vote in Argentina

several parties in recent years, at least in some provinces. Province-level elections, therefore, frequently pit multiple parties with unfamiliar names, and thus the PJ versus UCR results are difficult to disentangle. I therefore relied on careful watchers of the system (in particular, Mark Jones and Andy Tow), such that my data does reflect the trends in the province-level results for these two parties. Still, even the low levels of static and dynamic nationalization reflected in my data may be an overestimate of the degree of consistency in district-level voting.

The statistical measures of the two nationalization dimensions that I developed earlier in this book capture part of the dynamics and characteristics of the Argentine and Spanish party systems, but because they are summary measures, they do not capture all the detail of the graphs. Running the test on the three electoral years ending with the year where the crisis directly affected the election, the M&M model yields unadjusted[9] scores of 125 for Argentina's PJ and 52 for the UCR (for 1997–2001), while for Spain's (2004–11) parties, the scores were 43 and 144 for the PSOE and PP, respectively. In both countries, then, SN is relatively low, but it is significantly lower for one party than the other. On DN, the statistics show that the Spanish parties are much more

---

[9] These are raw scores; higher numbers imply more variance and thus less nationalization.

TABLE 8.2 *Peronist Support and Change, 1999–2001*

Province	1999	2001	Swing
San Luis	40.3	67.6	27.3
Corrientes	18.7	43.8	25.1
Santiago del Estero	34.2	54.1	19.9
Salta	42.3	53.5	11.2
Santa Cruz	45.6	56.4	10.8
Mendoza	21.6	28.8	7.2
San Juan	32.4	38.7	6.3
Neuquen	16.2	20.8	4.6
Formosa	40.9	45.1	4.1
Cordoba	24.6	27.2	2.6
Capfed	9.2	11.7	2.5
La Pampa	47.8	50	2.1
Santa Fe	32.6	34.6	2.0
Rio Negro	25.7	26.5	0.8
BA	36.7	37.4	0.7
Entre Rios	45.7	45.9	0.2
Chaco	34.5	34.5	−0.1
Tierra del Fuego	24.6	24.4	−0.2
Chubut	31.5	29	−2.6
Tucuman	41.5	36	−5.5
Catamarca	43.7	35.7	−8.1
Jujuy	45.7	36.9	−8.8
Misiones	53.9	44.2	−9.7
La Rioja	69	57.1	−11.9

dynamically nationalized than the Argentine parties, but they do not clearly capture the strongly parallel movement (in a negative direction) for the incumbents in the year of the crisis. For Argentina, the unadjusted DN values are 45 for the PJ and 82 for the UCR, and for Spain they are under 10 for both parties. The lower value for the PJ relative to the UCR is because the PJ did not experience a significant shift in its vote in most districts, in spite of the crisis. For Spain, the low (unadjusted) values on the dynamic dimension correctly indicate the strong parallel movement for the PSOE in all years, but an eyeball test suggests that the statistics understate the values for the PP. This low value is probably the result of a) generally parallel movements plus b) stable support between 2004 and 2008, which reduces the total variance that the model must parse.

PROSPECTIVE AND RETROSPECTIVE VOTING IN SPAIN AND ARGENTINA

These disparate patterns, both within the countries and among them, show why party nationalization and aspects of the party system should be pieces of economic voting analyses. Economics clearly affected voting in both countries, but a correlation of national economic variables and voting patterns would be weaker in Argentina. Further, it might show little effect on the challenger parties, although they too were affected in many of the electoral districts. Further, the nationalization context raises questions about which parties gain when the incumbent party loses (and vice versa). The answers here affect theories of prospective voting, and may have strong impacts on whether, for example, an economic crisis will empower regionalist or even separatist groups. In the two countries I considered here, analysis of economic voting within the context of nationalization uncovered the interesting finding that voters were more consistent in punishing an incumbent than in rewarding a challenger. In short, retrospective voting was much more nationalized than was prospective voting. And in Spain, the incumbent's fall did help the regional parties, since the other party with a national reach was not able to capitalize on the crisis situation.

Given the types of electoral patterns illustrated in these cases, plus the wide interest in federalism and regionalized politics, it is surprising that the literature on economic voting on these countries seems to ignore party nationalization.[10] In their studies on retrospective voting in Spain by Lewis-Beck and Fraile (Fraile and Lewis-Beck 2012, 2014; Lewis-Beck and Fraile 2013), for example, the authors' models test vote choice (for or against the incumbent) as a function of sociodemographic variables, left–right ideology, and economic issues (testing both objective and subjective versions). Region is not included among their controls.

Survey data does provide opportunities to incorporate geography into economic voting analyses. Latinobarometer data for 2001, for example, asked citizens about their views of the economy in 16 cities.[11] Unfortunately the Latinobarometer did not ask about party preferences, nor does it allow province-wide estimates that would completely pair with the electoral data. Still, it does allow a preliminary analysis.

---

[10] Some literature does consider nationalization and vote choice, but it does not look at retrospective voting. In their 2011 article, Lago-Peñas and Lago-Peñas are concerned with "contamination" of national with local elections. Rodden and Wibbels (2011) study "nationalization" in four federal countries, but they take a similar tack, considering the relation between national events and local elections. Lagos and Montero (2006), studying the effect of the terrorist attacks of 2004 on the Spanish elections, similarly ignore regions in their analysis, even though a) they do account for many sociodemographic variables, and b) the attacks were in Madrid and initially the Basque separatist group (ETA) was blamed for the attack.

[11] LAPOP data, which I use and discuss later in this chapter, are not available for Argentina until 2008.

Table 8.3 arrays the data according to the percentage of voters who judged the economy as "very bad." In each of these provinces the UCR (with coalition partners) saw its support fall, but the pattern does not seem to be consistent with how voters judged the economy. They did lose a relatively small percentage in one city in Misiones (Eldorado) where voters did not judge the economy too severely, but others in that state judged the economy more harshly. More tellingly, they lost a similar percentage in Santa Fe, in spite of 50 percent of voters in its city of Gran Rosario judging the economy as very bad. In sum, there is not a close correlation of economic evaluations and vote swings.

Evaluation of votes for the PJ yields a similar conclusion. In Eldorado, Misiones, the expectation is met, since the PJ (the challenger) fell by about 10 points. Further, at the other end of the table, more than one-half of Santa Fe residents judged the economy as very bad, and 11 percent of them switched to the PJ. While these two data points are consistent with an economic voting model, most of the other cities fail to support the theory. Over 30 percent of voters had a very negative view of the economy in eight provinces, but only in two did they also give many additional votes to the PJ.[12]

Overall, then, economics is only a part of the story in explaining the vote in Argentina. Other pieces of the explanations for the variance in how the vote shifted are embedded within the country's complicated party system. In La Rioja, for example, in 1999 there were just two parties on the ballot for the legislature, and the Peronists beat the Alianza (which included the Radicals) by 68 versus 31 percent. In 2001, with the economic collapse, four parties appeared on the ballot, including the Peronists, the Radicals (no longer in coalition), the Socialist Workers Party, and the "Front for All." The decline in the Peronist vote, therefore, did not reflect a rise of the UCR (which won 13 percent in 2001). Instead, the PJ change reflected a) the very high level at which it started and b) the loss of votes to new parties.

In Spain, a regional analysis yielded a similar result, showing that the economy had a more direct relation to the vote in some places than in others. The poor economy was universal, but other factors determined how voters reacted. As I described earlier, in the autonomous regions many voters chose to support the separatist parties rather than the PP, and others utilized the option of abstention. Individual-level data show that within Catalonia, for example, while economics drove people away from the PSOE, that variable cannot explain the prospective choice. Table 8.4 uses 2012 survey data from the Centro de Investigaciones Sociólogicas to show that most of those who continued to vote for the PSOE saw that the economy had fallen, and the

---

[12] The Latinobarometer does have a question about partisanship, but the parties are not identified. I requested a copy of the codebook, but did not receive a response. It appears that code 4 is the PJ and code 2 is the UCR, based on comparable frequencies in the database and the "codebook" (which is only a list of frequencies) that the Latinobarometer does make available. Note, too, that the on-line data analysis does not match the results from the database.

TABLE 8.3 *Citizen Views of the Economy and Vote Swings to the Parties, Argentina 2001*

Cty code	City/Province	Very good	Good	About ave	Bad	Very bad	Swing to UCR	Swing to PJ
114	Eldorado (Misiones)	0	0	55.81	30.23	13.95	-5.2	-9.7
112	Cutral Có- Plaza (Neuq)	0	4.65	30.23	48.84	16.28	-20.8	4.6
111	Chivilcoy (Bs.As)	0	0	11.63	67.44	20.93	-28.0	0.7
108	Córdoba Capital	0	3.53	24.71	49.41	22.35	-28.0	2.6
104	Mar del Plata	0	2.33	11.63	60.47	25.58	-28.0	0.7
113	Oberá (Misiones)	0	0	30.23	44.19	25.58	-5.2	-9.7
110	Cipolletti (Río Negro)	0	0	21.43	52.38	26.19	-16.6	0.8
116	Bragado (Bs.As.)	0	2.33	25.58	44.19	27.91	-28.0	0.7
106	Gran Mendoza	0	0	21.74	46.38	31.88	-17.8	7.2
103	Gran La Plata	0	2.33	20.93	39.53	37.21	-28.0	0.7
109	Villa María-V.Nv (Córd)	0	0	2.33	58.14	39.53	-28.0	2.6
107	Gran Tucumán	0	0	26.09	33.33	40.58	-19.0	-5.5
102	Gran Buenos Aires	0.69	0	15.46	42.61	41.24	-28.0	0.7
101	Capital Federal	0.6	0	17.26	36.9	45.24	19.5	2.5
116	J.María-Col Caro (Córd)	2.33	2.33	13.95	34.88	46.51	-20.3	2.6
105	Gran Rosario (Santa Fe)	0	0	11.76	37.65	50.59	-8.2	11.2

TABLE 8.4 *Catalonia 2012: Economic Evaluations and Vote Choice**

	PSOE	PP	CIU	ERC
Better	4.2	2.7	5.6	4.7
The Same	14.4	16.8	14.9	18.4
Worse	68.3	62.5	69.1	66.2
Much Worse	12.5	17.9	10.0	10.7
N	526	291	677	234

*Centro de Investigaciones Sociólogicas Survey: MD2965, questions P2 and P26A.

percentage of voters who saw that the economy had improved or stayed the same was higher for the PP and other opposition parties than for the PSOE.

There is no survey for Argentina at the time of their crises that includes enough respondents from any (or many) districts to allow for statistically valid comparisons. It is possible, however, to study the useful case of Bolivia using recent surveys by the Latin American Public Opinion Project (LAPOP).

BOLIVIA: REGION, ETHNICITY, AND A RISING INCUMBENT

Bolivia is interesting for its opposing experience to that of Spain and Argentina. Instead of a collapsing incumbent, concomitant to Bolivia's improving economy President Morales saw a sharp growth in his party's support from 2005 to 2009 (and then later, too). The case therefore allows analysis of how voters react to positive retrospective analyses. The case is also interesting because as noted elsewhere, Bolivian elections are highly regional, with voters in the four eastern departments of the "Half Moon" region much less prone to support indigenous leader Morales than in the five western "Andean" provinces, where a majority of the population is indigenous. For this case there is very good survey data to study individual-level response to the improved situation. The LAPOP survey of 2010 was conducted just a few months after the landslide victories of Evo Morales, and has several hundred observations in each province. Overall, the data (Table 8.5) show that voters' support of the Morales government depends on an interactive relation among economics, ethnicity, and region.

Adding more than 10 points to his support from 2005, Morales won re-election in 2009 with almost 65 percent of the vote. Regional patterns are clearly evident in the relation of economics to the electoral outcome. The table shows that the percentage of those who judged the current economic situation as good or very good was actually higher in the Half Moon region (column 2), but more Andean voters answered positively to prospective and retrospective questions, using either idiotropic or sociotropic questions. Voters, however, are clearly motived by more than economics, at least in the Andean provinces, which is shown by the much greater quantity of Andean-province voters who would

TABLE 8.5 *Bolivia: Support for Morales by Economic Evaluation and Region**

	Morales %	Current	Sociotropic % positive		Idiotropic % positive		Difference support-sociotropic
			Retro	Prosp	Retro	Prosp	Prosp
Andean							
Chuquisaca	58.1	19.3	4.0	4.0	7.7	18.6	54.1
Cochabamba	56.1	20.0	22.4	34.6	30.2	49.0	21.5
La Paz	69.3	19.8	32.5	49.3	26.4	51.7	20.0
Oruro	72.4	30.5	29.9	40.9	25.5	43.5	31.4
Potosí	68.7	24.7	19.7	38.0	21.6	40.2	30.7
Avg	64.9	22.9	21.7	33.4	22.3	40.6	31.5
Half Moon							
Beni	20.2	20.5	17.9	22.4	16.4	31.3	-2.2
Pando	49.8	40.1	11.0	16.4	10.4	15.8	33.4
Santa Cruz	28.4	22.6	15.1	27.8	15.7	41.9	0.6
Tarija	40.0	33.7	10.8	31.7	16.0	38.3	8.3
Avg	34.6	25.2	13.7	24.6	14.6	31.8	10.0

*2010 LAPOP survey; Economic evaluation questions IDIO2, IDIO3, SOCT1, SOCT2, SOCT3, and support question VB20. % positive is "good" or "very good" for current evaluation, "better" for prospective and retrospective evaluations.

TABLE 8.6 *Support for Morales by Race and Region**

	Indigenous who judged economy negatively		Whites who judged economy positively	
	Andean	Half Moon	Andean	Half Moon
Not vote	7.8	6.0	0	8.3
With president	30.5	8.2	84.6	50.0
Against president	33.6	66.5	7.7	16.7
Blank/null	28.1	19.2	7.7	25.0
Number obs	128	182	13	12

* Sociotropic evaluation (Soct2); race question ETID

support Morales even though they did not see an improved economic situation or did not expect improvements.[13] There is one exception in each group: the province of Pando gave more support to Morales than others in the Half Moon region, and voters in Chuquisaca gave the economy poorer marks than others from the Andean region. The patterns are similar for both pocketbook and sociotropic questions. Table 8.5 adds the prospective sociotropic evaluation and breaks the provinces into the two regions based on support for or against the current government. It shows that in the Andean region, there is much "off the equilibrium behavior" with 30 percent of voters supporting Morales in spite of seeing the economy in a negative light, but in the Half Moon over 40 percent expected better economic conditions and still would vote against Morales or spoil their ballots.

While some voters, especially in the eastern provinces, said they would vote against their economic interests, the most important message from the Bolivian case is that voters' use of economic cues has a decidedly regional element. Ethnicity also matters, but it too is conditioned by region. As shown in Table 8.6, almost all indigenous voters in the Half Moon who judged the economy positively said they support the Morales government, but they split their vote if they judge the economy poorly. The reverse is also true; among indigenous voters in the Andean region who view the economy poorly, 30 percent would still give their vote to Morales, while in the Half Moon region that number is under 10 percent. There were not many whites who judged the economy positively, but the regional influence is similarly evident. In that sample, only half responded that they would support Morales if they lived in the Half Moon, while in the other region that figure is 85 percent.

[13] The question asks whether voters would support the current government if an election were held this week. Options are: a) not vote, b) vote for the candidate or party of the current president, c) vote for a candidate or party different from the current president, or d) cast a null or blank ballot.

In sum, economic evaluations do play a role in Bolivian elections, but that impact is conditioned by region. This finding may not be surprising, given that Bolivian politics revolves around regional issues. It is surprising, however, that comparative studies of retrospective voting (Lewis-Beck and Stegmaier 2000; Singer 2010) – and even those that focus on Latin America (Benton 2005; Lewis-Beck and Ratto 2013; Singer and Carlin 2013) or Bolivia specifically (Singer and Carlin 2013) – ignore region in their analyses.

The Bolivian analysis allows one further comment. Morales's support rose sharply from 2005 to 2009 in all districts, regardless of his starting point. This implies a high level of DN, here related to a strong positive retrospective evaluation. Since his support was much smaller in some provinces, there is something of a fanning-in process for his party, and a more evident fanning-out for the rightist opposition (Podemos), as they suffered sharp losses in three Andean provinces but saw flat support in most of the Half Moon (see graphs in Appendix 2). These results do not fully mirror those of the MAS because there were also other competitors. In 2009 the National Unity Front, a party with ties to the cement industry, won 7 or 8 percent in three provinces, only two of which were in the Half Moon. And the biggest change from 2005 was the disappearance of the MNR, which had dominated Bolivian politics for decades. Its support, however, had been highly regional, with much more support in Beni and two of the other Half Moon departments. The case of Half Moon department Pando is particularly interesting. Prior to 2005 the MNR was relatively strong there, generally wining about 30 percent. But in 2005 the MNR's support evaporated in Pando (6.6 percent), even though it retained strong support in other parts of the east. Clearly, a mix of national and local forces has been driving changes in Bolivian parties' support. That said, retrospective voting is more nationalized than is prospective voting, as evidenced by the much more consistent changes in support for the governing party than for the other parties.

CANADA: ACCOUNTABILITY IN THE CONTEXT OF LOW NATIONALIZATION

Canada's combination of parliamentarism with single-member districts, plus a crisis of an incumbent party, provides a final opportunity to consider how voters hold parties accountable in the context of low levels of nationalization. Like Spain, Canada has a strong regional party, the Bloc Quebecois (BQ), but the DN for the national parties is relatively weak. The two longstanding parties, the Liberals and Conservatives (and their forerunner, the Progressive Conservatives), have done considerably worse in Quebec than in the rest of the country, at least since 1993 when the BQ first competed. These parties also have uneven support within and among other provinces, yielding more pillarized patterns and lower SN levels than in Spain. The dynamic levels are also lower – as evidenced in the Conservatives' declining share of the votes in Quebec between 2006 and 2011, even while rising in the rest of the

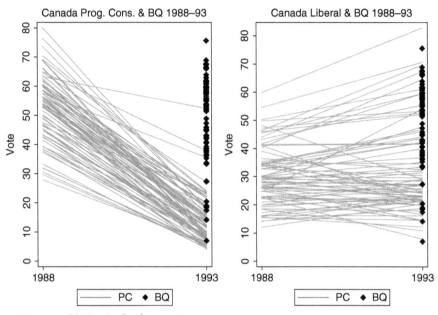

FIGURE 8.4 Voting in Quebec 1988–93

country – owed in part to the combination of regionalism, pillarization, and the large number of (single member) districts.

Due to the low level of both SN and DN for all parties, plus the country's majoritarian electoral system, accountability plays out very differently than in Spain. In particular, in addition to regional issues, district-level motives determine Canadian voters' choices. Further, with their single-member districts, even moderate changes in support can have dramatic changes in the seat swings. Still, while elections are not simple reflections of a national mood, there is evidence, as found in Argentina and Spain, of national trends with regards to retrospective evaluations, at least in critical years. As in the other countries, prospective voting is less reflective of a national mood.

The 1993 election produced a pattern similar to that of Spain and Argentina, with nationally oriented retrospective voting but prospective voting driven by local politics. In that election voters across the country turned against the ruling Progressive Conservatives, such that the party dropped from an average of 42 points in the average district to just 16. The spread among the districts dropped too (fanning-in), such that the PC won less than 20 percent in all but a few districts.[14] Figure 8.4 shows that even within Quebec the prospective vote, however, did not follow a consistent pattern. In the 75 Quebecois districts, most voters converged on

---

[14] Still, the low DN was evident, as the party actually gained in one district and fell only slightly in many others.

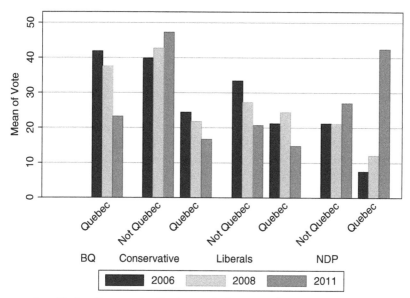

FIGURE 8.5 Voting Patterns in Quebec and the Rest of Canada 2006–11, Average Support across Districts

the decision to vote against the PC, but they did not coordinate on a new champion. The other nationally competitive party, the Liberals, grew in most districts, but in some places its support fell. Most impressively, support for the newly formed BQ, which competed (and competes) only in Quebec, was highly disparate, ranging from about 7 to 75 percent.

More recent elections allow an exploration of the prospective and retrospective patterns in years where there was not such a dramatic shift of voters. To depict the two types of nationalization, Figure 8.5 shows the evolution of votes for the main parties across the three elections from 2006 to 2011, separating their support in Quebec from the rest of the country. The low SN is evident in the different heights of the bars representing the parties' support in Quebec versus non-Quebec districts. The Conservative support in Quebec is less than half what it is outside of that province, the NDP support in 2011 was about 15 points higher on average in Quebec than out, and the Liberal support has been as much as 10 points weaker in Quebec. As the on-line appendix graphs show, the variance is also intra-regional (or pillarized).

The low DN is also evident, since the changes in support in Quebec are not at all parallel to what they have been for the rest of the country. Even though the two elections of 2008 and 2011 returned the Conservative party to government under the leadership of Stephen Harper, the complex voting pattern suggests that national politics or events are insufficient to explain retrospective voting. For its part, the Conservatives lost 3 percent in Quebec and gained a similar percentage in the rest of the country in 2008. The Conservatives then lost another 5 percent in Quebec in 2011, even while growing by that much elsewhere. The Liberals, meanwhile, saw their support fall both in (-9.5 percent) and out of Quebec (-6.6 percent) when comparing 2008 to 2011.

The decline of the Liberals was also uneven during those years; the average swing across the two electoral cycles was -5.6 points, but 106 of the 616 observations (308 districts for each election) show positive swings for the party. In almost one-half of these districts (43), the Liberals increased their vote by at least 5 percent. To an important degree this was a regional phenomenon, with the party gaining an average of 3 percent in Quebec's 75 districts and losing 6 percent in the other 233 districts for 2008.

The other significant party, the New Democratic Party (NDP), adds another dimension to the patterns. This party grew sharply from 2008 to 2011, rising from 19 to 30 percent of the vote. The statistics for SN suggest that it lacks the consistency of European parties, but it is more highly nationalized on this dimension than the other large parties in Canada. The statistics on DN, however, show that the change in its support is inconsistent around the nation. Perhaps most telling for the issue of accountability is that the fall of the BQ in 2011 benefited the NDP instead of one of the traditional parties. Alternatively, while the rise of the NDP was impressive around the country, the change was mostly in response to a regional shift in the vote; the NDP rose 30 points on average in Quebec's 75 districts, but only 6 points elsewhere (203 districts).

Canada uses a single-member district electoral system, which has translated the moderate vote shifts into large seat gains. In 2008, the Conservatives gained only one point on average, but they gained 19 seats (6 percent); then, in 2011, they gained 2 points in the vote and another 23 seats (7.5 percent). These examples are much less dramatic than what happened in 1993, when the Conservatives lost 27 percent from their previous vote share, but went from 156 to just 2 seats (of 295) in the parliament. The NDP's experience shows the pattern in reverse; in 2011 it gained about 12 percent nationally, and this translated into a change from 37 (12 percent) to 103 (33 percent) seats. Nationalization also plays a role in these vote-to-seat translation patterns, because the 12 percent increase ignores the distributional issues. In the NDP's case the vote gain was concentrated in Quebec, where it gained 30 percent in the average district, and it rose from just one seat there (of 75) in 2008 to 59 seats.

A final concern for accountability under the conditions of low DN and SN combined with a majoritarian electoral law is whether the parties concentrate their efforts in the most strategic districts. There is some evidence that the governing party was successful in doing just that. The Conservatives only gained two points on average in 2011, but there were 30 districts where it won seats that it had lost in 2008. In those 30 districts, it gained an average of nine points. Its efforts were imperfect, since it also lost seven districts in 2011 that it had won in 2008, but five of those were in Quebec.

Summary
While it is not controversial to argue that geography affects politics, nationalization has not usually been fully integrated into analyses of retrospective or prospective voting. Such analyses too often presume that all of a country's voters have the same options and act with a common purpose, but a comparative view of party nationalization shows that this is not always the case. The two dimensions of nationalization provide indicators for how well voters coordinate their choices, and, as I have argued here, when nationalization – especially of the dynamic type – is low, there cannot be a strong correlation of changing national conditions and voting responses.

Beyond this conditional argument, the examples across several crisis situations and one of improving national performance provided empirical evidence that voters have sometimes sent a clearer signal to the incumbent party than they have to the challengers. This provides some empirical backing to the thesis that even if retrospective voting is nationalized (on both dimensions), prospective voting may not be.

Perhaps it should be unsurprising that the incumbent party's DN will be high where the economy has shattered, since crises give all voters a focal point. Retrospective voting in these circumstances can appear as a coordinated and unified act. In the context of multipartism, however, DN for the challengers could still be low, because voters' views of the alternatives to the incumbent may vary across localities. Some parties, for example, could argue for more regional autonomy, while others give a prescription for a different economic model. Moves away from an incumbent would almost certainly generate inconsistent results among districts in countries where different parties compete in different regions (e.g. Canada, India, Spain) but inconsistent district-level changes are also possible (and perhaps likely) where the same parties are present everywhere (e.g. Mexico).

In sum, local factors are likely to drive prospective voting, even if national factors drive retrospective voting. The two dimensions of nationalization, at the party level, can reveal these patterns. While SN is an important piece of the context, DN provides a measure of the degree to which there is national unity in holding incumbents accountable for national conditions or coordination and a mandate for challengers. To reiterate, as nationalization statistics can indicate, these two types of voter decisions are not necessarily parallel; national context can drive voters views of the incumbent even while local factors can influence their prospective choices.

The following chapter takes up another challenge, looking at how nationalization affects co-sponsorship of legislative bills. As such, it shows how electoral institutions interact with nationalization in predicting a political process.

9

The Role of Party Nationalization on Collective Action and Dissent among Co-Partisan Legislators: Roll Call Voting and Bill Co-Sponsorship*

Most of this book has been about measuring differences among parties or considering how nationalization affects partisan behavior. By implication, party nationalization also has relevance for how individual legislators behave toward one another. Thus, while this chapter continues the exploration of the effects of nationalization, it takes a different tack than the others in this book by using individual legislators as the level of analysis rather than parties.

This book was inspired by questioning Cox and McCubbins's (1993) presumption that a weak tie among US legislators – which I have related to weak dynamic and perhaps static nationalization – is enough to generate collective action. After taking time to put the levels of party nationalization into a comparative context, it is now possible to return to the basic concern about whether electoral ties drive collective action among co-partisan legislators. To get at that question, I consider not just overall levels of party action or unity, but which individual legislators are prone to dissent. Are the legislators whose electoral fates are most closely tied to their parties' national trends also the most likely to cooperate with their partisan colleagues? Stated in reverse, are those legislators whose electoral fortunes are least attuned with those of other co-partisans the most likely to act independently?

To address these questions, the chapter considers two dependent variables: party unity on roll call votes and co-sponsorship among pairs of legislators. Though I do run some models on other countries in the second part of the chapter, the chapter focuses on the United States for several reasons. First, the Cox and McCubbins thesis is based on the US case. The US case is also a best test for the theory, given that I have shown in this book that party nationalization

* The third section of this chapter borrows from my paper, "Bill Co-Sponsorship and the Electoral Connection in Comparative Perspective" (n.d.) co-authored with Ernesto Calvo, Daniel Chasquetti, and Jose Manuel Magallanes.

there is relatively weak. There are, therefore, different electoral patterns within the party, and that variance assists the analysis. Finally, the data for the United States is particularly extensive, both for measuring party nationalization and for the two dependent variables (roll call voting and bill co-sponsorship).

Party Nationalization and Legislative Behavior

The root of *Legislative Leviathan* is the idea that electoral ties among a party's legislators yield incentives for the legislators to delegate power to the party leadership. Since some part of the legislators' electoral success is tied to a national movement, each has a common interest in building the party brand. They thus delegate to party leadership and build structures for that end. The leaders, in turn, use that power to discipline party members when necessary in the pursuit of common goals, which they define as developing a positive image for the party. They build from the perhaps apocryphal story (cited in Cheung [1983]) where boat pullers in China actually hired someone to whip their own members who were not fully contributing to the collective effort.

To substantiate their claim that US legislators share a common electoral fate, Cox and McCubbins examine vote swings at the district level of co-partisans. They find that the standard deviation of the swing is small, and thus argue that all legislators are affected by the overall support of the party. I have argued here that DN provides a more sophisticated measure of the degree to which a party's legislators share a common fate. Recall that I applied the term "local vote," the opposite of DN, to capture the degree to which a legislator's individual qualities or district characteristics drove voting. The local vote, therefore should allow a confirmation of the Cox and McCubbins thesis, and it allows me to put that thesis and the prime independent variable into a comparative context.

The Cox and McCubbins argument, and tests thereof, have important weaknesses, especially when considered from a comparative perspective. While they do show that there does exist a commonality in the fate of US legislators, they fail to discuss the relative strength of the common fate. They provide three tests of the purported relationship. For the first, they do not provide detailed results, only saying that "if party and year are included as main effects, along with their product as an interaction effect, all three factors are statistically significant in explaining interelection vote swings. This finding provides evidence that candidates of the same party do tend to be pushed in the same direction from year to year" (p. 112). They conduct a second test that measures the difference in the average swing to the two parties through a simple regression. The result confirms that there is a statistically significant difference in the swing to the average partisan. A third test, finally, looks at the probability of victory. Here, they also consider the legislators' previous margin of victory (which is important to the static nationalization). This too shows that the average swing to the party affects the probability of victory for each of that party's members. While these tests do suggest the existence of national electoral tides, they fail to quantify the strength of that tie. To provide that datum, we would also need information on the degree of spread in the swing. That is, if some of a party's members are less affected by (and thereby concerned with) the swing than others, then the average change could be insufficient to agglutinate all of a party's members.

From a comparative perspective, the types of tests that Cox and McCubbins provide do not answer the question of how strong the common electoral tie must be in order to conjoin the co-partisans. In a comparative model, the strength of the tie, not only its existence, could become a variable. Such a model, in turn, could shed light on how strong such a tie must be in order to generate the types of collective action that that Cox and McCubbins describe.

The model has another untested facet. It implies that while those co-partisan legislators who swing together should collaborate, those whose electoral fates are less dependent on the partisan swings should be more independent. This suggested relation touches both dimensions of nationalization. From the dynamic perspective, legislators with swings inconsistent with the partisan mode should be more independent. And from the static side, legislators from safer districts should be less concerned with contributing to the collective good than legislators whose fates do depend on partisan tides.

As argued in Chapter 3, the standard deviation of the swing is a one-dimensional measure of DN. To summarize, if that statistic is small for a given party, it would be denominated as having high DN and would suggest that all legislators in that party share a common electoral fate. Relating this back to Cox and McCubbins, if DN were very high, it would be reasonable to presume a high level of willingness to delegate on the part of the legislators. But is the level of DN in the United States sufficient to produce the delegation? The comparative measures I have provided in this book suggest that while the level of DN in the United States is higher than in most countries in Latin America, it is much lower than countries in Europe. Has the US crossed the threshold that supports delegation? Have the Latin American countries crossed that threshold? Would the US legislators offer a bit more power to their party leaders if the level of DN were a bit stronger?

These questions add one other subtle but important theoretical complication. They suggest the possibility of a threshold model of delegation; instead of assuming that a slightly tighter collective fate would produce a bit more collective action, they offer the possibility that the pursuit of common goals would lead legislators to delegate extensive powers to their leaders as long as the party's DN is above some (perhaps low) level. I do not fully explore this alternative model of politics, but its implications are important for this and other theories. Dividing variables into categories (i.e. at a threshold) is fraught, because the cutoffs are often arbitrary. But, scales are problematic too. A party that is able to hold 60 percent of its legislators on a roll call vote is not weaker than one that holds 70 percent; they are both weak in the sense that the leadership is unable to ensure collective action. It may also be reasonable to argue that a party unity score of 90 also suggest weakness, since that leadership too fails to rein in recalcitrants.

Thresholds and scales are also relevant when considering the logic of delegation (Kiewiet and McCubbins 1991). The model implies that party members delegate sufficient authority to the leaders to "whip the boatpuller." But the level of authority that they delegate to leadership could also be measured along a scale. Party members can give leaders only persuasive powers, or they can provide them with the tools to name candidacies, designate committee members, dole out perquisites, offer campaign support, direct pork, and use other tools to whip potential dissenters. If the common element in the electoral fate is weak, then it might be that party members would withhold some of these powers. Would leaders without some of these powers be able to assure collective actions? Do leaders need all of these powers to avoid dissent, or is one power sufficient?

These types of concerns highlight the difficulty and opportunities in creating valid hypotheses for both case studies and comparative analyses. In this chapter I do not attempt to address each of these issues. The tack I take is to go to the individual legislators, asking about the relation between their electoral incentives and their legislative behavior. As such, I hope to take the analysis back to its roots by looking at collective action as the result of individuals' decisions. I do this by looking at two dependent variables: roll call voting and bill co-sponsorship.

With regards to roll calls, I first test whether legislators who share collective fates – defined as a commonality in the dynamic dimension of nationalization – are more prone to vote together, and whether those legislators whose electoral fortunes are least tied to the rest of their party are most prone to dissent from the party line. These tests largely fail. Results do not improve much when taking electoral safety – which is related to SN – into account, but this variable does improve the results somewhat. I then use a regression analysis to test whether the two dimensions of nationalization are correlated with a legislator' ideological position (as measured by DW-NOMINATE[1] scores) or their propensity to dissent (as measured with Rice scores). These tests do not return strong results, thus straining the logic underlying the Cox and McCubbins' thesis.

The second question for this chapter regards patterns of bill co-sponsorship. If DN is high, then geography should not affect the patterns by which legislators choose co-sponsorship partners. If, however, legislators are concerned with promoting local rather than national politics, then co-sponsorship data could detect these interests by finding higher levels of intra-regional cooperation and a high propensity of legislators to co-sponsor with colleagues from different regions who share common electoral fates. Where both dimensions of nationalization are high, all legislators face similar fates, and thus there should be no strong geographic patterns evident in the co-sponsorship data. I

---

[1] On NOMINATE, see Poole and Rosenthal (1996). Scores are available at Poole's website, voteview.com.

test these hypotheses using data from the United States, Argentina, Peru, and Uruguay.

The preceding discussion yields two competing hypotheses, which allow empirical testing:

H1) If legislators are more concerned with their personal (local) electoral trends, then electoral experiences should be tied to patterns in how legislators vote on roll calls and with whom they co-sponsor.

H2) If (national) partisanship prevails over individualistic concerns, then there should be strong partisan patterns of intra-partisan cooperation on legislation and thus little evidence that legislators' personal electoral experiences influence with whom they co-sponsor or vote.

The first of these is closer in alignment with a Mayhewian version of politics, a model that virtually ignores parties. It is uncontested that legislators are more prone to vote and co-sponsor with members from their own parties than with those in the opposition, and thus the tests that I conduct assume a partisan context. The question is then less about tradeoffs between partisanship and personalism and more about whether personal incentives add to partisanship in shaping or explaining legislators' behavior. Stated differently, if partisanship gives a baseline expectation about cooperation, the test is whether legislators' personal electoral patterns change the probability of intra-party cooperation.

The second hypothesis stands in contrast, and evidence confirming it would support the Cox and McCubbins theory about the importance of partisan ties. Using the United States in the test would also confirm that even weak electoral ties are sufficient to generate cooperation on legislation. A full test would require not only that there is a lack of relationship between individual electoral experiences of the patterns of legislation, but also that the level of intra-partisan cooperation is high. There are no clear criteria for defining "high," however, and at any level of cooperation below unanimity it may be reasonable to argue about whether common electoral fates (or other mechanisms) have a causal effect. Still, the tests below follow conventional wisdom and assume that the level of cooperation is high, thus allowing a focus on whether or not personal electoral experiences shape roll call voting and co-sponsorship patterns.

Party Nationalization and Roll Call Voting

In this section I turn to testing how the strength of electoral ties among legislators affects patterns of roll call voting in the United States. Earlier, I showed that in a comparative frame DN is low in the United States, which implies that there should be only a weak notion of a collective fate among partisans. Here I look directly at the degree to which co-partisans share a common fate by considering how an individual legislator's level of the vote and swing affect their propensity to support their party. The expectation based on H1 is that those legislators whose electoral fates (in terms of swing or the level of the vote) are not parallel to the rest of their party should be least inclined to vote with their party. Or, legislators with similar electoral experiences should cluster in terms of their NOMINATE scores.

Because the Cox and McCubbins analysis focuses on swing, my first tests focus on the dynamic dimension of party nationalization. The implied test is whether the absolute size of the swing for each of a party's legislators is correlated with the absolute distance of each legislator's DW-NOMINATE score from the party's mean. In so doing, I am using NOMINATE more as a proxy for a legislator's voting tendency than as an ideological measure. Using just the first dimension of NOMINATE provides a left–right score for each legislator, which is based on their voting records on roll calls. Legislators grouped together, then, have similar voting predilections.

Absolute distances are most appropriate here, since those who are most distant, either above or below the mean, should be least likely to be concerned with the party's label. The tests fail; on tests for each of the 100th, 101st, and 102nd Congresses (elected in 1986, 1988, and 1990)[2] the correlation is no more than 0.05 for the Democrats, and for the Republicans it is under 0.03 for two years and it is about –0.2 for the third. Squaring the distances does not improve the relations (maximum correlation for the six observations is 0.15).

The next step in the analysis was to add the second (static) dimension of nationalization to the analysis. Adding the static dimension creates the expectation that supporting the party label (i.e. voting with party) would be most important to legislators who are most electorally vulnerable. Candidates in very safe districts, alternatively, should be less concerned with sacrificing personal interests for their party's goals. An alternative hypothesis that would still support the Cox and McCubbins theory is that those vulnerable legislators should be the least likely to support the party, since the party would be unwise to force them into difficult votes. If this were the case, then the data would show higher unity rates among the safe legislators. Neither of these hypotheses is confirmed in the data.

For the tests, I operationalized "safety" as the candidate's vote less 50 percent, and also took the square of that value. I then ran correlations of those values with the squared distance of the legislator's DW-NOMINATE score from the party's mean score. A high correlation would indicate that marginal legislators (i.e. those whose vote is close to 50 percent) would be more inclined to align closely with the mean of the party. While the correlations (regardless of whether the values are squared) are not particularly strong, they are above 0.20 for five of the six observations (three years, two parties; maximum value 0.33). Plots of these data suggest that while there are

---

[2] These three years provide a reasonable first test, because voting unity was a bit lower in that decade than in the 2000s, and thus the parties have significant variance on the Poole and Rosenthal scores. They also include one presidential election year. Perhaps Americanists will want to extend the time period.

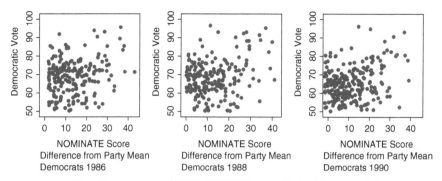

FIGURE 9.1 Vote Percentage and NOMINATE Scores, United States 1986–90

legislators from across the range in terms of vote totals who have NOMINATE scores close to the party mean, almost all legislators who have NOMINATE scores far from their party's mean also won strong electoral support (Figure 9.1). In sum, there is a bit of evidence for a relation between a legislators' electoral safety and the NOMINATE score, but the relation is weak.

Combining vote levels and swing into simple regressions, even including interaction terms, does not yield strong results, either. As suggested by the correlation analysis, there is some evidence that the vote level helps to explain how distant legislators are from their party's mean, but the swing does not have much explanatory power, and neither does the interaction. Specifically, the regressions show that the SN variable is generally positive and significant (five of six cases; again for each of the two parties for the three elections 1986–90), while the dynamic variable is only significant twice. Similar regressions using the percentage of votes in which legislators vote with their parties do not strengthen the results.[3]

In sum, the NOMINATE analysis gives more evidence to the second hypothesis: that local electoral factors do not significantly influence legislators' decisions on roll calls (at least beyond the influence of partisanship). If localism does matter, it does so most clearly among those legislators who are furthest from their party in terms of their electoral experiences.

As a more explicit test, I considered Rice scores (weighted by the degree to which votes divided the parties; Carey [2002]) as the dependent variable.[4] Tests on this variable again fail to yield strong results. Looking first at the dynamic variable, if the localism hypothesis is valid, those co-partisan legislators who share a common swing will vote together. In addition to testing for a linear relation (which did not yield strong correlations), I tried grouping legislators in terms of those who lost at least 5 points, those that gained at least 5 points, and

---

[3] These data are also available from Poole's website.
[4] Rice scores measure party unity. Simply, for a given party Rice=abs(%yea-%nay). A score of 1, then, implies all legislators voted together. A score of 90 would result from 95 percent voting together.

those whose inter-election swing was between –5 and 5 points. If the personal electoral experiences matter, then legislators within each of these groups would have had higher voting unity than was evident for the group as a whole. The differences among the groups were insignificant, however.[5]

For the next part of the test I defined marginal legislators as those who won with less than 55 percent of the vote, and again divided the swing into three categories as defined above. Tables 9.1 A and B show the results for the 100th and 101st Congresses. The safe Democrats who have sharply negative swings do have higher Rice scores in the 100th congress, but not in the 101st.[6] Overall, then, for the Democrats in those two Congresses, neither marginality nor the size of the swing has a strong impact on the propensity of members of any group to vote together. For the Republicans, who were in the opposition at that time, marginal legislators with a middle-level of swing were much more likely to vote together than other sub-groups. There are not many legislators in that group (6), but the result is relatively robust given that there were almost 900 votes. Still, the Rice score of 0.70 is low, implying that the party loses 15 percent of its members in any vote.

In sum, while it is possible that more sophisticated statistical analyses would find a more robust relationship between the commonality in electoral experiences and voting unity in the United States, this straightforward analysis found little evidence of such a relationship. This result could suggest that legislators work with co-partisans to preserve the party label and therefore are indiscriminate about with which co-partisans they will work. This would support the idea that (national) partisanship overrides (local) individual electoral concerns in the legislators' calculus. In so doing, however, the results tear at the micro-level logic of Cox and McCubbins by showing that legislators within a party who share a common experience or fate (as defined by safety and swing) are not more likely to join with one another than they are with others in their party. That is, collective fates do not generate higher levels of cooperation. This is inconsistent with the logic underlying the *Legislative Leviathan* model that is based on the need to preserve the electoral label due to the commonality in the electoral fate.

Party Nationalization and Bill Co-Sponsorship

The second set of tests considers whether legislators seek collaborators who have similar electoral fates. This analysis, based on work with my co-authors Calvo, Magallanes, and Chasquetti (2014), analyzes the relation of electoral

---

[5] The results were similarly unimpressive when using as the dependent variable the percentage of votes in which legislators supported their parties.
[6] Note that the swing might be of less importance to safe incumbents, and this is consistent the homogeneity in Rice scores for those legislators. It may be problematic to make this comparison, however, given the small number of observations in some categories.

TABLE 9.1A *Weighted Rice Scores by Marginality and Swing (100th US Congress)*

Democrats		<-5	-5 to 5	>5	Missing	n
			Democrats			
	No	0.82	0.80	0.76	0.67	181
		(9)	(64)	(80)	(28)	
	Yes	0.68	0.76	0.80	1	21
		(2)	(10)	(8)	(1)	
Marginal				Republicans		
(vote<55)	No	0.64	0.54	0.68	0.73	161
		(22)	(80)	(25)	(9)	
	Yes	0.56	0.71	0.64		15
		(3)	(9)	(12)		

Number of Votes: 939; number of legislators in each category in ( )
Most missing data is because the legislator ran unopposed in one of the two elections.

TABLE 9.1B *Weighted Rice Scores by Marginality and Swing (101st US Congress)*

Democrats		<-5	-5 to 5	>5	Missing	n
			Democrats			
	No	0.69	0.72	0.75	0.64	240
		(23)	(94)	(29)	(94)	
	Yes	0.74	0.73	0.67		18
		(8)	(6)	(4)		
Marginal				Republicans		
(vote<55)	No	0.48	0.52	0.55	0.60	161
		(13)	(76)	(40)	(32)	
	Yes	0.57	0.70	1		15
		(7)	(6)	(1)		

Number of Votes: 879; see Table 9.1A for details.

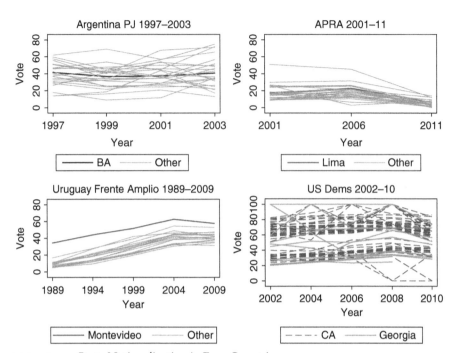

FIGURE 9.2 Party Nationalization in Four Countries

swings, the level of a legislator's vote, and bill co-sponsorship. Bill co-sponsorship is a particularly useful dependent variable, since signatures on bills show whom legislators rely on, without collapsing that collaboration into a single yes/no category as in roll call votes. The bottom line is that while the tests using NOMINATE and Rice scores did not yield significant results, the data suggest that common electoral patterns do influence legislators' co-sponsorship patterns in the United States and other countries.

To conduct these tests, my co-authors and I generated a dyadic database for co-sponsorship in the United States, Argentina, Uruguay, and Peru. For each bill, each co-sponsor is coded against every other co-partisan, thus creating a large network database. Our goal, then, is to test whether electoral fates affect the likelihood of co-sponsorship.

As I have shown in earlier chapters, some parties in Peru and Uruguay are highly nationalized on both dimensions of nationalization, while the main parties in the United States and Argentina score low on both dimensions. Figure 9.2 provides the comparison, showing the evolution of district-level votes for one party in each of the countries. For the United States, the graph portrays just districts in California and Georgia because adding more districts would blur the patterns. What is necessary to underline is that even in the countries where the parties are not nationalized as a whole, some legislators do share similar electoral experiences. For example, the Democrats receive almost the same percentage of the vote each year in some of Georgia's districts. In Argentina, not only do all intra-party legislators from a given province receive the same vote, but some of the provinces have very similar vote trends. The PJ won just over 50 percent in 1997 in both Salta and San Luis and fell to just over 40 percent in 1999. The goal of the tests, therefore, is to explore whether a) common swings or b) similar levels of support encourage legislators to co-sponsor legislation.

The models vary a bit by country, but each relies on two primary independent variables: Swing Difference and Vote Difference;[7] the former is the absolute difference in the change of the vote for the two legislators, and the latter is the absolute difference in the two legislators' level of support in the last election. Both variables take a value of zero for legislators who are on the same electoral (proportional representation) list. For the United States the vote difference is equivalent to the difference in the legislators' safety (and the regression model adjusts accordingly). If common electoral fates drive collaboration, then the regression should show more co-sponsorship among those legislators who had similar levels of the vote and, for example, big losses or big gains than between these two groups. If legislators are more concerned with partisanship than their own particular electoral situation, then the swing variable will have a small substantive impact. The smaller its substantive significance, the larger the support for H2, which highlights collective interest in building the party label over individual electoral concerns.

For the United States the swing variable requires a modification, because the uncontested elections distort its size. The solution here was to cut the value for the swing in half where either the previous or current race had only one competitor. This is tantamount to suggesting that an uncontested winner would have won 75 percent if a challenger had been present. The other possibility was to drop observations where one of the two main parties failed to win at least 10 percent of the vote. This lowered the number of observations significantly, but still did not affect the results dramatically.

Data for this chapter cover 1975–96 (the 94th–104th Congresses) for the United States, 1983–99 for Argentina,[8] 2006–11 for Peru, and 1995–2010 for Uruguay. This is all the data that is available for the Latin American countries, though we could extend the analysis for the United States. That 20-year period, however, covers much of what Cox and McCubbins analyzed. Further, party unity climbed after that period, and thus there is more variance to consider by not extending the analysis through the 2000s.

---

[7] The US model includes both the level of the vote and the difference in "safety" of legislators. This is less important in the countries that use PR, and the models thus test only the difference in the vote.

[8] We stop the analysis in 1999 for Argentina, because the 2001 economic and political crises generated significant volatility in party alignments which complicate the analysis.

Institutional Expectations

These four countries provide important variance on both the independent and dependent variables. First, Argentina and the USA are federal countries, while Peru and Uruguay are unitary. Unitary governments should help tie legislators together, and thus reduce the likelihood of using local cues for co-sponsorship. Legislators, in Argentina and the United States, therefore, should be more likely to co-sponsor with legislators based on the similarity of their electoral fates.

Given their primacy in studies of legislative behavior, we might expect electoral laws to drive co-sponsorship patterns. The particularities of proportional representation lead to several expectations. First, in closed-list systems, all legislators in a given district (state or province) will be on a single list, and they thus share a collective fate. They then should be prone to collaborate. If nomination control is at the district level, then there would not be expected cooperation across districts. In open-list systems the expectation is less clear-cut. All legislators on an open list have some collective interests, but they also must compete with one another (Morgenstern 2004). The countervailing pulls work against strong expectations about collaboration.

Among the countries under investigation, Argentina has the clearest expectation since it uses closed-list PR. The expectation, then, is for collaboration for co-partisans from each province. Peru used open lists during the period of investigation, and thus there are no strong expectations there. Uruguay uses a double-simultaneous vote, which has effects similar to an open list (Morgenstern 2001). The system also reinforces factionalism, and thus factionalism should combine with partisanship to drive co-sponsorship patterns. Finally, the single-member district system in the United States, plus federalism, should work against broad intra-partisan collaboration. The US case, therefore, is crucial to the Cox and McCubbins thesis, because electoral laws should not support intra-partisan cooperation.

Cox and McCubbins did not consider the static side of nationalization, but as I have argued throughout this book, theories are often improved by including both dimensions. In this case, adding that dimension allows a test of whether "safe" legislators behave differently from "marginal."

Bivariate Empirical Tests

The forthcoming tests are based on dyads of co-partisan legislators. Each pair is coded for the number of bills on which the two signed on as co-sponsors, plus the difference in the swing to and level of the vote for each legislator (and other information). To highlight the bivariate relations, the first panel of Figure 9.3 plots the number of bills that individual US Democrats co-sponsored with their co-partisans for one congressional session, the 104th, against the difference in the swings for each pair of legislators. Congruent with the expectation from H1, the plot yields a downward-slanting relationship, because as the swing difference increases, the number of co-sponsored bills should fall. There is much "noise" in the data, since many pairs of legislators co-sponsored few

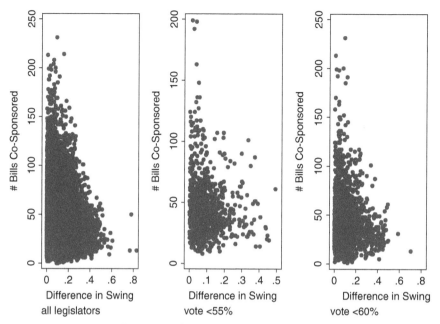

FIGURE 9.3 Swings and Number of Bills Co-Sponsored, US 104th Congress (1995–97)

bills together, but there are very few outliers where two legislators had high differences in the swing and also high numbers of co-sponsored bills. I have tested other congressional sessions, and each shows very similar patterns.

The second and third panels of the graph help to test the hypothesis that legislators with similar levels of electoral support might be more inclined to vote together. Those two graphs account for this by limiting the sample to those legislators with no more than 55 or 60 percent of the vote. The graphs keep the same shape, suggesting marginal legislators also consider the direction of the change in the vote. Further, note that all marginal legislators co-sponsor with each other; the minimum value on the count variable is 8 for the second graph, while the frequency of 0s is large in the other graphs. In giving evidence that the marginal legislators are most concerned with building a collective image, it calls into some question the blanket hypothesis proposed by Cox and McCubbins in which all co-partisans collaborate to promote their collective interest.

Moving to the Latin American cases, the overall scatter plot of co-sponsorship and the difference in the vote in Argentina (using only dyads where the number of bills co-sponsored is greater than zero) looks similar to that of the United States. Figure 9.4 shows the co-sponsorship swing difference relationship for nine provinces and shows that the pattern is upheld in most provinces; legislators very frequently co-sponsor with others from their own province, and are unlikely to co-sponsor with legislators from districts that have

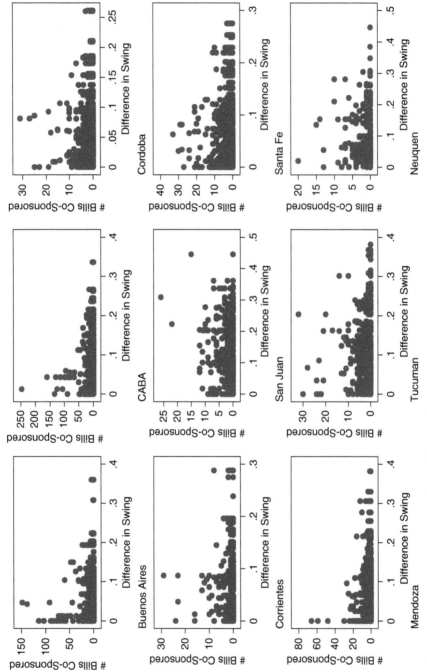

FIGURE 9.4 Argentina: Co-sponsorship and Swing, by Province

238

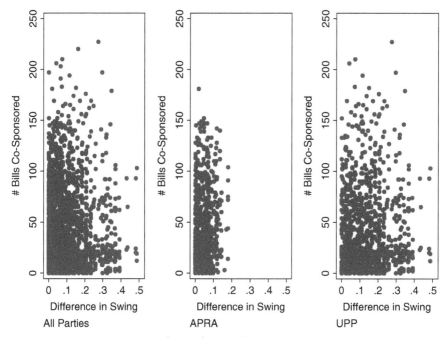

FIGURE 9.5 Peru: Co-Sponsorship and Swing, by Party

very different swings. The data has a potential bias based on the number of legislators from different provinces, but this does not drive the graph. For example, the two provinces that separate from Buenos Aires in terms of the swing are Neuquen and Tucuman, which have district magnitudes of 2 and 5 respectively (while Buenos Aires has a magnitude of 35). But, the graphs of Neuquen and Tucuman show the same general pattern; legislators from these provinces are most likely to co-sponsor with others that have similar swings.

Because Argentina has a closed-list proportional representation system, the level of the vote should have a strong impact on co-sponsorship. A similar set of graphs (not shown) confirms that relationship. There is one exception; PJ legislators from the city of Buenos Aires (CABA) and those from the Buenos Aires province are frequent collaborators, even though the PJ is much stronger in the surrounding area than in the city. Every one of the exceptions, however, involved one legislator from CABA (Alvarez).

Figure 9.5 portrays the results for Peru, first for the country as a whole and then for the two largest parties after the 2006 election, APRA and UPP. The graphs, however, show no apparent relation between co-sponsorship and swing. APRA is highly nationalized on the dynamic dimension, and the graph shows that all swing differences are less than 0.2. That small range, perhaps, leads APRA members to be equally likely to co-sponsor legislation with those of

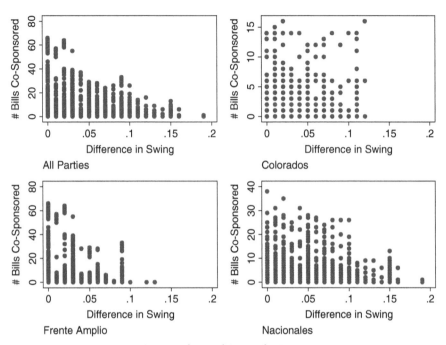

FIGURE 9.6 Uruguay: Co-Sponsorship and Swing, by Party

their own province (where swing=0) as with those who are from districts where
the swings are maximally different. For the UPP, there is frequent co-
sponsorship among legislators with very disparate swings, and many with
small differences in the swing fail to co-sponsor with one another. Overall,
then, the graph for all parties fails to show the downward-sloping trend as in the
graphs of the United States and Argentina. Unlike those cases, adding vote levels
does not yield a more shapely graph.

Uruguayan parties are highly nationalized on both dimensions, implying that
the differences in swings and vote levels are very small. The partial exception to
this fact is that the Frente Amplio is particularly strong in the capital city, and
the other two main parties do somewhat less well there. On the dynamic
dimension, however, the parties' votes track in an exceptionally parallel
manner. As a result, the swing differences should not be large enough to
produce effects on co-sponsorship rates, though the vote differences could
yield an effect. The first set of graphs (Figure 9.6) maps the swing and co-
sponsorship relation, and shows, to some surprise, a downward trend for the
Nacionales, which is also reflected in the graph for all parties. This trend is
driven by the lower rates of co-sponsorship where the swing differences were
greater than 0.1. The second set of graphs (Figure 9.7) shows no noticeable
impact of vote differences on co-sponsorship rates, even though there is a wider

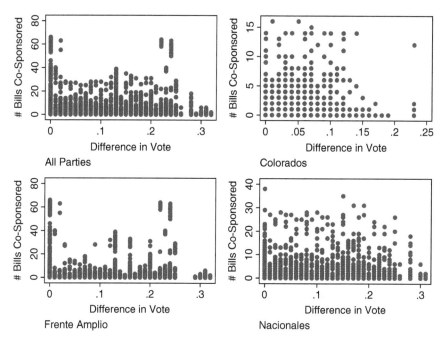

FIGURE 9.7 Uruguay: Co-Sponsorship and Vote Differences, by Party

range for that independent variable. Similar graphs (not shown) for the United States, Argentina, and Peru also fail to show any definitive pattern. The only partial exception is that for Argentina there is a negative-sloping trend after the vote difference reaches about 0.2.

Multivariate Tests

To test these ideas in a multivariate context, we applied negative binomial regressions, because the dependent variable is the number of times a pair of co-partisans co-sponsor legislation. The most critical independent variables are the Swing Difference and Vote (or Safety) Difference, as defined previously. To reiterate, H1 suggested that legislators who have small differences in their vote swings will have an incentive to work more closely together. If, on the other hand, the change in the district vote for one legislator is unrelated to the vote change for another, then policy signals from voters would depart from each other and those legislators would gain little from co-sponsoring legislation. The expectation for the Vote Difference variable is similar.[9]

Beyond the primary variables of interest, the model for the United States includes a control for differences in ideology, measured with NOMINATE

---

[9] I also considered the interaction of the variables. It is insignificant in the empirical tests and does not add much theoretically.

scores (Poole and Rosenthal [1996]). There is insufficient data to generate these values for the other countries, however. The model also includes a variable measuring the length of service (or at least whether both legislators are freshmen), the difference in the district magnitude for the two legislators' provinces, and faction membership for Uruguay.[10] Another variable for Uruguay was whether either legislator was a "substitute."[11] We also control for differences in the total number of bills sponsored by each legislator and cluster model errors by each pair of legislators. I focus below on pooled results that use fixed effects for parties and legislative sessions, but our paper includes analyses of individual sessions.

The pooled model on the US case (Table 9.2 and Figure 9.3, as well as the analysis of ten individual legislatures [the 94th to the 104th, excepting redistricting years]), provide support for our expectations, returning negative and significant coefficients for "swing difference."[12] Substantively, the results for the pooled model suggested that a one-unit increase in the swing difference would produce a 23 percent decrease in co-sponsorship.

While this measure of DN confirms the idea that DN is important in explaining collaboration among legislators, there was not strong evidence about the role of SN. The regression did return significant results in the expected direction for some years of the analysis, but for others years the variable suggested a negative relationship between the level of support and the propensity to co-sponsor. As suggested earlier, this should not be a surprise, since safe legislators may be willing to co-sponsor with those whose elections are less assured. There is not, then, a strong (linear) expectation about the relation of safety and co-sponsorship.

Other variables that we included as controls, including the number of bills sponsored and "same state," worked as expected. We also found some differences for variables measuring differences in ideology and seniority.

Figure 9.8 reproduces our predictive graph. There are two notable findings. First, the downward slopes indicate that as swing values for the two legislators increase, the predicted number of bills that they will co-sponsor decreases sharply. Here the change from no difference in the swing to the empirical maximum (which is about 1.3) would yield a difference of about 20 bills co-sponsored, for each of the four lines in the graph. The different intercepts of the four lines indicate that two legislators from safe districts will co-sponsor about ten bills less than two legislators who barely won their elections. That the regression did not return significance for the difference in the safety variable is

[10] Factions in Uruguay are formally defined through the electoral lists (Morgenstern 2001). Less formal membership, as is common elsewhere, would not allow an institutional test.
[11] "Suplentes" are a common feature of legislative politics in Uruguay. They are elected along with the title holder, and serve when the other is unavailable.
[12] Results for models on individual congresses, and more detailed description, are available in the original paper, which is posted on my website.

TABLE 9.2 *Explaining Collaboration in the US and Argentina Lower Houses*

	US Congresses 94–104[#]	Argentina 1985–99
Swing Difference	-0.257***	-1.300***
	(0.011)	-0.130
Vote 1	-0.119***	
	(0.011)	
Vote 2	-0.213***	
	(0.010)	
Vote (Safety) Diff	0.014	-0.819***
	(0.011)	-0.100
Magnitude Diff (ln)		-0.315***
		-0.009
#Sponsored1	0.006***	0.631***
	(0.000)	-0.008
#Sponsored2	0.005***	0.632***
	(0.000)	-0.008
Sponsor Diff (ln)		-0.360***
		-0.009
Party	-0.001***	-0.104***
	(0.000)	-0.016
Ideology Diff	-0.829***	
	(0.011)	
Shared Freshman		0.136***
		-0.014
Same state	0.396***	
	(0.009)	
Seniority Diff	-0.036***	
	(0.000)	
Constant	2.039***	-6.178***
	(0.011)	-0.012
/lnalpha	-0.916***	0.499***
	(0.004)	-0.072
Observations	419,896	77,340
LogLik	-1.960e+06	-106922

Robust standard errors in parentheses; fixed effects by congress
*** p<0.01, ** p<0.05, * p<0.1
[#] includes fixed effect

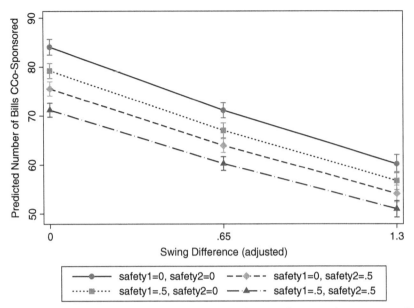

FIGURE 9.8 Absolute Differences in District-Level Vote Shares and Co-Sponsorship, USA, Pooled Results, 94th through 104th Congresses

evident in the middle two lines, which show that a mix of a safe and a marginal legislator are more likely to co-sponsor than two safe legislators, but not as likely to work together as two legislators who both might be worried about their jobs. In sum, like the bivariate analysis, these results suggest that legislators from tight districts might see added incentives to work together, even if there is no such obvious relation among the legislators who hold the safest seats.

The models for Argentina (Table 9.2 and Figure 9.9) also worked as expected, with the swing proving substantively and statistically significant.[13] The statistics confirm that legislators from a single province (vote difference=0) are likely to work together, but the model also suggests that legislators from different provinces with similar swings are also more likely to work together than are those who see their party's votes going along disparate paths. These results hold for both of the country's main parties, but the model suggested that the UCR legislators are more likely to seek co-partisan co-sponsors than are those from the PJ. We verified the results with several models, and continued to find evidence of a significant (negative) relation for co-sponsorship and SN; the tests showed that legislators from provinces where the party is strong are less likely to vote with those coming from areas where the party is weaker.

---

[13] These results are all available in the original paper.

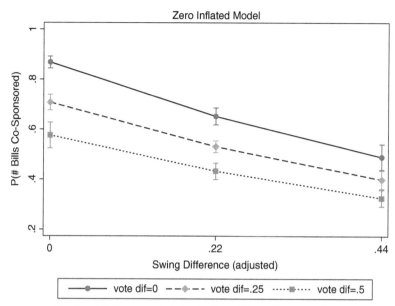

FIGURE 9.9 Absolute Differences in District-Level Vote Shares and Co-Sponsorship, Argentina

While the results for the US and Argentine parties worked as expected, the results for the two unitary countries, Peru and Uruguay, did not support the idea that common electoral experiences drove co-sponsorship. In those two countries the regressions confirmed that co-partisans collaborated without regard to the electoral fortunes of their collaborator. The unitary political system is probably only a piece of this story. Also driving the Peruvian result is the high level of electoral volatility, such that legislators may not have much faith that previous results will foretell the future. For Uruguay, factionalism is also important, and the overall high level of DN could mean that the legislators need not pay attention to small differences in the relative changes in the vote. Finally, since more than one-half of the legislators are from just two provinces, and parties have no more than one legislator in most other provinces, most are left with limited options when they want to co-sponsor.

Discussion

This chapter has taken a second look at the impact of party nationalization on legislative behavior, and has done so in the context of testing the Cox and McCubbins thesis about the effect of collective fates on collective action. Further, the chapter uses legislators' individual electoral experiences as independent variables, rather than the parties' overall nationalization. The empirical findings call the blanket theoretical framework of Cox and McCubbins into question in different ways. On one level, the roll call and NOMINATE data can support the idea that the parties' electoral experience drives legislative action, since there was no strong relation for the legislators' personal experiences and voting behavior. Theoretically, however, this finding strains the theory because it focuses on showing that many legislators' electoral fates are unrelated to that of their fellow partisans. The co-sponsorship data yield a different conclusion. They suggest that US legislators are sensitive to their personal electoral experiences and seek partners with similar concerns. These results, too, can be both supportive or not for the idea of collective fates. On the more positive side, while legislators with common electoral experiences are more likely to co-sponsor bills together, the results do not eliminate the high level of intra-party cooperation. As a simple comparison, the average level of co-sponsorship among co-partisan Democrats is about 72 bills, which is about 50 percent higher than the level of cross-partisan partnerships. But on the negative side the regression results suggested an even bigger range in comparing two co-partisan legislators with the most common electoral concerns with those who had the most disparate experiences.

A second goal for the chapter was to contribute to comparative theory. By using data from Argentina, Peru, and Uruguay, the chapter shows that the importance of collective electoral fates is contingent on electoral systems, federalism, and other institutions. In countries that use closed-list systems, for example, all legislators from a given district (provinces, for Argentina) have an identical experience in terms of swing and the level of the vote. In Peru, the unitary system might override concerns about shifting electoral winds, but the volatile party system also conspires against concerns about co-partisans' electoral fortunes. The Uruguay case suggested that the unitary government plus institutionalized federalism – and perhaps the concentration of legislators in just two districts – works against the idea that similar electoral experiences drive roll call voting patterns or bill co-sponsorship patterns.

PART IV

CONCLUSION

10

Summary and Conclusions

The motivation for this book was the timeless proclamation about the US Congress that "all politics is local." But, as this book has documented, this is truer in some countries, and at some times, than others. The book has also considered the causes and effects of varying the level of localism. To answer the descriptive questions – when, where, and how much localism – and to address theoretical concerns – such as the sources of the variation, and the impacts on electoral accountability and collaboration among legislators – the book has relied on extensive data and statistical models that facilitate analysis across a broad range of countries. Central to this effort was operationalizing "local politics" as the inverse of party nationalization, measured across two dimensions termed "static" and "dynamic."

The book has emphasized definitions and measurement, because the widely used term "nationalization" is imprecise. The first three chapters, therefore, provided conceptual and statistical definitions of the two types of nationalization, static and dynamic, in order to facilitate a broad comparative context. Chapter 1 provided the definitions. Static nationalization (SN) looks at the distribution of a party's support at any given time, and a party with high SN would have similar levels of support throughout a country. An election for a party is dynamically nationalized when a party's change in support is consistent throughout a country. The alternative, where support goes up in some areas and down in others, would be a party where local factors are more important. For this reason, low dynamic nationalization (DN) implies a high "local vote." Chapter 1 concluded by describing the book's empirical database, which is based on district-level electoral data. The dataset has broad geographic coverage, covering about 200 parties in 40 countries from Europe, Asia, the Pacific Basin, Africa, and the Americas.

Chapter 2 used the definitions to generate a typology of parties. DN and SN can combine to create three types: 1) *Nationalized* parties have homogeneous support across districts and local forces have limited impact on elections; 2)

Locally focused parties have heterogeneous support levels among the districts
and changes over time among the districts are also inconsistent. There are
several subtypes of locally focused parties; they can have a regional base, they
can compete nationally with variable outcomes, or a "pillarized" party can
compete in a limited set of districts that are not regionally concentrated; and 3)
Unbalanced parties have heterogeneous support across districts but because
national rather than local politics drive the changes in these parties' support,
across districts these parties have a similar electoral experience. The final
combination, where a party has homogenous support around the nation but
local factors drive inter-election changes would be 4) *unstable*.

Chapter 3 developed a statistical method for estimating the two dimensions
of party nationalization simultaneously. While I discussed other approaches, I
proposed a simple hierarchical model as the best available. Among other
problems, this method resolves the inherent bias within techniques that focus
on just one dimension. The technique also yields a precise measurement of the
"local vote." Measures of related concepts (such as the "personal vote"), by
contrast, are either unusable for comparative purposes or presume behavior by
examining *incentives* within electoral laws rather than actually measuring
behavior by examining patterns in electoral data. The chapter also discussed
weighting systems, based on the size of parties and other factors. Finally, the
chapter considered a number of issues that affect data analysis, especially the
issue of uncontested races.

Armed with the definitions and a statistical model for measuring the
concepts, Chapter 4 applied the statistical models and large database to
measure and categorize the parties into the typology developed in Chapter 2.
The empirical analysis showed wide variation in when and where politics
revolves around local rather than national affairs. The chapter shows that
politics are clearly more local in India, Japan, and much of South America
than in Germany, Austria, and much of Central America. Localism also drives
party politics in Canada, Spain, the United States, and the United Kingdom, but
elections there have a national element too. For these countries, the rise and fall
of support for at least some of the parties is consistent across the nation, even if
the parties have varied patterns of base-level support. Parties in these four
counties differ on a further dimension, however, in that those differences in
support are concentrated in regions for the first two countries, while it is
"pillarized" (and partially regionalized) for the latter.

In developing the descriptions of several exemplary parties and comparisons,
the chapter explores several substantive and methodological issues. As such, it
considers the face-validity of the statistical findings, intra-country variance, the
impact of changing the levels of analysis, and how to handle non-competitive
districts. The intra-country variance is of particular interest because it determines
when and whether analyses should focus on parties rather than the party system.
Through the analysis, the chapter noted difficulties in working with district level
electoral data but discussed means for tackling some of those challenges.

The second part of the book turned to explaining this variation. Chapters 5 and 6 built and tested explanatory models that grew from the idea that since the dimensions of nationalization are unrelated theoretically and (almost) unrelated empirically, they must reflect different causal models. Each hypothesis focused on a different institutional variable. In particular, while I expected the regime type (presidentialism versus parliamentarism) – but not the electoral system – to drive DN, the reverse should be true for SN, where the electoral system – but not regime type – should take prominence in the explanation. Finding different explanatory variables for the two aspects of nationalization is a key conclusion, because most previous studies assume that the same variables explain both dimensions. This is illogical, however, since the dimensions are independent. The chapters in this part also considered federalism and decentralization, ethnic heterogeneity, and the influence of time, as well as several interactions among these variables. Unlike the executive and electoral systems, these variables have predictable effects on both nationalization dimensions.

A novel aspect of this discussion was that it while it used electoral systems as an independent variable, it focused on how the number of electoral districts affected party nationalization (or politics generally), rather than standard variables such as district magnitude or the distinction between plurality and proportional representation. There is some relation between these variables, but I showed that the number of districts is a better predictor than standard explanations.

The third part of the book then asked why nationalization matters. The three chapters in that section were motivated by the surprising inattention in the political science literature to issues of party nationalization in studies of electoral accountability. This is an important oversight, because the geography of party support drives the extent to which voters use retrospective evaluations of national circumstances rather than their regional or ethnic identity when judging incumbents. Local politics also affects voters' prospective choices; as I show in several countries, even if voters can agree to throw out the bums, a heightened role of local politics undermines the voters' ability to coordinate on alternatives.

The first of the three chapters in that part was concerned with the relation of nationalization concepts to the responsible party model. Where static and/or dynamic nationalization is low, local politics or regional identities must play a role in explaining voting patterns. Voting based on identities rather than retrospective judgments of the accomplishments of the incumbent challenges the notion of accountability. In developing this discussion, the chapter took care to consider the different voting patterns that can generate low SN scores, thus discussing the differences between pillarized and regional (or state) parties. It also explains how to include states or regions into the statistical analysis.

Chapter 8 focused on the relation of party nationalization and retrospective evaluations of the national economy. The chapter used case studies to assess the degree to which voters entrust regional parties with economic management. More specifically, it asked how party nationalization and, in this case, the party system, condition voters' responses to economic change. High DN implies that voters act collectively. But in systems with low DN, accountability for national conditions is not straightforward. These points are almost definitional, but my case studies suggest two new twists: DN increases in bad times, but only for incumbent parties. The result is collective action among voters on retrospective voting, but a local focus for prospective voting. To pursue this line of thought, I focused on several countries where the incumbent party suffered dramatic drops in support: Spain, Argentina, and Canada. I also looked at Bolivia, where in 2009 the incumbent party experienced a significant national gain in spite of the traditional regionalism that divides the country's voters.

The last chapter in Part III continued the exploration of the effects of nationalization, but took a different tack in using individual legislators as the level of analysis rather than parties. This chapter returned to the basic concern about whether electoral ties – as defined by party nationalization – drive collective action among co-partisan legislators. To explore this concern, the chapter went beyond an exploration of overall levels of party action or unity to include an analysis of which individual legislators are prone to dissent. Are the legislators whose electoral fates are most closely tied to national trends also the most likely to cooperate with their partisan colleagues? Stated in reverse, are those legislators whose electoral fortunes are least attuned with those of other co-partisans the most likely to dissent?

To address these questions, the chapter considered two dependent variables: party discipline on roll call votes and co-sponsorship among pairs of legislators. The first part of the chapter analyzed several Latin American countries, and the second part of the chapter focused on the United States, which allowed a careful consideration of the hypothesis developed by Cox and McCubbins in their *Legislative Leviathan* (1993). The data showed that if the electoral fates of legislators from different districts are tied, they do co-sponsor legislation. But if local politics are predominant, they are less likely to build cross-district partnerships.

In sum, the book has emphasized the importance of party nationalization to understanding how democracy works – but understanding the concept requires care in terms of definitions and measurement.

GENERAL LESSONS

Beyond the specific hypotheses about the causes of and consequences for party nationalization, this book has revealed some general lessons, for both the particular concepts and broader issues about research and methodology. I am making final edits to this book just after the dramatic 2016 US election that will clearly be the subject of analyses for many years. Perhaps a first and overriding general lesson from this book is that the two dimensions of party nationalization can provide a framework for those analyses. DN, first, will help explore the degree to which there was a national trend that favored the Republicans in the vote or perhaps only in turnout. SN, then, will enter into the

discussion about differences among states and districts. This part of the analysis
will elucidate why the Democrats lost the presidency in spite in spite of winning
a majority of votes. The distribution of the congressional vote explains why the
Republicans won a proportionally larger share of seats (55.4) than votes (49.1).
These concepts are also applicable to patterns of party registration.

1 NATIONALIZATION SHOULD BE INCORPORATED AS A DESCRIPTIVE CATEGORY FOR POLITICAL PARTIES

This study has been dedicated to the idea that nationalization is a central party
trait. Traditional literature of parties and party systems, however, generally ignores
this characteristic, instead focusing on the number of parties, ideological diversity,
and perhaps coalitions. If the goal is to place parties into categories to facilitate
comparative analysis, analysts should not continue to ignore the geography of a
party's support, which is captured by nationalization. Multiparty systems in which
the parties all compete well across the whole country, for example, operate in very
different manners from those where some or all parties have a stronger regional
footing. Nationalization would also aid analysis of party or party-system change,
defining whether growth is consistent or regionally concentrated.

2 PARTY NATIONALIZATION HAS TWO DIMENSIONS

The most central focus of this book has been that party nationalization, which is
tied to the idea of local politics, has two dimensions: static and dynamic. Most
studies of party or party system nationalization (on this, see point 6 below) focus
only on what I have termed static nationalization. Studies using that concept have
contributed interesting theoretical findings, such as Caramani's suggesting that
[static] nationalization is an aspect of nation building, as countries overcome
regional divisions. But most studies have ignored the dynamic dimension, which
is perhaps more telling as an indicator of the degree to which regions are unified.
It is possible, as Katz (1973a) argued, that consistent movements of a party's
support across regions is the result of varying strategies, but such consistency is
most likely the result of a nationalized electorate. And when movements are
inconsistent, there is no doubt that local factors are central to the election.

The importance of localism to explaining politics has never been lost to
politicians or analysts. Distinct sets of literature have focused on regional
politics and candidate–party relationships. The former is interested in rural–
urban divides, separatist movements, and the ability of parties to transcend
regional or ethnic divides to attract voters across a country. The latter asks
whether legislators are bound by party dictates and how those ties affect party
discipline and the legislators' focus on local-level constituency interests. These
two literatures have a natural affinity, as they both speak to the degree to which
localism defines politics. A central goal of this book has been to explore the two
aspects of localism through the two dimensions of party nationalization.

Together, the two aspects of party nationalization qua localism provide a powerful lens on politics and elections. They can clarify the meaning of political tides, and more clearly define how regional electorates respond to national stimuli. For example, implications for how voters shift their support in the wake of an economic crisis would be different in areas where the incumbent already had limited support than for areas where the incumbent was strong. Each type of area could empower similar or distinct parts of the opposition, but where the incumbent was already weak the shift in support might not mean as much in terms of turnover. Further, economic crises facing countries fitting this example – where an incumbent's SN is low but DN is high – would be analytically distinct from others where the incumbent has more consistent regional support (higher SN) or the vote change is more uneven (higher DN). In short, the two dimensions provide a useful framework from which to analyze elections.

3 PARTY NATIONALIZATION PROVIDES A FRAMEWORK FOR ANALYZING ELECTIONS

Because nationalization is a defining party trait, it also frames elections. Election outcomes can be the result of national trends, but where localism is a prominent party or system trait, analyses should go beyond the national level in explaining the vote. There are questions, in short, not only about the degree of shifts in the vote, but in where it changed. Are all regions equally responsive to economic indicators such as inflation and unemployment rates? Do sociodemographic factors yield the same partisan ties in all parts of a country? Variance across the country in terms of a party's support and/or consistency in the change in those support levels – that is, a low level of one or the other dimension of party nationalization – thus contextualize models that seek to explain voting patterns. More specifically, establishing that a country's parties have high DN is a prerequisite for studying national voting tendencies. SN should also play a role in such studies, because the degree to which the level of the vote is consistent nationally also speaks to issues of voter allegiances or the representative process.

Overall, party nationalization provides a useful framework for analyzing electoral outcomes. The static dimension, first, provides a baseline of support for the parties across the country, which impacts their potential for change and perhaps gives a vantage point from which to understand the factors that influence their support. The dynamic dimension, then, could provide a means for analyzing trends in the vote, with an emphasis on whether parties are changing nationally or only in particular locales.

4 MEASUREMENT SYSTEMS MATTER

In support of the goal of studying party nationalization comparatively, this book has proposed a particular methodology. There are other tools for measuring one or the other dimension of the concept, but most face significant limitations. The principal tool that I have used throughout this book, which is based on a simple hierarchical (or components of variance) model, has multiple and significant advantages over other systems.

- The model measures the two dimensions of party nationalization simultaneously and thus provides statistically valid estimates of the variation in party support across time and space. That improves on models that measure one dimension of party nationalization at a time, which face an inherent bias, at least when electoral data provides the bases for operationalization.
- This measure is applicable to all countries where there are at least two electoral districts. The only important limitation is redistricting. Most other indicators, especially of the concept related to DN, limit comparisons by relying on country-specific factors in their operationalization. Surveys about legislators' behavior or voter knowledge, for example, are unavailable across time, and are non-existent for most countries. One study proposes a measure based on the differences in the vote for a national and regional office (Brady et al. 2000), but it is only applicable to the handful of countries that use midterm elections.
- It provides a direct *indicator* of voters' behavior for questions related to the personal vote. This facilitates studies of that phenomenon that too often rely on a rank ordering of electoral systems as an indicator of the *incentives* for candidates when the interest is in measuring the actual behavior.
- The model is simple to use, and the interpretation is intuitive. While the math behind the calculations have some complexity, standard statistical packages produce results from a short command.
- The values produced by the model have a statistically valid interpretation; most clearly, the SN is similar to the standard deviation of support across districts.
- The model produces wide variance among the empirical cases, thus facilitating statistical testing for the causes of difference. Models relying on variants of the Gini coefficient to measure SN show remarkably small differences among cases, even where the vote is highly skewed.
- The model is flexible in several ways, allowing for fanning patterns, further levels of variance (e.g. states), or different weighting schemes.

Of course, the proposed components of variance or hierarchical model cannot resolve all concerns with operationalization. It cannot differentiate checkerboard patterns of voting from those where a party's support is concentrated regionally. It has an implicit weighting of outliers that could be altered. Further, as discussed in some detail, neither this nor other methods – regardless of whether they include a weighting scheme – handle small parties in a manner that provides reasonable comparisons. Other methodologies face similar challenges, suggesting the need for researchers to tailor the methodologies to their research questions rather than applying the same method regardless of the question.

The choice of measures is crucial, however, since as emphasized in Chapter 3, different measures of party nationalization yield strikingly different results. The differences among the measures is strong enough to change the rankings among parties and where some measures find limited differences among parties, others measures find quite disparate results. The disparate results in the measurement techniques is the result of theoretical decisions. Theoreticians have generally done a good job in substantiating their methods, but many of the theoretical tradeoffs, such as how to weight outliers, become hidden in the math. To further advance the study of nationalization, researchers will continue to demand easily accessible methods, but expediency should not overwhelm theoretical rigor.

Another problem that my proposed methodology fails to resolve is how to translate party-level scores to a system-level value. That is the subject of the lesson 6.

5 FAILURE TO CONSIDER THE TWO DIMENSIONS WILL GENERATE MISLEADING INFERENCES

The preceding points add up to a fifth lesson: considering party nationalization as a single dimension, and/or measuring it without proper tools, will generate incorrect or misleading characterizations of the cases as well as impressions about causes and consequences of the concepts. In Chapter 1 I displayed graphs for three parties to highlight the different combinations of high and low levels of static and dynamic nationalization. The Japanese LDP scores highly on both dimensions, the Socialists in Portugal have a high dynamic score but are low with respect to static nationalization, and the Chilean Concertación are low on both measures. Comparing the Democrats and Republicans in the USA and the Liberals and Conservatives in the United Kingdom yields another contrast; all these parties are low in terms of SN, but those in the United Kingdom have higher DN. Further, the US parties have increased in DN since the 1970s, but the SN has remained stable during that period. And, while DN differentiates US presidential and congressional elections, with the former showing a much stronger national component, the SN indicates these two types of elections have similarly high levels of localism when considering the spread of the vote. These changes and contrasts would be lost if the analysis focused solely on one dimension. If the analysis looked solely at SN, as is common in many studies, then the parties in the United States, the United Kingdom, Portugal, and Chile would all look similar. In turn, the consistency in the change in support that links cases such as Portugal's Socialists and Japan's LDP would be lost.

Characterizing a party's level of nationalization based on only one dimension would necessarily lead to incorrect analyses about causes and consequences. Most clearly, because the dimensions are (mostly) independent, there must be different factors that explain each dimension and different impacts of the two dimensions on politics. This does not mean that some forces, such as foreign wars or universal access to education or particular institutions (e.g. federalism) cannot impact both dimensions. But ignoring the separable impacts misses important aspects of the analysis and could miss important relationships among variables. Relating the executive system to SN or the electoral system to DN, for example, could produce null results. It would be wrong to conclude, however, that these two key institutions are unimportant to nationalization, because the electoral system does drive SN and the executive system has a strong impact on DN.

6 NATIONALIZATION IS A PARTY, NOT ONLY A SYSTEM CONCEPT

While a motivating factor in studying parties is to understand systems of which they are a part, this book has explicitly focused on party nationalization rather than party-system nationalization. A party is a team of people who run candidates for political office. A party "system" is more than the sum of these individual parts; its definition includes the number of parties, but it also considers the interactions among them. Similarly, while party nationalization characterizes the political geography of a particular party, party-system nationalization implies the totality of the interactions in terms of political geography. An average (even if weighted) would ignore the interactions, which could be in different flavors. Overall, the problem is that nationalized parties can appear in systems that are not nationalized, and thus the average of the party-level scores would be a poor indicator of how parties operate. Spain or Canada provide good examples; in each of these countries some parties compete nationally (yielding high SN), but there are also parties that compete only in proscribed regions (thus having low SN). A weighted average of the scores, then, would yield a moderately nationalized system – but that would be very different from systems where all parties have moderate nationalization.

Dynamic nationalization is also a party-level concept. As I showed in Chapter 8, the fall of the incumbent party, for example, does not foretell which party or parties will rise. As I explained for the case of Spain, although the PSOE fell in a dynamically nationalized pattern, the prospective choices were not nationalized. It would be misleading, then, to summarize system-level nationalization as either high, low, or middling.

These measurement issues yield a deterrent to a comprehensive study of party systems, but they should not preclude such an analysis. When studies use only one value to summarize a system, it is analogous to describing a group of numbers with an average but no standard deviation. System-level analyses of the party system, similarly, should account for the diversity of parties within a given system.

7 NATIONALIZATION CONTEXTUALIZES DEMOCRACY, BUT THERE IS NOT A LINEAR RELATION OF NATIONALIZATION AND THE STABILITY OR QUALITY OF DEMOCRACY

The goal of this book has not been to attempt to test a model of democracy which might pretend that a particular level of nationalization – on either dimension – will generate higher-quality or more stable democracy. Analogous to the balance democracies must strike between representation and efficiency, different societies use – but also find tension in – the levels of dynamic and static nationalization.

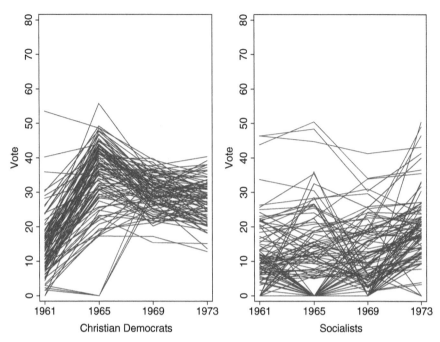

FIGURE 10.1 Party Nationalization in Chile 1961–73

The variety of combinations shown in the empirical examples in this book then confirm that democracy is sustainable under varying degrees of localism. This is not to say that all forms of representation are equally propitious for democracy, at least in all circumstances. Consociational theory implies acceptance of low SN because it supports differential representation of regional groups. Horowitz (1985) and Caramani (2005), alternatively, propose the importance of cross-cutting cleavages, which would suggest higher levels of party nationalization. This book is not set up to resolve these theoretical questions, as it does not include a long enough timeline (as Caramani does) or cases where democracy is not the only game in town. Still, the methodology would allow such tests, at least in the epoch where authoritarians have included elections. An interesting thesis about the downfall of democracy in Chile in the early 1970s is that constitutional changes led to more fights over national policy instead of localized pork. Did this lead to more nationalized elections? Preliminary analysis does not suggest that it did. The Socialist president, Salvador Allende, won the 1970 election (with just over one-third of the vote) and his coalition won about 44 percent of the vote in the congressional election of 1973. His own Socialist party was still relatively small, winning about 18 percent that year. Even that vote, however, does not look particularly nationalized, on either dimension, as shown in Figure 10.1. The vote for the main opposition party, the Christian Democrats, shows more party nationalization as compared to the Socialists, but there is not a marked change from the previous election.

In sum, it may be that democracy is feasible with or even well served under a wide range of party nationalization schemes. Extreme values clearly challenge representation, but perhaps the level of party nationalization indicates the need for different mechanisms of democratic management. Countries such as Canada and Belgium can attest to the difficulties facing democracies with low levels of party nationalization, but they also indicate the potential for successful democratic management.

CONCLUSION

In a *New York Times* editorial (Edsall 2015) titled "What if all politics is national?" Thomas Edsall reflects on recent political science research and largely bemoans the loss of localism in US politics. Most concerning is the strong correlation between polarization among the parties and the move toward more nationalized elections. Earlier literature on party nationalization, as identified by Schattschneider or popularized by Tip O'Neil, highlighted the opposite concern: that politics was too local. As such, these authors were worried about wasteful localized spending and the inability of disparate politicians to generate coherent policy. The purpose of this book has been to bring these debates to the comparative field. Where are politics local? Why are they more local in some places (or at some times) than others? How can we measure that localism? What are some of the effects of that localism?

I have offered more specific answers to some of these questions than others, and have clearly left much work for the future. The methodological tools have allowed precise measurements of different aspects of localism, and as such they have facilitated categorization of parties. Neither the tools nor the categories, however, are without flaws. They cannot, for example, differentiate pillarized from regional parties or resolve the debates about how to weight different observations. In the realm of explanation, I have focused on institutions, showing that the number of electoral districts, other aspects of the electoral system, and federalism correlate with one or the other dimensions of party nationalization. Institutional explanations, however, are largely unable to explain variation among a country's parties, or why nationalization levels change over time. Finally, I have developed ideas about the relation of party nationalization and accountability, shown the relevance of nationalization to retrospective voting and how it can change in response to national events, and tested how SN and DN affect legislators' interest in working with their co-partisans. But because party nationalization qua localism is central to politics, future work will have much to explore in terms of these issues plus coalition formation, polarization, campaign strategies, inter-governmental relations, and parties' orientation toward nationalism.

Appendices

Other supplementary materials, including databases of district-level electoral data, additional (and color-coded) graphs, and notes about cases, are available at www.polisci.pitt.edu/person/scott-morgenstern.

APPENDIX I

Party-Level Graphs

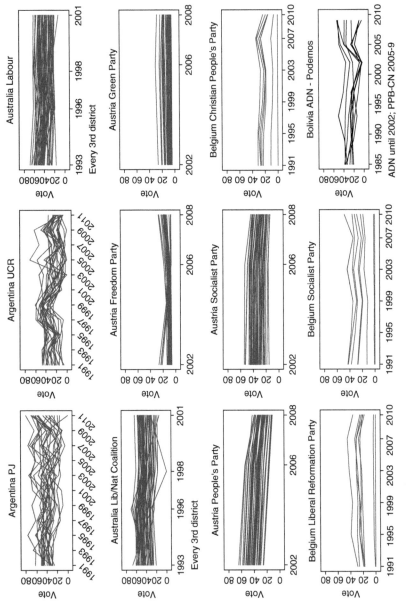

FIGURE A1.1 Party-Level Graphs

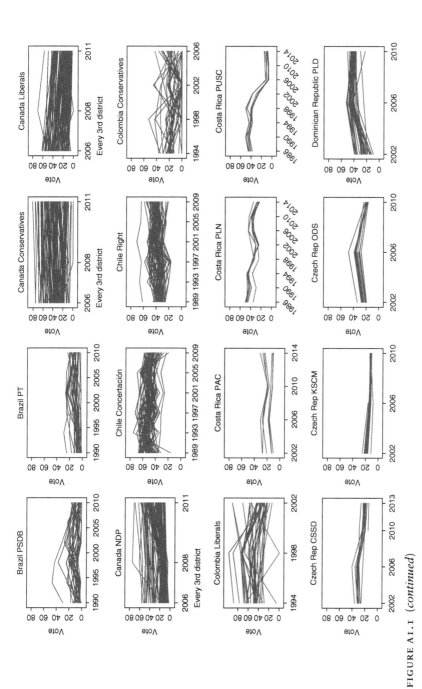

FIGURE A1.1 (*continued*)

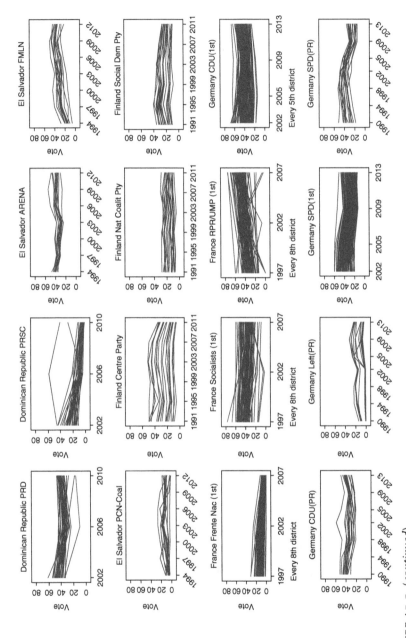

FIGURE A1.1 *(continued)*

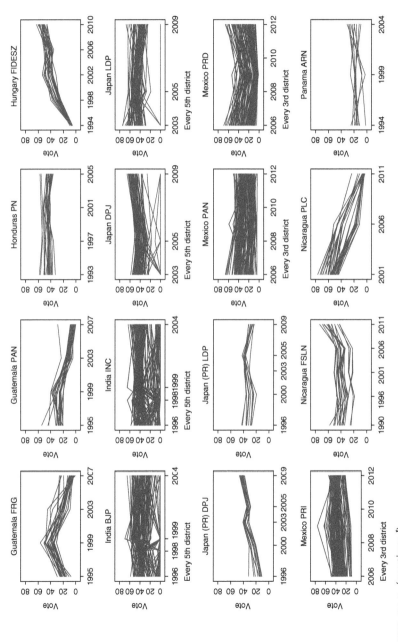

FIGURE A1.1 (*continued*)

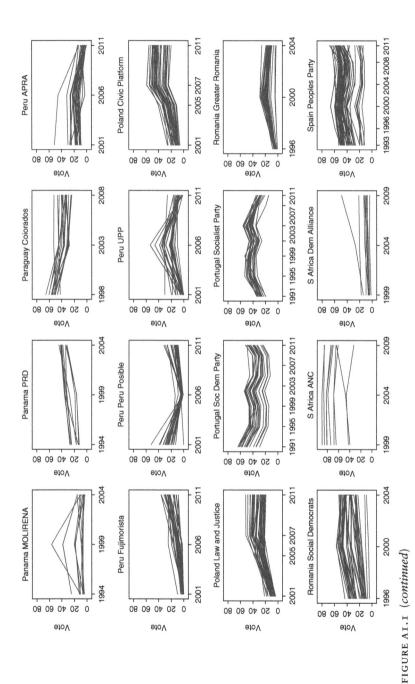

FIGURE A1.1 (*continued*)

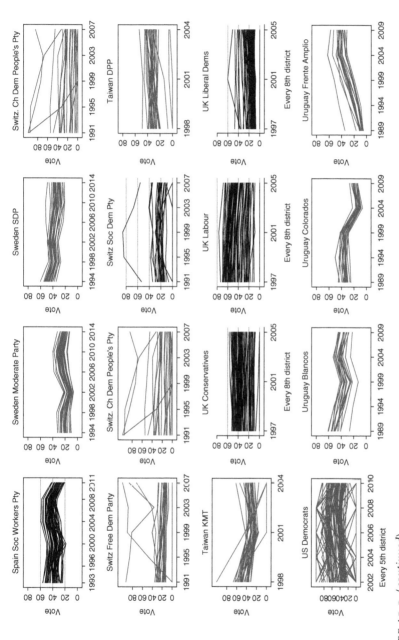

FIGURE A1.1 (*continued*)

APPENDIX 2

Parties Analyzed and Variables in Regression Analysis

TABLE A2.1 *Parties Analyzed and Variables in Regression Analysis*

Country	Party	Yrs in Analysis	Restricted Model	Static	Dynamic	Pres	Semi-pres	# Dists	Fed	Ethnic seg	In Cabinet?	Party Age	Size	Extreme	Pers. Vote
Argentina	PJ	2003–07	R	0.0	0.0	1	0	24	1	0.01	1	4.0	39.9	2.4	0.05
Argentina	UCR	2003–07	R	25.1	0.0	1	0	24	1	0.01	0	4.7	21.3	0.0	0.05
Australia	Coalition	1993–98	R	0.0	83.1	0	0	147	1	0.07	1	4.3	43.6	2.8	0.10
Australia	Labour	1993–98	U	0.0	95.8	0	0	147	1	0.07	1	4.5	41.3	0.3	0.10
Austria	FPO	2002–08	U	85.3	97.1	0	0	43	1	0.05	0	3.8	12.7	3.6	0.28
Austria	Green	2002–08	U	72.5	99.6	0	0	43	1	0.05	0	2.2	10.5	2.1	0.28
Austria	OVP	2002–08	U	0.0	98.0	0	0	43	1	0.05	1	4.0	34.3	1.3	0.28
Austria	SPO	2002–08	U	14.6	99.3	0	0	43	1	0.05	1	4.7	32.9	0.3	0.28
Belgium*	CD&V	2003–10	R	0.0	90.5	0	0	11	1	0.20	1	0.7	11.1	1.0	0.50
Belgium*	MR	2003–10	U	0.0	96.2	0	0	11	1	0.20	0	0.0	15.7	2.3	0.50
Belgium*	PS	2003–10	R	0.0	94.7	0	0	11	1	0.20	1	3.2	15.7	1.0	0.50
Bolivia	ADN	1993–02	R	15.6	82.4	1	0	9	1	0.09	1	2.6	21.6	3.6	0.05
Bolivia	MAS	2002–09	R	0.0	54.1	1	0	9	1	0.09	1	1.9	35.8	.	0.05
Bolivia	MNR	1997–05	R	45.1	85.1	1	0	9	1	0.09	1	4.0	20.0	3.3	0.05
Brazil	DEM(PFL)	2002–10	U	0.0	80.3	1	0	27	1	0.05	0	2.8	11.1	1.4	0.78
Brazil	PMDB	2002–10	R	72.3	75.2	1	0	27	1	0.05	0	3.0	15.8	0.3	0.78
Brazil	PSDB	2002–10	U	31.2	88.2	1	0	27	1	0.05	0	2.6	10.5	1.0	0.78
Brazil	PT	2002–10	U	55.5	94.2	1	0	27	1	0.05	1	3.1	13.6	2.8	0.78
Canada*	Conserv.	2006–11	U	0.0	88.7	0	0	305	1	0.12	1	1.1	39.1	2.3	0.10

TABLE A2.1 (*continued*)

Country	Party	Yrs in Analysis	Restricted Model	Static	Dynamic	Pres	Semi-pres	# Dists	Fed	Ethnic seg	In Cabinet?	Party Age	Size	Extreme	Pers. Vote
Canada*	Liberal	2006–11	U	0.0	83.0	0	0	299	1	0.12	0	4.9	29.2	0.1	0.10
Canada*	NDP	2006–11	U	17.9	48.9	0	0	307	1	0.12	0	3.8	25.6	2.1	0.10
Chile	Concertac	2001–09	R	79.2	57.7	1	0	60	0	0.02	1	2.6	50.4	0.9	0.47
Chile	Right*	2001–09	U	54.2	89.5	1	0	60	0	0.02	1	2.6	38.6	2.8	0.47
Colombia	Conserv.	1994–02	R	67.0	0.0	1	0	33	1	0.28	1	5.0	13.1	3.2	0.38
Colombia	Liberal	1994–02	R	10.7	0.0	1	0	33	1	0.28	1	5.0	48.3	1.2	0.38
Costa Rica	PAC	2006–14	R	72.7	93.3	1	0	7	0	0.04	1	1.8	20.0	1.0	0.05
Costa Rica	PLN	2006–14	R	90.2	97.0	1	0	7	0	0.04	1	4.0	34.4	3.3	0.05
Costa Rica	PUSC	2006–14	R	94.6	99.3	1	0	7	0	0.04	0	3.4	9.8	2.3	0.05
Czech Rep.	CSSD	2002–10	R	91.6	98.5	0	0	14	0	0.01	1	4.8	28.2	2.2	0.11
Czech Rep.	KSCM.	2002–10	U	91.3	99.8	0	0	14	0	0.01	0	2.6	14.5	3.7	0.11
Czech Rep.	ODS	2002–10	U	80.8	97.4	0	0	14	0	0.01	1	2.4	26.3	2.3	0.11
Domin Rep.	PLD	2002–10	U	55.4	79.3	1	0	32	0	0.01	1	3.7	36.5	0.1	0.06
Domin Rep.	PRD	2002–10	R	81.6	74.9	1	0	32	0	0.01	1	4.1	38.7	1.9	0.06
Domin Rep.	PRSC	2002–10	R	60.8	60.3	1	0	32	0	0.01	0	3.7	14.9	3.2	0.06
El Salvador	ARENA	2006–12	R	76.8	94.9	1	0	14	0	0.22	1	3.2	38.9	4.1	0.06
El Salvador	FMLN	2006–12	U	60.7	97.8	1	0	14	0	0.22	0	3.3	36.9	3.8	0.06
El Salvador	PCN-CN	2006–12	U	68.7	95.1	1	0	14	0	0.22	0	3.8	11.7	2.1	0.06
Finland	Kesk	2003–11	U	0.0	99.0	0	1	14	0	0.06	0	2.6	25.1	1.5	0.77
Finland	Kok	2003–11	R	67.9	98.1	0	1	14	0	0.06	1	4.4	18.4	2.4	0.77
Finland	SDP	2003–11	U	54.5	98.9	0	1	14	0	0.06	0	2.6	22.6	1.5	0.77

Country	Party	Years	Type												
France*	FN	1997–07	U	0	64.8	97.5	0	571	0	0.02	0	3.2	10.2	5.0	0.20
France*	PS	1997–07	U	1	5.7	75.1	0	575	0	0.02	1	3.3	37.8	0.9	0.20
France*	RPR/UMP	1997–07	U	1	51.0	56.1	0	577	0	0.02	1	3.7	40.5	2.3	0.20
Germany PR	CDU/CSU	2005–13	U	0	56.9	97.5	0	16	1	0.00	1	4.1	33.8	1.9	0.03
Germany	CDU/CSU (1st)	2005–13	U	0	10.2	96.0	0	243	1	0.00	1	4.1	42.0	1.9	0.10
Germany PR	Linke	2005–13	U	0	16.7	94.8	0	16	1	0.00	0	0	14.3	3.5	0.03
Germany PR	SPD	2005–13	U	0	80.3	96.1	0	16	1	0.00	1	4.9	27.5	1.2	0.03
Germany	SPD (1st)	2005–13	U	0	20.9	97.0	0	243	1	0.00	1	4.9	33.2	1.9	0.10
Guatemala	FRG	1999–07	R	1	92.5	51.8	1	23	0	0.50	0	2.3	24.8	3.7	0.06
Guatemala	PAN	1999–07	R	1	92.3	81.1	1	23	0	0.50	1	2.3	15.5	3.2	0.06
Honduras	PN	1997–05	R	1	82.3	92.8	1	18	0	0.22	1	4.6	45.1	.	0.05
Hungary PR	FIDESZ	2002–10	R	0	87.1	88.0	0	20	1	0.07	1	2.6	46.7	0.0	0.05
India*	BJP	1998–04	U	0	8.7	59.5	0	384	1	0.19	1	2.9	39.1	3.2	0.10
India*	Ind. Nat. Cong	1998–04	U	0	1.0	32.1	0	437	1	0.19	1	4.7	27.0	0.8	0.10
Japan PR	DPJ	2003–09	R	0	97.2	95.9	0	11	1	0.03	1	1.6	37.2	0.3	0.03
Japan PR	LDP	2003–09	R	0	96.4	94.7	0	11	1	0.03	1	3.9	35.5	3.4	0.03
Japan SMD*	DPJ	2003–09	U	0	17.5	78.7	0	300	0	0.03	0	4.4	43.2	2.9	0.10
Japan SMD*	LDP	2003–09	U	0	33.0	51.5	0	293	0	0.03	1	3.9	46.0	3.4	0.10
Mexico	PAN	2006–12	U	1	0.0	69.5	1	300	1	0.16	1	4.2	29.8	2.0	0.10
Mexico	PRD	2006–12	U	1	0.0	62.6	1	300	1	0.16	0	2.8	24.0	1.7	0.10
Mexico	PRI	2006–12	U	1	26.3	51.0	1	300	1	0.16	1	4.1	35.6	1.2	0.10
Nicaragua	FSLN	2001–11	R	1	46.9	85.2	1	17	0	0.12	1	3.7	45.1	.	0.06

TABLE A2.1 (*continued*)

Country	Party	Yrs in Analysis	Restricted Model	Static	Dynamic	Pres	Semi-pres	# Dists	Fed	Ethnic seg	In Cabinet?	Party Age	Size	Extreme	Pers. Vote
Nicaragua	PLC	2001–11	R	56.3	52.9	1	0	17	0	0.12	1	3.5	30.5	.	0.06
Panama	ARN/PP	1994–04	R	100.0	59.0	1	0	10	0	0.19	1	4.1	17.3	1.0	0.60
Panama	MOLIRENA	1994–04	U	64.1	29.0	1	0	10	0	0.19	0	2.5	12.6	2.9	0.60
Panama	PRD	1994–04	R	78.3	86.5	1	0	10	0	0.19	1	2.7	28.7	0.5	0.60
Paraguay	Colorados	1998–08	R	74.2	80.7	1	0	18	0	0.02	1	4.7	42.2	.	0.07
Peru	APRA	2001–11	U	24.9	82.0	1	0	25	1	0.02	1	4.3	14.1	.	0.66
Peru	Fujimorista	2001–11	U	99.8	85.1	1	0	25	1	0.02	0	2.2	11.3	.	0.66
Peru	Peru Posible	2001–11	U	62.5	70.0	1	0	25	1	0.02	1	1.9	15.1	.	0.66
Peru	UPP	2001–11	R	96.6	42.2	1	0	25	1	0.02	0	1.9	14.1	.	0.66
Poland	Civic Plat	2005–11	U	51.2	87.1	0	1	41	0	.	.	2.2	33.7	.	0.74
Poland	Law & Justice	2005–11	U	76.1	93.0	0	1	41	0	.	.	2.2	29.6	.	0.74
Portugal	PPD/PSD	2005–11	R	30.6	97.6	0	1	20	0	0.02	1	3.4	33.6	1.4	0.04
Portugal	PS	2005–11	R	82.0	93.7	0	1	20	0	0.02	1	3.5	36.1	0.1	0.04
Romania	Greater Roma	1996–04	R	92.3	93.6	0	1	42	0	0.03	0	1.6	12.3	1.0	0.05
Romania	Social Dems.	1996–04	R	0.0	84.5	0	1	42	0	0.03	1	1.8	32.1	0.5	0.05
South Africa	African Nat.	1999–09	U	0.0	90.7	0	0	9	0	0.25	1	4.5	69.8	1.1	0.03
South Africa	Democ. Al.	1999–09	U	79.9	97.8	0	0	9	0	0.25	0	0.0	11.4	0.4	0.03
Spain	PP	2004–11	R	0.0	91.8	0	0	52	1	0.24	1	2.7	43.6	2.5	0.05
Spain	PSOE	2004–11	U	56.5	94.7	0	0	52	1	0.24	1	4.8	37.8	1.0	0.05
Sweden	Moderates	2006–14	U	67.1	99.2	0	0	29	0	0.00	1	4.6	24.6	3.3	0.16
Sweden	Social Democ.	2006–14	R	60.2	98.5	0	0	29	0	0.00	1	4.8	34.5	0.9	0.16

Switzerland	CVP	1999–07	R	0.0	81.5	0	1	26	1	0.09	1	4.5	21.5	0.6	0.50
Switzerland	FPD	1999–07	R	0.0	48.9	0	1	26	1	0.09	1	4.7	21.6	1.0	0.50
Switzerland	SP	1999–07	U	0.0	94.6	0	1	26	1	0.09	1	4.7	21.1	2.4	0.50
Switzerland	SVP	1999–07	R	10.7	31.4	0	1	26	1	0.09	1	3.3	16.7	1.3	0.50
Taiwan*	DPP	1998–04	R	69.6	82.2	0	1	27	1	0.04	1	2.5	33.0	0.4	0.80
Taiwan*	KMT	1998–04	R	58.9	22.1	0	1	29	1	0.04	1	4.4	37.7	0.9	0.80
UK*	Conservatives	1997–05	U	0.0	96.3	0	0	559	0	0.17	0	4.5	33.6	2.7	0.10
UK*	Labour	1997–05	U	0.0	94.0	0	0	565	0	0.17	1	5.1	43.1	0.6	0.10
UK*	Lib. Demo	1997–05	U	0.0	93.8	0	0	558	0	0.17	0	4.6	20.8	0.2	0.10
US*	Dems	2006–10	U	0.0	80.5	1	0	429	1	0.07	1	5.2	51.7	0.9	0.60
Uruguay	Blancos	1999–09	R	58.5	95.2	1	0	19	1	0.01	0	5.1	37.3	2.2	0.74
Uruguay	Colorados	1999–09	R	89.0	97.0	1	0	19	1	0.01	1	5.1	22.5	1.8	0.74
Uruguay	Frente Amp	1999–09	R	33.3	96.5	1	0	19	1	0.01	1	3.3	37.5	2.2	0.74

*excludes districts where parties did not compete.

Variable names: Static and dynamic nationalization; as defined in text (reversed scales, truncated at 100); Pres=Presidential dummy; Semi-pres=Semi-presidential; Fed=Federal or Decentralized; Ethnic seg=Maximum of Ethnic/linguistic/religion segregation index; Pers Vote =Personal Vote, as coded in Appendix 3. Others as defined in text and summarized in Appendix 4; See also the on-line appendix at www.polisci.pitt.edu/person/scott-morgenstern, which explains inclusion of cases. Restricted refers to Unrestricted and Restricted models, based on significant LR test.

Countries with two tiers identified by PR (proportional representation) and SMD (single member districts).

APPENDIX 3

Operationalizing the Personal Vote

Carey and Shugart (1995) define the incentives to "cultivate a personal vote" by three variables: ballot, pooling, and vote (BPV). They define the coding as follows:

Ballot

    0: Leaders present a fixed ballot, voters may not "disturb" list;
    1: Leaders present party ballots, but voters may "disturb" list;
    2: Leaders do not control access to ballots, or rank.

Pooling

    0: Pooling across whole party;
    1: Pooling at sub-party level;
    2: No pooling.

Vote

    0: Voters cast a single vote for one party;
    1: Voters cast votes for multiple candidates;
    2: Voters cast a single vote below the party level.

Using this system, a closed list system – with fewer incentives to cultivate a personal vote – would get scores 0,0,0 (for BPV, respectively) and a personal-vote motivating open list system would be a 2,0,2. They then call for interacting these scores with the district magnitude, but do not operationalize that part of the model, though Hallerberg and Marier take up that challenge (as described in Chapter 6).

    Following Hallerberg and Marier (2004) and Hallerberg (2004) I coded all countries for BPV and then interacted this with the district magnitude. I used information and coding from these papers, and updated it (e.g. for Austria and

Belgium) using information gleaned from other published papers and databases, including Golder (2005), Saiegh (2010), the Pilet and Renwick's Electoral System Change in Europe (ESCE) project, and other sources. Many of these datasets, however, have significant errors. There are also theoretical problems for the coding. For example, several European countries have open lists, but voters do not frequently use the opportunity to indicate the individual candidates that they prefer, perhaps because a large number of personal votes is necessary to alter the lists as given by the party. I therefore followed Carey and Shugart (1995) and coded the BPV for Finland as 2,0,2 but Netherlands as 1,0,2.[1] Two-level systems create other problems. I coded them as having two levels only if voters had two votes (as in Germany). Votes are distributed for two levels in Mexico and Sweden, but because the voters only vote once, I coded the level at which the voters are distributed into smaller units.

My coding for the different countries is in Table A3.1. The table includes columns to define ballot, pool, and vote; then a column that calculates using the Hallerberg method; and finally a column where I revised the model for several cases (as described in Chapter 6: "Alternative Variables and Further Bi- and Tri-Variate Tests on Executive and Electoral Systems"). Among the differences are those for Austria and Belgium. Hallerberg coded these two countries as 0,0,0, though he acknowledges that Austria had changed. Now (since 1995) Belgium has changed, too. It has increased the importance of personal votes, and ESCE calls it a semi-open list, because while parties' list ordering has importance, personal votes take precedence if they reach a threshold. This was also true in the old system, but the threshold was very high. Hallerberg gives Switzerland a 0,0,0, but based on ESCE, I prefer 1,0,1. The ESCE states: "Parties are allowed to present several lists within the same district, and then to link them through an apparentement for a common counting of their votes during the process of allocation of seats." Another difference is with Bolivia; Hallerberg and Marier list 12.5 for the average magnitude, but it has 62 plurinominal seats distributed in 9 districts, yielding an average of 6.8.[2]

France is also problematic. Hallerberg scores it as 0,0,1, but 0,0,0 is also justifiable given the single member districts. Also, 1,0,1 is reasonable, since 2 allied parties compete and voters choose among them.

For Peru, Saiegh lists Peru as 1,0,1, while I list 2,0,2, and could accept 2,0,1. This difference is based on interpretation of access to the ballot.

My coding for Uruguay is quite different than that for Hallerberg. His coding is based on the closed list formula (which divides by the log of M), even though he codes it as a 1,0,2, which implies something closer to open list (which necessitates adding the log of M instead of dividing by it). I code the case as 1,1,2, and use the open list formula.

[1] I had to exclude the Netherlands from the analysis, however, because it has one national district.
[2] Hallerberg uses the average magnitude for the senate and the house. I focus on the house. It also seems that sometimes his models use the log and other times use the natural log in the calculations.

TABLE A3.1 *Scoring for Personal Vote Incentive Systems*

Country	Ballot	Pool	Vote	Avg M	Hallerberg method	Revised
Argentina	0	0	0	8.70	0.05	0.05
Australia	0	0	0	1.00	0.10	0.10
Austria	1	0	2	4.26	0.54	0.28
Belgium	1	0	1	7.10	0.50	0.50
Bolivia	0	0	0	6.78	0.05	0.05
Brazil	2	0	2	16.80	0.78	0.78
Canada	0	0	0	1.00	0.10	0.10
Chile	1	0	2	2.00	0.47	0.47
Colombia	2	1	2	4.91	0.76	0.38
Costa Rica	0	0	0	8.14	0.05	0.05
Czech Rep.	1	0	1	14.30	0.57	0.11
Dom Republ.	0	0	0	5.72	0.06	0.06
El Salvador	0	0	0	6.00	0.06	0.06
Finland	2	0	2	14.29	0.77	0.77
France	0	0	1	1	0.20	0.20
Germany	0	0	0	1.00	0.10	0.10
Germany PR	0	0	0	37.38	0.03	0.03
Guatemala	0	0	0	5.52	0.06	0.06
Honduras	0	0	0	7.11	0.05	0.05
Hungary PR	0	0	0	7.60	0.05	0.05
India	0	0	0	1.00	0.10	0.10
Japan PR	0	0	0	18.18	0.03	0.03
Japan	0	0	0	1	0.03	0.10
Korea	0	0	0	1.00	0.10	0.10
Mexico	0	0	0	1.00	0.10	0.10
Nicaragua	0	0	0	5.06	0.06	0.06
Panama	1	0	2	7.10	0.60	0.60
Paraguay	0	0	0	4.44	0.07	0.07
Peru	2	0	2	4.80	0.66	0.66
Poland	2	0	2	11.2	0.74	0.74
Portugal	0	0	0	11.50	0.04	0.04
Romania	0	0	0	7.81	0.05	0.05
South Africa	0	0	0	22.22	0.03	0.03
Spain	0	0	0	6.70	0.05	0.05
Sweden	1	0	2	12.00	0.65	0.16

TABLE A3.1 *(continued)*

Country	Ballot	Pool	Vote	Avg M	Hallerberg method	Revised
Switzerland	1	0	1	7.69	0.50	0.50
Taiwan	1	2	2	7.76	0.80	0.80
UK	0	0	0	1.00	0.10	0.10
US	2	2	1	1.00	0.60	0.60
Uruguay	1	1	2	11.40	0.74	0.74

For Panama, Hallerberg codes 0,0,0, but with M=1.8, the country has lots of single-member districts. There is also preference voting, so I treat the case as open list 1,0,2. Also, my data suggests M=7.1 for the PR seats, thus yielding a final score of 0.6 instead of the 0.4 that Hallerberg uses.

Colombia also avoids easy coding. I have data for the five elections between 1994 and 2010, but Colombia revised its system for the 2006 election. In order to have three consistent elections, most analyses therefore use the data from 1994 to 2002, at which time the country used a Single Non-Transferable Vote (SNTV) system, which yields the BPV coding of 2,1,2. The coding problem here is that both Hallerberg and Marier, as well as Saiegh, list M as 42, presumably because the Senate has a magnitude of 100. Using just the lower house, the value is about 5.0.

For 2006, 2010, and future elections, I would apply 1,0,2, though 1,0,1 or 1,0,0 are also defensible. Under the new system, some departments do allow open lists, but the system is much less open than in the past. Pachon and Shugart (2010) suggest the system does not promote a personal vote very much, and call it a system of "listization."

APPENDIX 4

Independent Variable Operationalization

TABLE A4.1 *Independent Variable Operationalization*

Regime type	Dummy; 1=presidential
Federalism	Dummy; 1=federal or decentralized
Number of districts	Count of number of electoral districts
Regime*number of districts	Interaction of regime and number of districts
Ethnic heterogeneity and segregation	Maximum of ethnic, religious, or language segregation, as coded by Alesina and Zhuravskaya (2011)
Federalism*segregation	Interaction of Federalism and maximum of segregration
Personal vote	Modified from Hallerberg and Marier (2004); See Appendix 3
Party age	Years since party founded to first year in regression
Ideology	Score on left–right scale
Party size	Average percent won, across districts and included years
Governing experience	Was the party in government during any year of series?

APPENDIX 5

SUR Models with One Observation/Country

TABLE A5.1 *SUR Models with One Observation/Country*

	Model 1		Model 2	
	Static/ Distributional (1)	Dynamic (2)	Static/ Distributional (3)	Dynamic (4)
Presidential	15.75	−27.19**	−10.43	−25.78**
Semi-Presidential	−34.32**	−30.04**	−30.03	−26.73**
Number of Districts	−0.07**	0.00	−0.07**	−0.00
Federal or Decentralized	−35.39**	−0.30**	−36.41**	−3.93
Max Segregation	−23.94	13.54	−20.91	11.61
Federal*Segregation	59.58	148.36*	62.64	140.70*
Extremism	−4.34	−3.62		
Governing Experience	14.37	9.30	12.46	9.87**
Ln (Party age)	−4.60	−5.14	1.93	3.07
Average Vote	−0.75	−0.55	−0.77	−0.37*
Constant	105.02**	132.80**	92.02**	114.93**
N	33	33	38	38
R² adj	0.58	0.41	0.56	0.36

** p≤.05 * p≤.1

Bibliography

Ajenjo, Natalia, and Ignacio Molina. 2011. "Spain: Majoritarian Choices, Disciplined Party Government, and Compliant Legislature." In *The Role of Governments in Legislative Agenda Setting*, eds. Bjorn Erik Rasch and George Tsebelis. Rurh University Bochum, Germany: Routledge/ECPR Studies in European Political Science.

Alemán, Eduardo, and Marisa Kellam. 2008. "The Nationalization of Electoral Change in the Americas." *Electoral Studies* 27: 193–212.

Alesina, Alberto, Arnaud Devleeschauwer, William Easterly, Sergio Kurlat, and Romain Wacziarg. 2003. "Fractionalization." *Journal of Economic Growth* 2: 155–94.

Alesina, Alberto, and Ekaterina Zhuravskaya. 2011. "Segregation and the Quality of Government in a Cross Section of Countries." *American Economic Review* 101: 1872–911.

Alford, John, and David Brady. 1988 "Partisan and Incumbent Advantages in US House Elections, 1846–1986." *Working Paper 11, Center for the Study of Institutions and Values. Rice Univ.*

Allison, Paul D. 1978. "Measures of Inequality." *American Sociological Review* 43: 865–80.

American Political Science Association, Committee on Political Parties. 1950. *Toward a More Responsible Two-Party System.* New York: Rinehart and Company, Inc.

André, Audrey, Sam Depauw, and Shane Martin. 2015. "Electoral Systems and Legislators' Constituency Effort: The Mediating Effect of Electoral Vulnerability." *Comparative Political Studies* 48: 464–96.

Bagashka, Tanya. 2012. "The Personal Vote and Economic Reform." *Electoral Studies* 31: 562–75.

Bartolini, Stefano, and Peter Mair. 1990. *Identity, Competition, and Electoral Availability: The Stabilisation of European Electorates 1885–1985.* Cambridge: Cambridge University Press.

Bax, Erik H. 1990. *Modernization and Cleavage in Dutch Society. A Study of Long Term Economic and Social Change.* Avebury: Ashgate Publishing.

Bax, Erik Hans. 1995. "Cleavage in Dutch Society: Changing Patterns of Social and Economic Discrimination." Paper presented at the Conference on Political, Economic and Social Racism, Thessaloniki, Macedonia, Greece, May 14–18.

Beck, Thorsten, George Clarke, Alberto Groff, Philip Keefer, and Patrick Walsh. 2001. "New Tools in Comparative Political Economy: The Database of Political Institutions." *WorldBank Economic Review* 15: 165–76.

Benton, Allyson L. 2005. "Dissatisfied Democrats or Retrospective Voters?" *Comparative Political Studies* 38: 417–42.

Birnir, Johanna Kristin. 2007. *Ethnicity and Electoral Politics*. Cambridge: Cambridge University Press.

2008. "Party Regulation in Central and Eastern Europe and Latin America: The Effect on Minority Representation and the Propensity for Conflict." In *Political Parties in Conflict-Prone Societies: Regulation, Engineering and Democratic Development*, ed. Benjamin Reilly and Per Nordlund. New York: United Nations University Press. 158–81.

Blais, André. 2005. "Accounting for the Electoral Success of the Liberal Party in Canada: Presidential Address to the Canadian Political Science Association." *Canadian Journal of Political Science* 38: 821–40.

Blais, André, Elisabeth Gidengil, Agnieszka Dobrzynska, Neil Nevitte, and Richard Nadeau. 2003. "Does the Local Candidate Matter? Candidate Effects in the Canadian Election of 2000." *Canadian Journal of Political Science* 36: 657–64.

Blalock, Jr., Hubert M. 1972. *Social Statistics*. Second edn. New York: McGraw-Hill Companies.

Bochsler, Daniel. 2010. "Measuring Party Nationalization: A New Gini-Based Indicator That Corrects for the Number of Units." *Electoral Studies* 29: 155–68.

Brady, David W., Robert D'Onofrio, and Morris P. Fiorina. 2000. "The Nationalization of Electoral Forces Revisited." In *Continuity and Change in House Elections.*, eds. David W. Brady, Robert D'Onofrio, and Morris P. Fiorina. Stanford: Stanford University Press. 130–48.

Brancati, Dawn. 2008. "The Origins and Strength of Regional Parties." *British Journal of Political Science* 38: 135–59.

"Brizuela Del Moral Se Diferenció De Cobos Para No 'Nacionalizar La Elección'." 2011. *INFOBAE*, 3/13.

Butler, David E., and Donald E. Stokes. 1969. *Political Change in Britain: Forces Shaping Electoral Choice*. New York: Palgrave Macmillan.

Cain, Bruce, John Ferejohn, and Morris Fiorina. 1984. "The Constituency Service Basis of the Personal Vote for U.S. Representatives and British Members of Parliament." *American Political Science Review* 78: 110–25.

1987. *The Personal Vote: Constituency Service and Electoral Independence*. Cambridge: Harvard University Press.

Calmes, Jackie, and Michael D. Shear. 2010. "Obama Aides Weigh Bid to Tie the GOP To the Tea Party." *New York Times*, 9/19/2010.

Calvo, Ernesto, and Marcelo Leiras. 2012. "The Nationalization of Legislative Collaboration: Territory, Partisanship, and Policymaking in Argentina." *RIEL – Revista Ibero-Americana dde Estudios Legislativos* 2: 2–19.

Canavan, Mark. 2014. *The Impact of Localism on Public Goods and Services Provision*. Ireland: PhD Dissertation: Trinity College, Dublin.

Caramani, Daniele. 2000. *Elections in Western Europe since 1815: Electoral Results by Constituencies*. London: Macmillan Reference.

2004. *The Nationalization of Politics: The Formation of National Electorates and Party Systems in Western Europe*. Cambridge Studies in Comparative Politics. Cambridge: Cambridge University Press.

2005. "The Formation of National Party Systems in Europe: A Comparative-Historical Analysis." *Scandinavian Political Studies* 28: 295–322.

2015. *The Europeanization of Politics: The Formation of a European Electorate and Party System in Historical Perspective*. New York: Cambridge University Press.

Carey, John. 2002. "Parties, Coalitions, and the Chilean Congress in the 1990s." In *Legislative Politics in Latin America*, eds. Scott Morgenstern and Benito Nacif. Cambridge: Cambridge Univeristy Press. 222–53.

Carey, John, and Matthew S. Shugart. 1995. "Incentives to Cultivate a Personal Vote: A Rank Ordering of Electoral Formulas." *Electoral Studies* 14: 417–39.

Carlson, Matthew M. 2006. "Electoral Reform and the Evolution of Informal Norms in Japan." *Asian Survey* 46: 362–80.

Carreras, Miguel. 2014. "Outsiders and Executive-Legislative Conflict in Latin America (1980–2007)." *Latin American Politics and Society* 56: 70–9.

Castañeda-Angarita, Nestor. 2013. "Party System Nationalization, Presidential Coalitions, and Government Spending." *Electoral Studies* 32: 783–94.

Centellas, Miguel. 2010. "Bolivia's Radical Decentralization." *Americas Quarterly* Summer.

Chang, Eric C. C., and Miriam A. Golden. 2007. "Electoral Systems, District Magnitude and Corruption." *British Journal of Political Science* 37: 115–37.

Cheung, Frederick Hok-Ming. "From Military Aristocracy to Imperial Bureaucracy: Patterns of Consolidation in Two Medieval Empires." PhD Dissertation, University of California, Santa Barbara, 1983.

Chhibber, Pradeep, and Ken Kollman. 1998. "Party Aggregation and the Number of Parties in India and the United States." *American Political Science Review* 92: 329–42.

2004. *The Formation of National Party Systems: Federalism and Party Competition in Canada, Great Britain, India, and the United States*. Princeton: Princeton University Press.

Cho, Wendy K. Tam, and James H. Fowler. 2010. "Legislative Success in a Small World: Social Network Analysis and the Dynamics of Congressional Legislation." *The Journal of Politics* 72: 124–35.

Claggett, William, William Flanigan, and Nancy Zingale. 1984. "Nationalization of the American Electorate." *American Political Science Review* 78: 77–91.

Converse, Philip E. 1969. "Survey Research and the Decoding of Patterns in Ecological Data." In *Quantitative Ecological Analysis in the Social Sciences*, eds. Mattei Dogan and Stein Rokkan. Cambridge, MA: MIT Press. 459–85.

Coppedge, Michael. 1998. "The Dynamic Diversity of Latin American Party Systems." *Party Politics* 4, 4: 547–68.

Cox, Gary W. 1987. *The Efficient Secret: The Cabinet and the Development of Political Parties in Victorian England*. Cambridge, New York: Cambridge University Press.

1990. "Centripetal and Centrifugal Incentives in Electoral Systems." *American Journal of Political Science* 34: 903–35.

1997. *Making Votes Count. Strategic Coordination in the World's Electoral Systems.* Cambridge: Cambridge University Press.

Cox, Gary W., and Mathew D. McCubbins. 1993. *Legislative Leviathan: Party Government in the House.* Berkeley: University of California Press.

2001. "The Institutional Determinants of Economic Policy Outcomes." In *Presidents, Parliaments and Policy*, eds. Stephan Haggard and Mathew McCubbins. New York: Cambridge University Press.

Cox, Gary W., and Scott Morgenstern. 2001. "Latin America's Reactive Assemblies and Proactive Presidents." *Comparative Politics* 33: 171–89.

Craig, Fred, ed. 1989. *British Electoral Facts, 1832–1987.* England: Parliamentary Research Services, Gower Publishing Company Limited.

Craig, Fred, ed. 1972. *Boundaries of Parliamentary Constituencies, 1885–1972.* Chichester: Political Reference Publications.

Crisp, Brian F., Kristin Kanthak, and Jenny Leijonhufvud. 2004. "The Reputations Legislators Build: With Whom Should Representatives Collaborate?" *American Political Science Review* 98: 703–16.

Crisp, Brian F., Santiago Olivella, and Joshua D. Potter. 2013. "Party-System Nationalization and the Scope of Public Policy: The Importance of Cross-District Constituency Similarity." *Comparative Political Studies* 46: 431–56.

Cross, William, and Lisa Young. 2013. "Candidate Recruitment in Canada: The Role of Political Parties." In *Parties, Elections, and the Future of Canadian Politics*, eds. Bittner Amanda and Royce Koop. Vancouver: UBC Press. 24–45

Downs, Anthony. 1957. *An Economic Theory of Democracy.* New York: Harper & Row.

Duverger, Maurice. 1954. *Political Parties, Their Organization and Activity in the Modern State.* New York: Wiley.

Eagles, Munroe. 2013. "Constituency and Personal Determinants of Mps' Positions on Social Conservative Issues in the 37th and 38th Canadian Parliaments." In *In Parties, Elections, and the Future of Canadian Politics*, eds. Amanda Bittner and Amanda Koop. Vancouver: UBC Press.

Eaton, Kent. 2002. "Fiscal Policy Making in the Argentine Legislature." In *Legislative Politics in Latin America*, eds. Scott Morgenstern and Benito Nacif. Cambridge: Cambridge University Press. 287–314.

Edsall, Thomas. 2015. "What If All Politics Is National?" *New York Times*, September 30.

Ersson, Svante, Kenneth Janda, and Jan-Erik Lane. 1985. "Ecology of Party Strength in Western Europe." *Comparative Political Studies* 18: 170–205.

Feierherd, Germán. 2012. "El Tamaño De Las Coaliciones Legislativas En La Argentina." In *Los Legisladores En El Congreso Argentino*, eds. Ana María Mustapic, Alejandro Bonvecchi, and Javier Zelaznik. Buenos Aires: Instituto Torcuato di Tella. 113–40.

Fenno, Richard F. 1978. *Home Style: House Members in Their Districts.* Boston: Little Brown.

Ferejohn, John, and Brian Gaines. 1991. "The Personal Vote in Canada." In *Representation, Integration and Political Parties in Canada*, ed. Herman Bakvis. Vol. 14. Toronto and Oxford: Dundurn Press. 262–78

Filippov, Mikhail, Peter C. Ordeshook, and Olga Shvetsova. 2004. *Designing Federalism: A Theory of Self-Sustainable Federal Institutions.* New York: Cambridge University Press.

Fraile, Marta, and Michael S. Lewis-Beck. 2012. "Economic and Elections in Spain (1982–2008): Cross-Measures, Cross-Time." *Electoral Studies* 31: 485–90.

2013. "Multi-Dimensional Economic Voting in Spain: The 2008 Election." *Electoral Studies* 32: 465–69.

2014. "Economic Vote Instability: Endogeneity or Restricted Variance? Spanish Panel Evidence from 2008 and 2011." *European Journal of Political Research* 53: 160–79.

Geddes, Barbara. 1991. "A Game Theoretic View of Reform." *American Political Science Review* 85, 2.

Gelman, Andrew, and Gary King. 1990. "Estimating Incumbency Advantage without Bias." *American Journal of Political Science* 34, 4: 114–64.

1994. "A Unified Method of Evaluating Electoral Systems and Redistricting Plans." *American Journal of Political Science* 38: 514–54.

Gerber, Linda M. 2006. "Urban Diversity: Riding Composition and Party Support in the Canadian Federal Election of 2004." *Canadian Journal of Urban Research* 15: 105–18.

Gervasoni, Carlos. 2010. "A Rentier Theory of Subnational Regimes: Fiscal Federalism, Democracy, and Authoritarianism in the Argentine Provinces." *World Politics* 62: 302–40.

Gold, Matea, and Paul Kane. 2016. "The GOP – and Its Big Funders – Scramble to Insulate Congress from Trump." *Washington Post*, 3/23/16.

Golden, Miriam A. 2003. "Electoral Connections: The Effects of the Personal Vote on Political Patronage, Bureaucracy and Legislation in Postwar Italy." *British Journal of Political Science* 33: 89–212.

Golder, Matt. 2005. "Democratic Electoral Systems around the World, 1946–2000." *Electoral Studies* 24:1, 103–21.

Goldman, Ralph M. 1959. "Party Committees and National Politics." *Midwest Journal of Political Science* 3: 306–09.

Green, Andrew, and Scott Morgenstern. 2009. "Peru: Assessment Report for Political Parties and Party Systems." United States Agency for International Development (USAID).

Greene, William H. 1997. *Econometric Analysis* Upper Saddle River, New Jersey: Prentice-Hall, Inc.

Grofman, Bernard, and Arend Lijphart, eds. 1986. *Electoral Laws and Their Political Consequences.* New York: Agathon Press.

Haggard, Stephan, and Robert R. Kaufman. 1995. *The Political Economy of Democratic Transitions.* Princeton: Princeton University Press.

Hallerberg, Mark. 2004. "Electoral Laws, Government, and Parliament." In *Patterns of Parliamentary Behavior: Passage of Legislation across Western Europe*, eds. Herbert Doring and Mark Hallerberg. England: Ashgate. 11–33.

Hallerberg, Mark, and Patrik Marier. 2004. "Executive Authority, the Personal Vote, and Budget Discipline in Latin American and Caribbean Countries." *American Journal of Political Science* 48: 571–87.

Harbers, Imke. 2010. "Decentralization and the Development of Nationalized Party Systems in New Democracies: Evidence from Latin America." *Comparative Political Studies* 43: 606–27.

Harell, Allison 2013. "Revisiting the 'Ethnic' Vote: Liberal Allegiance and Vote Choice among Racialized Minorities." In *Parties, Elections, and the Future of Canadian Politics*, eds. Amanda Bittner and Royce Koop. Vancouver UBC Press.

Hicken, Allen, Ken Kollman, and Joel W. Simmons. 2016. "Party System Nationalization and the Provision of Public Health Services." *Political Science Research and Methods* 4, 3: 573–94.

Hloušek, Vít, and Lubomír Kopecek. 2008. "Cleavages in the Contemporary Czech and Slovak Politics between Persistence and Change." *East European Politics and Societies* 22: 518–52.

Hooghe, Liesbet, Gary Marks, and Arjan H. Schakel. 2010. *The Rise of Regional Authority: A Comparative Study of 42 Democracies (1950–2006)*. London: Routledge.

Horowitz, Donald L. 1985. *Ethnic Groups in Conflict*. Berkeley: University of California Press.

Hoschka, Peter, and Hermann Schunck. 1978. "Regional Stability of Voting Behaviour in Federal Elections: A Longitudinal Aggregate Data Analysis." In *Elections and Parties*, eds. Max Kaase and Klaus von Beyme, Volume 3 of Sage Studies in International Sociology. Thousand Oaks: Sage Publication.

Huber, John, and Ronald Inglehart. 1995. "Expert Interpretations of Party Space and Party Locations in 42 Societies." *Party Politics* 1, 1: 73–111.

Ishiyama, John T. 2002. "Elections and Nationalization of the Vote in Post-Communist Russian Politics: A Comparative Perspective." *Journal of Communist Studies and Transition Politics* 18: 29–40.

Jacobson, Gary C. 1987. "Running Scared: Elections and Congressional Politics in the 1980s." In *Congress: Structure and Policy*, eds. Mathew McCubbins and Terry Sullivan. Cambridge: Cambridge University Press. 39–81.

Jacobson, Gary C., and Samuel Kernell. 1983. *Strategy and Choice in Congressional Elections*. New Haven and London: Yale University Press.

Jaffrelot, Christophe, and Frederic Grare. 2012. "The Regionalization of Indian Politics and the Challenge of Coalition-Building." *Carnegie Endowment for Internatonal Peace*, 8/11/2013.

Johnson, Joel W., and Jessica S. Wallack. 2012. "Electoral Systems and the Personal Vote." Harvard Dataverse, V1: https://dataverse.harvard.edu/dataset.xhtml? persistentId=hdl:1902.1/17901.

Johnston, Richard. 2002. "Prime Ministerial Contenders in Canada." In *Leaders' Personalities and the Outcomes of Democratic Elections*, ed. Anthony King. Oxford: Oxford University Press.

Johnston, Ronald John. 1981. "Testing the Butler-Stokes Model of a Polarization Effect around the National Swing in Partisan Preferences: England, 1979." *British Journal of Political Science* 11: 113–17.

Jones, David R., and Monika L. McDermott. 2004. "The Responsible Party Government Model in House and Senate Elections." *American Journal of Political Science* 48: 1–12.

Jones, Mark P. 2002. "Explaining the High Level of Party Discipline in the Argentine Congress." In *Legislative Politics in Latin America*, eds. Scott Morgenstern and Benito Nacif. Cambridge: Cambridge University Press. 147–84.

2008. "The Recruitment and Selection of Legislative Candidates in Argentina." In *Pathways to Power: Political Recruitment and Candidate Selection in Latin*

America, eds. Peter Siavelis and Scott Morgenstern. University Park, Pennsylvania: The Pennsylvania State University Press.

Jones, Mark P., and Scott Mainwaring. 2003. "The Nationalization of Parties and Party Systems: An Empirical Measure and an Application to the Americas." *Party Politics* 9: 139–66.

Jurado, Ignacio. 2014. "Party System Nationalisation and Social Spending." *European Journal of Political Research* 53: 288–307.

Karvonen, Lauri. 2004. "Preferential Voting: Incidence and Effects." *International Political Science Review* 25: 203–26.

Kasuya, Yuko, and Moenius Johannes. 2008. "The Nationalization of Party Systems: Conceptual Issues and Alternative District-Focused Measures." *Electoral Studies* 27: 126–35.

Katz, Jonathan N., and Gary King. 1999. "A Statistical Model for Multiparty Electoral Data." *American Political Science Review* 93, 1: 15–32.

Katz, Richard S. 1973a. "The Attribution of Variance in Electoral Returns: An Alternative Measurement Technique." *American Political Science Review* 67: 817–28.

    1973b. "Rejoinder to 'Comment' by Stokes." *American Political Science Review* 67: 832–34.

Kawato, Sadafumi. 1987. "Nationalization and Partisan Realignment in Congressional Elections." *American Political Science Review* 81: 1235–50.

Kerevel, Yann. 2010. "The Legislative Consequences of Mexico's Mixed-Member Electoral System, 2000–2009." *Electoral Studies* 29: 691–703.

Key, V.O. 1959. "Secular Realignment and the Party System." *Journal of Politics* 21, 2: 198–210.

    1966. *The Responsible Electorate: Rationality in Presidential Voting 1936–1960.* Cambridge, Massachusetts: The Belknap Press of Harvard University Press.

Kiewiet, D. Roderick, and Mathew D. McCubbins. 1991. *The Logic of Delegation.* Chicago: University of Chicago Press.

King, Gary, Michael Tomz, and Wittenberg Jason. 2000. "Making the Most of Statistical Analyses: Improving Interpretation and Presentation." *American Journal of Political Science* 44: 347–61.

Kitschelt, Herbert, Kirk A. Hawkins, Juan Pablo Luna, Guillermo Rosas, and Elizabeth J. Zechmeister. 2010. *Latin American Party Systems.* Cambridge: Cambridge University Press.

Kitschelt, Herbert, and Steven Wilkinson. 2007. "Citizen-Politician Linkages: An Introduction." In *Patrons, Clients and Policies in Patterns of Democratic Accountability and Political Competition*, eds. Herbert Kitschelt and Steven I. Wilkinson. Cambridge: Cambridge University Press. 1–49.

Koellner, Patrick. 2009. "Japanese Lower House Campaigns in Transition: Manifest Changes or Fleeting Fads?" *Journal of East Asian Studies* 9: 121–49.

Kopecky, Petr 2006. "The Rise of the Power Monopoly: Political Parties in the Czech Republic." In *Post Communist Eu-Member States: Parties and Party Systems.*, ed. Suanne Jungerstam-Mulders. Burlington, VT: Ashgate.

Kunicová, Jana, and Susan Rose-Ackerman. 2005. "Electoral Rules and Constitutional Structures as Constraints on Corruption." *British Journal of Political Science* 35: 573–606.

Lago, Ignacio, and José Ramón Montero. 2006. "The 2004 Election in Spain: Terrorism, Accountability, and Voting." *Taiwan Journal of Democracy* 2: 13–36.
2013. "Defining and Measuring Party System Nationalization." *European Political Science Review First View* 6, 2: 1–21.
Lago-Peñas, Ignacio, and Santiago Lago-Peñas. 2009. "Does the Nationalization of Party Systems Affect the Composition of Public Spending?" *Economics of Governance* 10: 85–98.
Lago-Peñas, Ignacio, and Santiago Lago-Peñas. 2011. "Descentralización Y Voto Económico En España." *Reis* 136: 111–26.
Lee, Adrian. 1988. "The Persistence of Difference: Electoral Change in Cornwall." Paper presented at the Political Studies Association Conference, Plymouth.
Leithner, Christian. 1997. "Electoral Nationalisation, Dealignment and Realignment: Australia and the Us, 1900–88." *Australian Journal of Political Science* 32: 205–22.
Lewis-Beck, Michael S., and Marta Fraile. 2013. "Multi-Dimensional Economic Voting in Spain: The 2008 Election." *Electoral Studies,* 32: 465–69.
Lewis-Beck, Michael S., and Maria Celeste Ratto. 2013. "Economic Voting in Latin America: A General Model." *Electoral Studies* 32: 489–93.
Lewis-Beck, Michael S., and Mary Stegmaier. 2000. "Economic Determinants of Electoral Outcomes." *Annual Review of Political Science* 3: 183–219.
Lijphart, Arend. 1969. *The Politics of Accommodation: Pluralism and Democracy in the Netherlands*: University of California Press.
1977. *Democracy in Plural Societies: A Comparative Exploration*. New Haven: Yale University Press.
1999. *Patterns of Democracy: Government Forms and Performance in Thirty-Six Countries*. New Haven: Yale University Press.
Lin, Lawrence I-Kuei. 1989. "A Concordance Correlation Coefficient to Evaluate Reproducibility." *Biometrics* 45: 255–68.
2000. "A Note on the Concordance Correlation Coefficient." *Biometrics* 56: 324–25.
Linz, Juan J., and José R. Montero. 2001. "The Party Systems of Spain: Old Cleavages and New Challenges." In *Party Systems and Voter Alignments Revisited*, eds. Lauri L. Karvonen and Stein Kuhnle. London: Routledge. 150–96.
Llanos, Mariana. 1998. "El Presidente, El Congreso, Y La Politica De Privatizaciones En La Argentina (1989–97)." *Desarrollo Economico* 38: 743–70.
Lundberg, Thomas Carl 2005. "Second-Class Representatives? Mixed-Member Proportional Representation in Britain." *Parliamentary Affairs* 59: 60–77.
Madrid, Raul. 2012. *The Rise of Ethnic Politics in Latin America*. Cambridge: Cambridge University Press.
Mainwaring, Scott, and Timothy Scully. 1995. *Building Democratic Institutions: Party Systems in Latin America*. Stanford: Stanford University Press.
Mainwaring, Scott, and Edurne Zoco. 2007. "Political Sequences and the Stabilization of Interparty Competition." *Party Politics* 13: 155–78.
Manin, Bernard, Adam Przeworksi, and Susan C. Stokes. 1990. "Elections and Representatio." In *Democracy, Accountability, and Representation*, eds. Adam Przeworksi, Bernard Manin, and Susan C. Stokes. Cambridge: Cambridge University Press.
Mayhew, David. 1974a. *Congress: The Electoral Connection*. New Haven: Yale University.
1974b. "Congressional Elections: The Case of the Vanishing Marginals." *Polity*: 295–317.

McCubbins, Mathew, and Frances Rosenbluth. 1995. "Party Provision for Personal Politics: Dividing the Vote in Japan." In *Structure and Policy in Japan and the United States*, eds. Peter F. Cowhey and Mathew McCubbins. Cambridge: Cambridge University Press.

Michels, Robert. 1915. *Political Parties: A Sociological Study of the Oligarchical Tendencies of Modern Democracy*. Translated by Eden and Cedar Paul. New York: Collier Books.

Montero, Alfred P. 2007. "The Limits of Decentralisation: Legislative Careers and Territorial Representation in Spain." *West European Politics* 30: 573–94.

Moraes, Juan Andres. 2008. "Why Factions? Candidate Selection and Legislative Politics in Uruguay." In *Pathways to Power: Political Recruitment and Candidate Selection in Latin America*, eds. Peter Siavelis and Scott Morgenstern. University Park: University of Pennsylvania. 164–86.

Morgenstern, Scott. 2001. "Organized Factions and Disorganized Parties: Electoral Incentives in Uruguay." *Party Politics* 7: 235–56.

2004. *Patterns of Legislative Politics: Roll call voting in Latin America and the United States*. Cambridge: Cambridge University Press.

Morgenstern, Scott, Ernesto Calvo, Daniel Chasquetti, and Jose Manuel Magallanes. 2014. "Bill Co-Sponsorship and the Electoral Connection in Comparative Perspective." Paper prepared for American Political Science Association Meeting. Washington, DC.

Morgenstern, Scott, John Polga Hecimovich, and Peter Siavelis. 2012. "Ni Chicha Ni Limoná: Party Nationalization in Pre- and Post-Authoritarian Chile." *Party Politics* 20: 751–65.

Morgenstern, Scott, and Richard F. Potthoff. 2005. "The Components of Elections: District Heterogeneity, District-Time Effects, and Volatility." *Electoral Studies* 24: 17–40.

Morgenstern, Scott, John Polga Hecimovich, and Peter Siavelis. 2012. "Ni Chicha Ni Limoná: Party Nationalization in Pre- and Post-Authoritarian Chile." *Party Politics* 20: 751–65.

2014. "Seven Imperatives for Improving the Measurement of Party Nationalization with Evidence from Chile." *Electoral Studies* 33: 186–99.

Morgenstern, Scott, Stephen Swindle, and Andrea Castagnola. 2009. "Party Nationalization and Institutions." *Journal of Politics* 71:4, 1322–41.

Morgenstern, Scott, Noah Smith, and Alejandro Tresses. 2017. "How Party Nationalization Conditions Economic Voting." *Electoral Studies*. 47: 136–45.

Morgenstern, Scott, and Stephen Swindle. 2005. "Are Politics Local? An Analysis of Voting Patterns in 23 Democracies." *Comparative Political Studies* 38: 143–70.

Morgenstern, Scott, and Javier Vázquez-D'Elía. 2007. "Electoral Systems, Parties and Party Systems in Latin America." *Annual Review of Poltiical Science* 10: 143–68.

Moser, Robert G., and Ethan Scheiner. 2012. *Electoral Systems and Political Context*. Cambridge: Cambridge University Press.

Mustillo, Thomas, and Yoo-Sun Jung. 2016. "Distinguishing Territorial Structure from Electoral Adventurism: The Sources of Static and Dynamic Nationalization." *Electoral Studies*.

Mustillo, Thomas, and Sarah Mustillo. 2012. "Party Nationalization in a Multilevel Context: Where's the Variance?" *Electoral Studies* 31: 422–33

Nielson, Daniel. 2003. "Supplying Trade Reform: Political Institutions and Liberalization in Middle-Income Presidential Democracies." *American Journal of Political Science* 47: 470–91.

Pachon, Monica, and Matthew Shugart. 2010. "Electoral Reform and the Mirror Image of Inter-Party and Intra-Party Competition: The Adoption of Party Lists in Colombia." *Electoral Studies* 29: 648–60.

Panebianco, Angelo. 1988. *Political Parties: Organization and Power.* Cambridge and New York: Cambridge University Press.

Pekkanen, Robert, Benjamin Byblade, and Ellis S. Krauss. 2006. "Electoral Incentives in Mixed-Member Systems: Party, Posts, and Zombie Politicians in Japan." *American Political Science Review,* 100: 188–93.

Persson, Torsten, and Guido Tabellini. 2003. *The Economic Effects of Constitutions.* Cambridge: Massachusetts Institute of Technology Press.

Persson, Torsten, and Guido Tabellini. 2004. "Constitutions and Economic Policy." *The Journal of Economic Perspectives,* 18: 75–98.

Persson, Torsten, Guido Tabellini, and Francesco Trebbi. 2003. "Electoral Rules and Corruption." *Journal of the European Economic Association* 1: 958–89.

Pilet, Jean-Benoit, and Alan Renwick. "Electoral System Change in Europe since 1945." Université libre de Bruxelles, University of Reading.

Polga Hecimovich, John. n.d. "Thinking Strategically: A Theory of Party (De-)Nationalization, with Evidence from Latin America."

Poggi, Nicolás. 2013. "Cristina Presentó a Sus Candidatos Con Una Fuerte Apuesta Para 'Nacionalizar' La Elección." *Agencia Nova: Noticias de Provincia de Buenos Aires,* 6/29.

Polga Hecimovich, John. 2014. "Hacía Una Superación Del Clivaje Regional? La Evolución De La Nacionalización De Los Partidos Políticos Ecuatorianos Desde El Retorno a La Democracia." *América Latina Hoy* 67: 91–118.

Poole, Keith T, and Howard Rosenthal. 1996. *Congress: A Political-Economic History of Roll Call Voting.* New York: Oxford University Press.

Powell, G. Bingham. 2000. *Elections as Instruments of Democracy: Majoritarian and Proportional Visions.* New Haven: Yale University Press.

Powell, G. Bingham, and Guy Whitten. 1993. "A Cross-National Analysis of Economic Voting: Taking Account of the Political Context." *American Journal of Political Science* 37: 391–414.

Preece, Jessica R. 2014. "How the Party Can Win in Personal Vote Systems: The 'Selectoral Connection' and Legislative Voting in Lithuania." *Legislative Studies Quarterly* 39: 147–67.

Pridham, Geoffrey. 1973. "A 'Nationalization' process? Federal Politics and State Elections in West Germany." *Government and Opposition* 8: 455–72.

Primo, David M., and James M. Snyder Jr. 2010. "Party Strength, the Personal Vote, and Government Spending." *American Journal of Political Science* 54: 354–70.

Randall, Vicky, and Lars Svasand. 2002. "Party Institutionalization in New Democracies." *Party Politics* 8: 5–29.

Ranney, Austin. 1954. *The Doctrine of Responsible Party Government: Its Origins and Present State.* Urbana: University of Illinois Press.

Reed, Steven 2003. *Japanese Electoral Politics: Creating a New Party System.* London: Routledge.

Reed, Steven, Ethan Scheiner, and Michael Thies. 2012. "The End of LDP Dominance and the Rise of Party-Oriented Politics in Japan." *Journal of Japanese Studies* 38: 353–76.

Reilly, Benjamin. 2002. "Electoral Systems for Divided Democracies." *Journal of Democracy* 13: 156–70.

Roberts, Kenneth M. 2014. *Changing Course in Latin America: Party Systems in the Neoliberal Era.* Cambridge: Cambridge University Press.

Roberts, Kenneth M., and Erik Wibbels. 1999. "Party Systems and Electoral Volatility in Latin American: A Test of Economic, Institutional, and Structural Explanations." *American Political Science Review* 93: 575–90.

Rodden, Jonathan, and Erik Wibbels. 2011. "Dual Accountability and the Nationalization of Party Competition: Evidence from Four Federations." *Electoral Studies* 17: 629–53.

Rokkan, Stein. 1970. *Citizens, Elections, Parties; Approaches to the Comparative Study of the Processes of Development,* Comparative Studies of Political Life, 1. New York: McKay.

Rose, Richard, and Derek W Urwin. 1975. *Regional Differentiation and Political Unity in Western Nations.* Ed. Richard Rose, Contemporary Political Sociology Series. London: Sage Publications.

Rosenbluth, Frances, and Michael Thies. 2010. *Japan Transformed: Political Change and Economic Restructuring.* Princeton: Princeton University Press.

Saiegh, Sebastian. 2010. "Active Players or Rubber Stamps? An Evaluation of the Policymaking Role of Latin American Legislatures." In *How Democracy Works: Political Institutions, Actors, and Arenas in Latin American Policymaking,* eds. Carlos Scartascini, Ernesto Stein, and Mariano Tommasi. Washington, DC: Inter-American Development Bank.

Samuels, David. 2002. "Pork Barreling Is Not Credit Claiming or Advertising: Campaign Finance and the Sources of the Personal Vote in Brazil." *Journal of Politics* 64: 845–63.

Schattschneider, E.E. 1960. *The Semisovereign People: A Realists View of Democracy in America.* Hinsdale: Dryden Press.

Scheiner, Ethan. 2006. *Democracy without Competition in Japan: Opposition Failure in a One-Party Dominant State.* Cambridge; New York: Cambridge University Press.

  2012. "The Electoral System and Japan's Partial Transformation: Party System Consolidation without Policy Realignment." *Journal of East Asian Studies* 12: 351–79.

Sengupta, Somini. 2009. "Local Issues Dominate as India Votes." *New York Times,* 4/16.

Shin, Jae Hyeok. 2017. "The Choice of Candidate-Centered Electoral Systems in New Democracies." *Party Politics* 23:2, 160–71.

Shugart, Matthew S., and Martin P. Wattenberg, eds. 1993. *Mixed-Member Electoral Systems.* Oxford: Oxford University Press.

Shugart, Matthew S., and John Carey. 1992. *Presidents and Assemblies.* Cambridge: Cambridge University Press.

Siavelis, Peter M. 1997. "Continuity and Change in the Chilean Party System: On the Transformational Effects of Electoral Reform." *Comparative Political Studies* 30: 651–74.

Simon, Pablo. 2013. "The Combined Impact of Decentralisation and Personalism on the Nationalisation of Party Systems." *Political Studies* 61: 24–44.

Simmons, Joel, Allen Hicken, Ken Kollman, and Irfan Nooruddin. 2011. "Dividing the Spoils: Party Nationalization, Credibility, and Foreign Direct Investment." *Unpub.*

Singer, Matthew M. 2010. "Who Says 'It's the Economy'? Cross-National and Cross-Individual Variation in the Salience of Economic Performance." *Comparative Political Studies* 44: 284–312.

Sorauf, Frank J. 1980. *Party Politics in America.* Boston: Brown, Little.

Steele, Abbey. 2011. "Electing Displacement: Political Cleansing in Apartadó, Colombia." *Journal of Conflict Resolution* 55: 423–45.

Stokes, Donald. 1965. "A Variance Components Model of Political Effects." In *Mathematical Applications in Political Science,* ed. J. M. Claunch. Dallas: Southern Methodist University.

　1967. "Parties and the Nationalization of Electoral Forces." In *The American Party Systems: States of Political Development,* eds. Chambers W. N. and W. D. Burnham. New York: Oxford University Press. 182–202.

Strom, Kaare. 1990. *Minority Government and Majority Rule* Cambridge: Cambridge University Press.

Su, Yen-Pin. 2013. "Party Registration Rules and Party Systems in Latin America." *Party Politics* 21, 2: 295–308.

Summers, Lawrence H. 1994. "Forward." In *Voting for Reform: Democracy, Political Liberalization, and Economic Adjustment: Democracy, Political Liberalization, and Economic Adjustment,* eds. Stephan Haggard and Steven B. Webb. World Bank and Oxford University Press. ix–xii

Sundquist, James L. 1973. *Dynamics of the Party System: Alignment and Realignment of Political Parties in the United States.* Washington, DC: The Brookings Institution.

Thames, Frank C. 2001. "Legislative Voting Behavior in the Russian Duma: Understanding the Effect of Mandate." *Europe-Asia Studies* 53: 869–84.

　2005. "A House Divided: Party Strength and the Mandate Divide in Hungary, Russia, and Ukraine." *Comparative Political Studies* 38: 282–303.

Vertz, Laura L., John P. Frendreis, and James L. Gibson. 1987. "Nationalization of the Electorate in the United States." *The American Political Science Review* 81: 961–66.

Wallack, Jessica Seddon, Alejandro Gaviria, Ugo Panizza, and Ernesto Stein. 2003. "Particularism around the World." *World Bank Economic Review* 17.

Weber, Eugen. 1976. *Peasants into Frenchmen: The Modernization of Rural France, 1870-1914.* Stanford: Stanford University Press.

Wittenberg, Jason. 2008. "How Similar Are They? Rethinking Electoral Congruence." Paper presented at the Annual Meeting of the MPSA, Chicago.

Zelaznik, Javier. 2012. "Agenda Presidencial Y Apoyo Legislativo: El Peronismo Como Partido De Gobierno." In *Los Legisladores Den El Congreso Argentino,* eds. Ana María Mustapic, Alejandro Bonvecchi, and Javier Zelaznik. Buenos Aires: Instituto Torcuato Di Tella. 61–112.

Zellner, Arnold. 1962. "An Efficient Method of Estimating Seemingly Unrelated Regression Equations and Tests for Aggregation Bias." *Journal of the American Statistical Association* 57: 348–68.

Author Index

Subject Index